Religion and Ethnic
Minorities and Social Change in

Rohit Barot (ed.)

Religion and Ethnicity

Minorities and Social Change in the Metropolis

Kok Pharos Publishing House
Kampen – the Netherlands

CIP-GEGEVENS KONINKLIJKE BIBLIOTHEEK, DEN HAAG

© 1993, Kok Pharos Publishing House,
P.O. Box 5016, 8260 GA Kampen, The Netherlands
Cover Design by Rob Lucas
ISBN 90 390 0061 1
NUGI 631

Contents

Acknowledgements

The collection of essays in this volume is based on a conference entitled 'Religion, Minorities and Social Change'. The Centre for the Study of Minorities and Social Change, Department of Sociology at the University of Bristol was the venue for this gathering in September 1991. As co-ordinators of the Centre, Dr. Rohit Barot, Dr. Steve Fenton, Dr. Charles Watters and Ms Azra Sadiq organised the conference. We are most thankful to all the participants for their contributions which made the conference a stimulating event and the production of this volume possible.

I am grateful to all my colleagues in the Department of Sociology for their support and encouragement in the preparation of this volume. I would like to express my warm thanks to Professor Theo Nichols for his encouragement, support and continued interest in the volume. Dr Kieran Flanagan undertook the laborious task of copy editing for which I am most grateful to him. Mrs. Madeleine Chinnick of University of Bristol Computer Centre assisted me with disk conversion and various queries about the reprocessing of the disks. I am thankful for her assistance. Finally, my debt to Mrs. Jackie Bee, our departmental secretary, is very special. She carefully proof-read the manuscript and assisted me in producing a camera ready copy of the book.

My gratitude to Dr. Kristin De Troyer of Kok Pharos Publishing House is immense for her encouragement, support and patience throughout the preparation of this volume.

For their kindness and understanding, I dedicate this book to Tejas and Sonal.

Rohit Barot
Department of Sociology
Centre for the Study of Minorities and Social Change
University of Bristol
BRISTOL
July 1993

1

Religion, Ethnicity and Social Change: An Introduction

Rohit Barot

This volume explores the relationship between religion and ethnicity in the context of global social changes with a particular focus on ethnic minority communities now living as permanent settlers in leading European Community countries. Historians, sociologists and anthropologists have argued that one of the key factors in explaining the presence of this distinctive and visible minority population is the rapid process of globalisation associated with economic and political changes. It is these changes which have created conditions necessary for the movement of men, women and children to the centres of wealth and prosperity in Europe. Studies of these changes usually focus on migration, settlement and changing conditions of the European labour markets which determine forms of marginality and exclude the population of non-European ethnic origin in particular. This brief introduction examines the concept of ethnicity and its relationship to religion with reference to changes that ethnic minority communities face in contemporary European societies.

Numerous studies now provide valuable information about objective factors which influence the position of the ethnic minority population in different societies. In Britain, a wide range of research and government reports and especially the PEP and PSI studies of racial discrimination (Daniel, 1968; Smith, 1977; Brown, 1984) provide reliable information on the extent of discrimination in employment, housing and various other fields. In all probability, the situation is similar in other European countries even if they have not produced such detailed information on patterns of discrimination and disadvantage. Although these studies depend on actual interviews with ethnic minority individuals, they rarely focus on what Badr Dahya identified as the 'actor's frame of reference' (1984) or, from the point of view of anthropologists, the self-consciousness of the migrants and their communities.

Studies which take account of the 'actor's frame of reference' or his or her self-consciousness provide us with valuable data on migration and settlement of particular groups and development of their social and cultural organisation. A number of important anthropological studies of ethnic minority communities in Britain have been carried out throughout 1960s, 1970s and 1980s with notable pioneering contributions by scholars like Michael Banton (1955), Sheila Patterson

(1961) and Rashmi Desai (1963).   Such community studies were valuable in providing an overall profile of the migrant population in question.

Concerned as they were with the welfare of migrants, their families and their eventual integration into British society, sociologists and anthropologists were keen to show the patterns of adaptation that were being developed by the newcomers. This approach was not incompatible with views on successful integration, which, to some extent, were jointly shared by the migrants and the authorities for entirely different reasons; the migrants being concerned with their successful adaptation and the authorities being concerned with the potential social cost of disruption created by the process of migration.

As Roger and Catherine Ballard have illustrated in their study of Sikh settlement in Britain (1975), as soon as working men were joined by their wives and children and started to form residential communities, the question of religious values and practices began to feature prominently in their lives. Although the Sikhs had already established a *gurdwara* as their place of worship in Hammersmith, London in mid 1930s, the construction of places to carry out collective and communal worship received greater impetus after families began to settle in Britain to form communities after 1960s. European countries like Holland, Germany, France and Sweden appear to have followed a similar pattern. Although migrants had regarded their belief system, religious values and the practices associated with them as a vital part of their new settlement, this concern with religion was insufficiently reflected in sociological and anthropological accounts of ethnic minority communities in the 1960s. The new settlers began to express their concern for establishing communities, institutions and organisations to sustain their religion and the study of religion and ethnicity began to receive more attention during the 1970s and 1980s in Britain. A relatively similar pattern appears to have occurred in Holland and Sweden and by implication, equally in France and Germany.

Ethnicity and Social Change

Developments which brought ethnicity and religion into a sharp focus depended on social and political changes as well as on growing interest among both sociologists and anthropologists in the concept and phenomenon of ethnicity.

In Britain, these social and political changes were marked on the one hand, by immigration control and on the other, by the introduction of legislation against racial discrimination to ensure that minorities had remedies in law to protect themselves from the effects of overt and covert discriminatory practices. Integration as assimilation has been seen as 'a unidimensional one-way process in which the outsiders relinquished their own culture in favour of the dominant society' (Abercombie, Hill and Turner, 1984 (1988): 14). In contrast to this in an address he gave to a meeting of Voluntary Liaison Committees on 23rd May 1966, the Home Secretary Roy Jenkins had defined integration as 'not a flattening process of assimilation but as equal opportunity accompanied by cultural diversity, in an atmosphere of mutual tolerance' (Rose, 1969: 25). This definitive statement which underlined cultural diversity and equal opportunity was to influence policy developments on minorities throughout 1970s with increasing acceptance of the fact that the ethnic minorities would retain their own religion, language and culture and participate in British life just as the Jews had done before.

Jennifer Williams had noted in her study in mid 60s that immigrant children were subject to 'dual socialisation' (Rex and Moore, 1967: 230-257). In her research she had noted a clear conflict between the school as an agent of socialisation and the radically different kind of socialisation immigrant children would receive in their family and in their community. As a consequence, conflict between the values of the dominant society and those of marginal ethnic minority communities was not unlikely. As parents became more and more aware of the educational goal of anglicisation for their children, there was a self-conscious opposition to this process, especially from the parents of young Muslim girls. They had begun demanding separate schools for their daughters from as early as 1970 in Bradford. South Asian groups began to express a well-focused concern for sustaining their religion, language and cultures at a time when they were creating religious associations and institutions for their particular group or community. From my own London fieldwork on a particular Swaminarayan sect[1], it was evident that some Hindus were deeply concerned with sustaining their religious identity and protecting their young from what they saw as the undesirable influence of the school, the peer group and the wider society.

Conceptions of race used in popular discourse as well as in academic studies had a powerful influence on the research concerned with migrants of non-European origin in Britain. Books with the title 'race' or 'racial' were not uncommon such as Michael Banton's 1972 book *Racial Minorities*. However although the conception of 'race' and 'race relations' had hardly disappeared from the debates on non-European minorities, what was remarkable was the emergence of ethnicity as a concept in opposition to theories of stratification.

Ethnicity as an Explanatory Conception

In his essay 'Some Theoretical Considerations on the Nature and Trends of Change of Ethnicity', Talcott Parsons had noted rather incisively that ethnicity 'is, however, an extraordinarily elusive concept and very difficult to define in any precise way' (Glazer and Moynihan, 1975: 55-83). Most contemporary sociologists and anthropologists recognise the difficulty of defining ethnicity and therefore argue that it is much more a concept rather than a theory with a set of interrelated propositions.

The word ethnicity derives from the Greek word *ethnos*, meaning people and appears to have been used from the dawn of Christianity, originally to distinguish 'a rustic or village people as opposed to those dwelling in organised cities'[2] (Souter, 1916: 72). The new edition of *The Compact Oxford English Dictionary* (1991) refers to ethnic as 'pertaining to nations not Christian or Jewish'. Ethnic is also referred to as 'pertaining to or having common racial, cultural, religious or linguistic characteristics especially designating a racial or other group within a larger system'. It refers to an ethnic minority as a 'group of people differentiated from the rest of the community by racial origins or cultural background and usually claiming or enjoying official recognition of their group identity' (Simpson & Weiner, 1991: 535).

From about 1953, sociologists and social anthropologists alike have used the concept of ethnic group to identify culturally distinctive groups. Recently social science scholars have developed a variety of conceptions which relate to ethnicity. The word ethnogenesis has been used to identify the process of change according to which a population may forge a new identity in a given society. It is a relatively common practice among scholars to distinguish ethnic group from ethnic category; the former refers to a corporate group while the latter applies to a population which may share common cultural features and social institutions without necessarily forming a corporate group.

A number of well-known works have influenced studies of ethnicity and ethnic groups in last thirty years or so. In the United States, Nathan Glazer and Daniel P. Moynihan's book *Ethnicity: Theory and Experience* stimulated interest in ethnic phenomena at the time when the groups like the Blacks and Chicanos were actively involved in campaigning for their civil rights and in reconstructing their own history and culture to increase their self-esteem. The authors not only questioned the ability of stratification theorists to explain and account for solidarity of cultural groups, but also argued that ethnicity was a more fundamental source of stratification than property-based class relations (1975: 16-18). A similar theme was explored in an edited study of British ethnic groups by James L Watson (1977). The Glazer and Moynihan study was influential and became particularly well-known for introducing the distinction between ethnicity which was primordial and that which was circumstantial. Primordial ethnicity is about divisions between men with roots in deep historical experience. Circumstantial ethnicity refers 'to specific and immediate circumstances to explain why groups maintain their identity' (Glazer and Moynihan, 1975: 19-20). The extent to which such simple propositions about ethnicity constitute a proper foundation for a systematic study of the ethnic phenomenon is a matter for further debate. Most contemporary analysts of ethnicity are less likely to argue for the kind of primordial ethnicity which may imply intellectually and morally dubious and unacceptable forms of determinism.

As the readers of this volume will no doubt know, British social anthropologists began to use the concept of ethnicity instead of tribe in their research in African towns. Abner Cohen's book *Custom and Politics in Africa* (1969) was influential in showing that when groups compete for specific aims and gains, ethnicity can emerge as a distinctive feature of group identity. In this study, he shows that in their dealings with Yorubas, Hausas deploy cultural distinctiveness to retain their monopoly over cattle and Kola trading just as some Bengalis in Britain may use cultural symbolism to maintain their control over the Indian restaurant trade in a particular city.   Abner Cohen makes his clearest theoretical statement in his 'Introduction: the lessons of ethnicity' in his *Urban Ethnicity* (1974a) and his book *Two Dimensional Man* (1974b).   The core of his argument about ethnicity relates to the connection between symbolism and power and the emergence of ethnicity as a political phenomenon in competition between groups for control over scarce resources.   From this perspective, contact and interaction between groups for economic and political rewards is a necessary condition for political ethnicity to arise.

In contrast to Abner Cohen's focus on competition and conflict as a critical focus for ethnicity to develop, the Norwegian social anthropologist Fredrik Barth has pursued a more interactionist approach in advancing the study of ethnicity in his book *Ethnic Boundaries: The Social Organisation of Culture and Difference* (1969).   Like Cohen, Barth recognises the importance of culture but argues that the continuity of the ascriptive and exclusive character of ethnic groups depends not merely on the culture itself but, importantly, on the maintenance of a boundary which marks both belonging and non-belonging at the same time (Barth, 1969: 14).   As he suggests, 'the critical focus from this point of view becomes ethnic *boundary* that defines the group, not the cultural stuff that encloses it' (Barth, 1969: 15). This facilitates the dichotomisation of those with whom one shares or does not share critical features of culture which defines who one is.   In broad terms, the concept of ethnicity has come to refer to shared cultural heritage, common descent, interaction between groups and the construction of boundaries to sustain those identities which members of the groups know, understand and use in response to their own life and more particularly in response to non-belongers who are regarded as being 'different' and even inferior.

While American scholars have often used the word ethnic without distinguishing it from race, in the European context, especially in Britain, sociologists and anthropologists have attempted to sustain a distinction between race and ethnicity to divorce the latter from the former.   Although the word race has no meaning in science, its use in social science is persistent.   For example Sammy Smooha's entry on ethnic groups in Adam Kuper and Jessica Kuper's *The Social Science Encyclopedia*   notes that 'one significant distinction is between race and ethnicity.   A racial group is composed of people who are believed to share the same biological make-up, while a non-racial ethnic group is identified by a cultural marker' (1985: 267-269).

In Britain, using Fredrik Barth's conception of the boundary, it was Michael Lyon who attempted to provide a conceptual marker between race and ethnicity in the early 70s.   He introduced categorical difference between race as a boundary of exclusion, a boundary defined and imposed by a dominant group (often, but not always in the majority) and ethnicity as a boundary of inclusion to mean the way members of a particular group would define themselves (Lyon, 1972-3: 1-11; 1973: 1-24).   Although this conception helps to sustain the difference between race and ethnicity, in both folk and analytical traditions, the boundary between the two concepts has remained blurred, especially when the words ethnic and ethnicity have been used to express some idea about race and racial differences.

In Britain, the legal difficulties in making a categorical distinction between race and ethnicity were sharply highlighted in the case of Mandla vs Dowell Lee reported in *All England Law Reports* of 1982(3) and 1983(1). The case concerned a thirteen year old Sikh boy, Gurinder Singh, who had been refused entry at a Birmingham private school. A case was brought against the school for discrimination. In the first instance, the Birmingham County court found that Sikhs were a religious but not an ethnic group. The Court of Appeal, Lord Denning and two other judges upheld the County Court judgment. But in the House of Lords, Lord Fraser of Tullybelton held that if members of groups shared a history, a distinctive cultural tradition, a common geographical origin or descent, common language and literature, a common religion and minority status, then the group could constitute an ethnic group if it also saw itself as a distinct community and was so regarded by others. The Lords emphasised the cultural dimension of the ethnic group and at the same time they argued that the notion of common descent gave members of an ethnic group something akin to a racial aspect. Lord Templeman asserted that although Sikhs did not qualify as a separate race, they were more than a religious sect, 'almost a race, almost a nation'. This case illustrates the degree to which the boundary between race and ethnicity is likely to be blurred in law.

The blurring of ethnicity and culture on the one hand and biological race and culture on the other could present itself as a methodological problem unless the connection between the two was clearly and logically conceptualised. An insightful observation from Talcott Parsons provides some way forward followed by Michel Wieviorka's illuminating paper 'Ethnicity as Action' (1992). In relation to the distinction between race and cultural tradition (which can be read as ethnicity if its cultural component was emphasised more), Parsons says, '. . . with respect to the distinction between race and cultural tradition, it is pertinent to point out that designations of racial groups by colour are themselves cultural symbols' (1985: 74).

Parsons does not pursue the extent to which the pseudo-science of racial typology and hierarchy can be regarded as a cultural expression which symbolised the global rise of the European power. However, his contention that identification of colour has to do with culture rather than with objective facts is an important starting point for an understanding of racial categorisation as a social and cultural process. The history of the Nazi ideology of Aryan superiority and Jewish inferiority provides most extraordinary accounts of the construction of racial differences even when physical differences between groups are not always obvious.

Michel Wieviorka's contribution brings ethnicity and race together in a single conceptual framework. He argues that 'ethnicity refers to a combination of characteristics from the realms of both culture and nature'. Rooted in mechanical solidarity, these groups are identified by an underlying process of ascription. As he explains further, 'when clearly formulated, such characteristics refer to seemingly biological categories such as blood, phenotype or, ultimately race'. The process of differentiation may depend upon the interplay of categories deemed to be natural and cultural[3]. When Wieviorka says, 'ethnicity tends to convey a twofold principle of inferiorisation and differentiation' (1992: 1-2), he encompasses the processes of exclusion and inclusion in his formulation. The Other is both different and inferior at the level of exclusion and also capable of self-esteem and pride in the context of inclusion. The principle of differentiation and inferiorisation refers to marginal and minority statuses of ethnic minorities. In response to exclusion, ethnic minorities mobilise collectively and reactively to campaign for their civil rights - a theme of growing importance throughout Europe.

Ethnicity and Religion

The fallacy of a causal relationship between race and culture can equally apply to assumptions about the relationship between ethnicity and religion. Sociologists and anthropologists who identify ethnicity as a phenomenon of prime importance may argue that the religion members of a group pursue is integral to their ethnicity. The legacy of ideas about the connection between race and culture continues to exert a powerful influence on the construction of this link and leads many to argue, not so much about the religions of ethnic minority groups but about ethnic religion (Burghart, 1987). Although it is perfectly possible to show that links do exist between a particular group and their religion in specific cases, there is no more a one-to- one relationship between ethnicity and religion than there ever was between race and culture. However, the discredited legacy of connection between race and culture continues to influence ideas about the relationship between ethnicity and culture and, by implication, the link between ethnicity and religion. Studies of the religions of minority groups clearly show that their belief systems may encompass a variety of ethnicities especially when members of an ethnic group or an ethnic category may define themselves with reference to some conception of shared descent and similarity of outward appearance as well as common culture.

In the metropolitan societies of Europe, the majority identification of the ethnic minority population and the various categories and groups within it clearly shows that Wieviorka's two-fold principle of differentiation and inferiorisation immediately comes into play underpinned by the 19th century conception of race and typology. As a consequence, the position of minorities is defined with reference to immediately visible differences of colour and appearance in the first instance with the conception of cultural difference implied in it or explicitly related to it even in those situations where differences in colour and appearance may not correspond with any real cultural differences.

As Michael Banton has explained in his lucid essay 'Changing conceptions of race' (1983: 32-59), the word race initially meant descent or lineage. But it acquired a distinctive meaning as a fixed and permanent type throughout the course of 19th century. Physical anthropologists studied a variety of racial types, organised them in hierarchies and attributed to them different degrees of savagery and civilisation. Although more refined and sophisticated knowledge of human societies and cultures disproved racial theories, the heritage of this particular mode of thinking was to sustain itself in social science circles as well as in popular thinking. As Banton has pointed out, the folk concept of race 'draws heavily upon the Typological Theory which has been superseded in science but is not easily expelled from the popular mind because of its appealing simplicity and the ease with which it can be twisted to deal with conflicting evidence' (Banton, 1983: 53).

Besides the hierarchical differentiation between a white majority and a non-white minority, the dominant majority stigmatises ethnic minority groups and their cultures as inferior to what is conventionally regarded as European culture. The process of inferiorisation generates emotionally charged stereotypes about population of non-European origin which, in turn, work to their social, cultural, economic and political disadvantage. The status of marginality and even exclusion from the normal benefits of the civil society including denial of citizenship rights to men, women and their families create grievance, protest and what has now come to be known as the process of ethnic mobilisation (Banton, 1985; Rex, 1992) in which the notion of group solidarity based on common religion may have an important part to play. For a group which is defined as being both different and inferior and denied opportunities to assume identity and status relevant to the main stream of the metropolitan society, self-conception and self-esteem may increasingly focus on religious belief and practices and its reconstruction in a less friendly and even an 'alien milieu' to use an expression from the title of Richard Burghart's study of Hinduism in Britain (1987). These new surroundings, however, have a great deal of influence on culture, social organisation, and identity of individuals from ethnic minority background.

The arguments about the extent to which belief in religion and rituals has declined is a topic of considerable debate among scholars. Theories of modernisation assume that societies have changed from mechanical solidarity to organic solidarity with the social organisation increasingly being marked by both individualism and association to use Durkheimian distinctions (1964: 70-132). To what extent does the validity of this proposition about change apply to non-European populations of ethnic origin in Europe?

Religion Ethnicity and Social Change

Theories of modernisation and paradigms of social change often assume a unilinear direction and a unitary outcome. Dichotomous classification of key categories such as from traditional to modern, from simple to complex, from kinship to association, from status to contract, from multiplex to simplex and from religious to secular often point to directions which are assumed to be unavoidable on the basis of the long term historical development of modern European societies. Influenced by the notion of development and progress as the rationally planned improvement of human condition, these theories are appropriate tools of analysis although they do not provide a full explanation of the complex events of our time which appear to defy the logic of social change regarded as being inherent in the rational unfolding of modernity.

The sociologists and anthropologists who contribute to this volume examine the relationship between religion and ethnicity in the framework of modernity and change but rightly shy away from a simple one-way conception of social change. They recognise the complexity of the relationship between religion, ethnicity and social change and analyse it from a variety of perspectives.   John Rex's essay 'Religion and Ethnicity in the Metropolis' applies distinctions from the sociology of religion to the religions of ethnic minorities.   He uses Britain as an example to illustrate the historical complexity of ethnicity and religion that has gone into British social structure, which, now, incorporates a wide range of groups from ex-colonial societies of the Indian subcontinent, Africa and the Caribbean.   Although the British social structure cannot necessarily mirror the position of ethnic minorities in other European societies, it is doubtless that most European societies share certain common patterns of differentiation and inferiorisation which apply to ethnic minorities of non-European origin in particular.

Chapters which concentrate on Islam in this volume highlight the complex ideological and political processes which create hierarchical differences between the dominant majority and Islamic minorities in Britain and Sweden.   John Eade and Kirsti Kuusela provide detailed accounts of the relationship between dominant institutions and Islamic groups with a particular reference to the need Muslims have felt for the creation of religious space for worship in the construction of mosques. John Eade outlines the case of Bengali Sunni Muslims in Tower Hamlets and the case of Dawoodi Bohras, a Gujarati speaking Shia sect. In both instances, the local whites mounted a campaign to emphasise the other or even foreign character of Islamic groups to put a stop to 'their' alien invasion.   Muslims in Tower Hamlets appear to have been more successful in mobilising themselves to achieve their objective more than the Dawoodi Bohras, who, being dispersed all over the Metropolis, were less effective in putting forward a demand for their own religious space.   There is a remarkable change in the political discourse in which, through the electoral complexity of the local politics, Bengalis moved from a wider secular politics of class and socialist values to a position where they increasingly argued for the Islamic needs of their local community.

Kirsti Kuusela's chapter discusses a similar case for Gothenburg in Sweden. Her account of ethnic residential segregation of Turkish immigrants in Gothenburg is reminiscent of the inner city settlement of Indians and Pakistanis in Birmingham or Bradford.   Although an Ahmaddiya mosque had been built in the city ten years earlier without any local protest, the contemporary Turkish Muslim demand for a mosque of their own has aroused strong opposition.   Rising unemployment and declining welfare provision coupled with growing hostility towards visible foreigners goes some way towards explaining strong local opposition to the construction of a mosque. In both the instances the Other and alien character of Islam and its tacit inferiority to Western and Christian liberal values is supplemented by highly emotive and aggressive campaign against Iran throughout the 1980s followed by the Rushdie affair and the Gulf War.

In contrast to the case for preservation of Islamic values in the utilisation of physical space, Haleh Afshar's study of Muslim women in Yorkshire shows their commitment to the best possible education for their children for professional employment. In her analysis, she argues that the third generation of women face constraints of discrimination, obligation to uphold family morality and duties of motherhood which curtail their advancement. As Muslims feel more threatened, the women not only cocoon themselves into their *biraderi* kinship group but return to Islam to belong to the universal community the *umma*. This return to an Islamic fold is similar to the desire of Sunni Bengalis in Tower Hamlets to emphasise the value of Islam more than the principle of universal political participation.

The question of political organisation among the Muslims in Europe has become highly significant here. Ahmed Andrews describes the foundation of the Jamat-i-Islami party in Britain to examine the extent to which it represents the grass root Islamic communities of the Indian subcontinental origin. His study and analysis show that the middle class and literate followers of Maulana Maududi, who founded the Jamaat, have managed to position themselves to influence both the local as well as the institutional view of Islam without being representative of the tradition of ordinary Muslims. Recent Studies show that Islamic organisations have proliferated in Europe (Shadid and van Konnisveld, 1991; 1992) and Muslims in Britain have seen the founding of both an Islamic Political Party as well as Kalim Sidiqui's Islamic Parliament which evoked many negative reactions[4]. How far such bodies represent views and feelings of ordinary Muslims is a question which needs further investigation.

Roger Ballard and Darshan Singh Tatla provide chapters on the question of religion, ethnicity and modernity in relation to Sikhism and Sikhs. Roger Ballard's account of the politicisation of religion in Punjab raises certain methodological issues. The relationship between Europe and the Indian subcontinent has a depth of several centuries through colonial connections. Now a significant number of Punjabi Sikhs, Hindus, Muslims and Christians have settled in Europe from the beginning of this century. Their contemporary position in Europe or North America is much less comprehensible without an understanding of their historical background shaped and formed by British influences in particular. Both Ballard and Tatla emphasise this point. Given the influence which events in Punjab has on Sikhs in Britain and America - a theme more explicitly explored by Darshan Singh Tatla, it is possible to have an appreciation of the forces which have structured Sikh religious identity since 1984. Ballard provides an incisive overview of social changes in Punjab during precolonial and colonial times to argue that the interaction between the Sikhs and the followers of Dayanand Saraswati's Arya Samaj was a critical precondition for the emergence of a more distinctive Sikh identity.

Interaction between groups and a complex construction of boundaries involving the Sikhs, Arya Samajists and the British provides a backdrop against which more recent developments in Punjab can be assessed and evaluated.   Darshan Singh Tatla's account of the mobilisation of Sikhs in Britain shows the powerful effect of events outside Europe on an ethnic minority community resident in Europe.   The Indian government's invasion of the Golden Temple in Amritsar made a strong impact among the Sikhs and brought about, at least initially, a collective political mobilisation among them to protest and to strengthen the campaign for the establishment of the state of Khalistan.   Ballard's study is particularly valuable for showing how changes in ethnicity and ethnic identity, far from being primordial, are contingent upon conditions of modernity.

Although Hindus and Hinduism have not featured as prominently as Muslims and Islam and Sikhs and Sikhism in the West, there has been a Hindu presence in Britain for nearly as long as the length of the British Raj in India (Visram, 1986; Barot, 1988).   The contributors to the study of Hindus in Europe explore the connection between religion and ethnicity in relation to migration and change, which, instead of indicating conventionally assumed patterns of acculturation, show the   reconstruction of tradition, even when the Hindus concerned have been distanced in time and space from India as in the case of Surinam Hindus.

Both Helen Kanitkar and Malory Nye focus on ethnicity and ethnic identity. From her detailed personal and anthropological knowledge of the Maharashtrian Hindus living in Britain, Kanitkar provides a comprehensive account of the *upanayana* ceremony which is usually performed for young boys (and not girls) of the twice-born caste groups.   Accepting the sacred thread to be worn at all times, the young Hindus make a formal entry into being a *brahmachari* student who is assigned to a guru.   Many modern Hindus regard this rite as an ancient custom with little relevance in the modern world.   Kanitkar argues that Maharashtrian Hindu families with middle class background and a comfortable lifestyle, who had not paid much attention to this rite in 1950s and 1960s, now return to the *upanayana* ceremony as an important marker for the young of the fact that they are Hindus and that the *upnayana* marks an important stage in their life and that they cannot enter the next stage of being a householder or a *grihastha* unless they had donned the sacred thread which she sees as an additional element   giving distinctiveness to Hindu identity in Britain.   I have also noted the growing importance of *upanayana* among Gujarati Hindus.   Ceremonies which bring together hundreds of young men for accepting *janoi*, the sacred thread are organised in British cities (*Gujarat Samachar*, 1992 & 1993).

For those social anthropologists who may regard a rite like the *upanayana* as an example of reactive ethnicity, with ethnic minorities asserting pride and self-esteem in a situation where the majority defines their inferiority, Malory Nye's study of the Hindus in Edinburgh has a few comments to offer.   From his recent ethnographic fieldwork, Nye provides an account of the settlement of Gujarati and Punjabi Hindus in Edinburgh.   In British towns and cities where the South Asian population is small, it is not uncommon for Hindus coming from different parts of India to form a single Hindu religious association. Nye's study provides such an example and shows how Hindus from different parts of India establish a temple community which may combine different Hindu rites in the daily routine of religious activities. He also argues with some justification that when the Hindus reproduce their religious institutions in Britain, they do not do so merely to react to the wider white community. They create their religious institutions to reinforce their own culture and identity. Nye makes an important point in conveying the relative degree of autonomy of religion and identity among Hindus with the argument that it is not merely a function of external pressure and circumstances.

In contrast, the settlement of Hindus in Surinam and their migration to the Netherlands when Surinam became independent provides a profile of Hindus who have gone through a series of social, economic and cultural transformations with a keen sense of commitment to their religious identity. Corstiaan van der Burg provides an account of Surinam Hinduism using Louis Dumont's distinction between 'group religion' and 'religion of choice'. The group religion is very much a part of a hierarchical system of statuses while devotional religion offers individual values of choice and equality. In highlighting socio-economic and cultural changes which the Surinam Hindus go through, their sense of affiliation to a religion of social order and hierarchy is nearly replaced by a religion of choice which, to some extent, transcends tradition, and, in the Netherlands in particular, enables them to choose belief and practices which do not replicate their old Hindu tradition. This change is very much a product of migration, displacement, state intervention and modernity. This model of Hinduism which van der Burg has outlined explains social change in terms of ideas about constraints which a religious system imposes on the one hand and the element of choice which arises out of social changes. To what extent this particular model of Surinam Hinduism would apply, for example, to the Hindus in Britain and America is a question which will attract much attention in future.

Both Eleanor Nesbitt and Marianne Freyne-Lindhagen explore the relationship between Christianity and ethnicity for both European and non-European ethnic groups. Nesbitt reports a comparative study of religious nurture among Irish Catholics, Greek Cypriots of Orthodox persuasion, Ukrainian Catholics and finally, Punjabi Christians. Her comparative approach explores a number of distinctive themes. She shows that there is a spectrum of distance that each of these ethnic categories maintains from the mainstream of the Christian tradition in Britain. She also shows that each of these groups has its own religious culture which is distinctive and, at least potentially capable of sustaining a boundary with other Christian denominations. The case of Punjabi Christians is most interesting in showing that their ethnicity and religion are shrouded in a complex web. It can generate stress when, although they identify with the religion of the dominant majority, they nevertheless have to contend with the definition of the otherness which implies stigma and inferiorisation.

Lindhagen presents a fascinating case study of a single Suryoyo woman whose settlement in Sweden is largely determined by immigration and the social policy of the state and its welfare agencies. She analyses the case of Inci with the kind of empathy which allows her to gain an understanding of two conflicting models of Inci's needs. There is the Swedish welfare model which is assumed to provide equal opportunity for the full development of each individual. Lindhagen points out that the presenters of this model are impervious to what it is that Inci considers to be her significant others, especially her mother, whose presence will make her existence more meaningful. If Kirsti Kuusela's analysis is any guide to recent developments in Sweden, it is doubtful if the kind of compassionate understanding Lindhagen advocates is likely to emerge in the current economic and political climate of European states. The immigration policy of most states is unlikely to respond to the needs of those who seek refuge in Europe.

In the final chapter of this volume, Bernard Ineichen examines the connection between mental illness, religion and social change. If the proposition that religion promotes social solidarity is accepted, his findings for British Asians raise more questions which call for further research and analysis. Perhaps the most important finding concerns the rate of suicide amongst women of South Asian origin which can be explained with reference to the institutions of patriarchy and migration. However, the difference in the rate of suicide between Hindus and Muslims requires detailed investigation supplemented by statistical analysis as well as in-depth qualitative studies to isolate the causes of difference between two religious groups. The extent to which religion and differences in the belief systems of the groups are a critical factor in the desire to end life needs further research.

Conclusion

To return to Michel Wieviorka's themes of differentiation and inferiorisation, contributions to this volume on Islam, Sikhism, Hinduism and Christianity do refer to experience of resentment and hostility, especially against people of colour, usually based on racism and prejudice. Although some minority communities may have lived in Europe for a long time, as in Britain, France and Germany, they continue to experience prejudice, exclusion and marginality. Although some states provide legal remedies for the protection of minority rights, it is doubtless that men and women from minority background have suffered humiliating experiences of harassment, abuse and violence. The final writing of this Introduction coincides with Roger Boyes's report 'Blinkered Germans trapped in vicious circle of racism'[5] which gives an account of the neo-Nazi incineration of five Turks in Solingen and the state of marginality among Turks and their exclusion from basic civil rights in reunified Germany. Racism is on rise in Europe with growing levels of xenophobia against 'foreigners'.   As some minorities like Turks become structurally more and more marginal with persistent threats to their well-being, it is certain that this change will increase prospects of civil disorder and mayhem which occurred in British inner cities throughout the earlier part of 1980s. Policies which protect the minorities and honour their rights to living peacefully will be more successful than the policy which calls for aggressive policing and unfair treatment.

Now a vast number of migrants and their families live in secular European democracies in which religion is a matter of the private domain and not a matter of public focus as far as individual belief and practice are concerned. Both sociological as well as social expectations that the importance of religion will begin to decline among minority communities may prove to be untrue. Most of these communities are forming and developing their particular institutions. They are concerned with building temples and mosques and places of worship which are appropriate for their religious needs. Manifestation of their belief system culturally as well in the urban space will increase as they consolidate their settlement in Europe. Unless state policies are correctly directed to reducing social tensions which often underlie the relationship between the dominant majority and ethnic minorities, intolerance and oppression will prevail. The final reflection on the question of the position of ethnic minorities must come from John Rex's contribution to this volume. As for social policy on religion and ethnicity, he argues for a framework of a multicultural society which will allow for a private and communal sphere within which different religious beliefs and customs may be tolerated and fostered. As he rightly concludes, 'it goes without saying that such policies can only be expected to work in a society where there is perceived equality of opportunity for all and in which religion and ethnicity have ceased to be markers of inequality, oppression and exploitation'.

Footnotes

1   See Pocock 1965 and Barot 1980, 1987.
2   I am most grateful to Dr Ian Hamnett for his comments and assistance in highlighting this early use of the Greek word *ethnos*.
3   At one level, the distinction between nature and culture may appear to be obvious. However, whether one is using the category of nature in an objective scientific sense or as an expression of culture may be relevant to a systematic analysis of ethnicity.
4   Iqbal Wahhab reported 'Muslims to set up separate "parliament"' in *The Independent* on Saturday 5 January 1991, p.6. As this report explains, Muslims saw 200 year old British Board of Jewish Deputies as providing a model for a similar organisation for Muslims. The popular media misconstructed the use of the word 'Parliament' to imply that the Muslims wanted to have their own law making body (thus expressing disrespect for the proper British Parliament).
5   *The Times*, June 2, 1993, No.64,660 p.10.

References

Abercombie, A., Hill, S. and Turner, B. S. (1988) *The Penguin Dictionary of Sociology*, Harmondsworth: Penguin Books Ltd.

Ballard, R. and Ballard, C. (1977) in Watson, James L. *Between Two Cultures: Migrants and Minorities in Britain*, Oxford: Basil Blackwell, pp.21-56.

Banton, M. P. (1955) *The Coloured Quarter: Negro Immigrants in an English City*, London: Jonathan Cape.

Banton, M. P. (1972) *Racial Minorities*, London: Fontana.

Banton, M. P. (1983) *Racial and Ethnic Competition*, Cambridge: Cambridge University Press.

Banton, M. P. (1985) *Promoting Racial Harmony*, Cambridge: Cambridge University Press.

Barot, R. (1980) *The Social Organisation of a Swaminarayan Sect in Britain*, London: University of London School of Oriental and African Studies Ph.D. thesis.

Barot, R. (1987) 'Caste and Sect in the Swaminarayan Movement' in Burghart, Richard (ed.) *Hinduism in Great Britain: The perpetuation of religion in an alien milieu*, London: Tavistock Publications, pp.67-80.

Barot, R. (1988) *Bristol and the Indian Independence Movement*, Bristol: University of Bristol Historical Association.

Barth, F. (1969) *Ethnic Groups and Boundaries: The Social Organisation of Culture Difference*, Boston: Little Brown & Co.

Brown, C. (1984) *Black and White Britain: The Third PSI Survey*, London: Heinemann Educational Books Ltd.

Burghart, R. (ed.) (1987) *Hinduism in Great Britain: The perpetuation of religion in an alien milieu*, London: Tavistock Publication.

Cohen, A. (1969) *Custom and Politics in Urban Africa*, London: Routledge.

Cohen, A. (1974a) *Urban Ethnicity*, London: Tavistock Publications.

Cohen, A. (1974b) *Two Dimensional Man: An Essay on the Anthropology of Power in Complex Society*, London: Routledge.

Dahya, B. (1974) 'The nature of Pakistani Ethnicity in Industrial Cities in Britain' in Cohen, Abner (ed.) *Urban Ethnicity*, London: Tavistock Publications, pp.77-118.

Daniel, W. W. (1968) *Racial Discrimination in England: Based on the PEP Report*, Harmondsworth: Penguin Books Ltd.

Desai, R. (1963) *Indian Immigrants in Britain*, London: Oxford University Press for the Institute of Race Relations.

Durkheim, E. (1964) *The Division of Labour in Society*, New York: The Free Press.

Glazer, N. and Moynihan, D. P. (1975) *Ethnicity: Theory and Experience*, London: Harvard University Press.

Lyon, M. (1972-73) 'Ethnic Minority in Britain: the Gujarati tradition', *New Community* 2, pp.1-11.

Lyon, M. (1973) 'Ethnic Minority Problems: an overview of some recent research', *New Community*, 7, pp.1-24.

Parsons, T. (1975) 'Some Theoretical Considerations on the Nature and Trends of Change of Ethnicity' in Glazer, N. and Moynihan, D. P. (eds.) (1975) *Ethnicity: Theory and Experience*, London: Harvard University Press, pp.53-83.

Patterson, S. (1961) *Dark Strangers: A Study of West Indians in London*, Harmondsworth: Penguin Books.

Pocock, D. (1976) 'Preservation of the Religious Life: Hindu Immigrants in Britain', *Contributions to Indian Sociology*, New Series, 10(2), pp.342-365.

Rex, J. and Moore, R. (1967) *Race, Community and Conflict: A Study of Sparkbrook*, London: Oxford University Press.

Rex, J. (1991) *Ethnic Identity and Ethnic Mobilisation in Britain*, Coventry: University of Warwick Centre for Ethnic Relations.

Rose, E. J. B. (1969) *Colour and Citizenship: A Report on British Race Relations*, London: Oxford University Press for the Institute of Race Relations.

Sammy, S. (1985) 'Ethnic Groups' in Kuper, A. and Kuper, J. (eds) *The Social Science Encyclopedia*, London: Routledge, pp.267-272.

Shadid, W. A. R. and van Koningsveld, P. S. (eds) (1991) *The Integration of Islam and Hinduism in Western Europe*, Kampen: Kok Pharos Publishing House.

Shadid, W. A. R. and van Koningsveld, P. S. (eds.) (1992) *Islam in Dutch Society: Current Developments and Future Prospects*, Kampen: Kok Pharos Publishing House.

Simpson, J. and Weiner, E. (1991) *The Compact Oxford English Dictionary*, Oxford: Oxford University Press.

Smith, D. (1977) *Racial Disadvantage in Britain: The PEP Report*, Harmondsworth: Penguin Books Ltd.

Souter, A. (1916) *A Pocket Lexicon to the Greek New Testament*. Oxford: The Clarendon Press.

Visram R. (1986) *Ayahs, Lascars and Princes: The Story of Indians in Britain 1700-1947*, London: Pluto Press.

Watson, J. L. (1977) *Between Two Cultures: Migrants and Minorities in Britain*, Oxford: Basil Blackwell.

Wieviorka, M. (1992) 'Ethnicity as Action'.   A paper presented at Ethnic Mobilisation in Europe in the 1990s Conference, University of Warwick Centre for Research in Ethnic Relations.

Williams, J. (1967) 'The Younger Generation' in John Rex and Robert Moore's (1967) *Race, Community and Conflict: A Study of Sparkbrook*, London: Oxford University Press, pp.230-257.

Newspapers:

Gujarat Samachar 1992/1993: London

2

Religion and Ethnicity in the Metropolis

John Rex

It has become increasingly clear that in any mapping of the ethnic minority populations in Britain and Europe religion is an important differentiating factor. It divides groups with shared geographical, national, linguistic and ethnic origins, and sometimes unites groups with different origins of these other sorts. In the European context, Britain provides a very good example of the kind of complexity which is typical of ethnic minority population. Thus Indians are divided between Hindus, Sikhs, Muslims, Christians and others. Pakistani Muslims are divided into different Muslim sects and West Indians are divided in terms of their different Christian beliefs and practices. On the other hand Muslims with different ethnic and national origins may be united by their sectarian religious affiliation and West Indian Christians may be united with groups of fellow believers in the indigenous British population. Such divisions and unities may rest upon shared beliefs and world views only, or they may be expressed in shared congregational organisation around a place of worship.

The Theory of Religion and Ethnicity

Religion and Group Formation

Religious diversity has been shown in the sociology of religion to have important economic and political consequences. Thus Weber, who was primarily concerned with the affinity between capitalist behaviour and Calvinism sought to place that affinity within a wider comparative context in his *Sociology of Religion* (1963), while Troeltsch, dealing with Christianity, suggested that a belief in the Kingdom of God resulted in a variety of politically relevant attitudes to the institutions of 'The World'. Even though the focus of these studies was on Christianity, the theorisations to which they led have been extended and are further extendible to the analysis of the problem of the relation between non-Christian beliefs and social organisation.

Weber made a four-fold distinction between the World Salvation religions (1968: 399-634) (setting on one side Confucianism, which he saw as a religion, not of salvation, but of adaptation to the world). These were religions based on Other-Worldly Mysticism, which sought to flee the world of which the principle exemplar was Hinduism, Inner-worldly Mysticism which sought detachment from the world while remaining within it, as is exemplified by Buddhism, Other-Worldly Ascetism involving self-mastery in the pursuit of Other-worldly goals, as is found in some forms of Christian Monasticism, and Inner-Worldly Ascetism, involving living in the world but seeking to master it.

Inner-Worldly Mysticism was most completely represented for Weber by Calvinism, but this is a relative matter and, compared with Hinduism and Buddhism, the whole of the Judaeo-Christian tradition as well as Islam are to be thought of as falling under the heading of Inner-Worldly Mysticism. Weber also makes a distinction, however, between the sphere within which World Mastery occurs. It might relate to the economic, the political, the sexual or the aesthetic sphere. Calvinism expresses itself through economic activity as well as through sexual self-discipline, while Islam addresses itself more to the world of social and political organisation.

According to Troeltsch, Christ had no social teachings as such but, in talking of the Kingdom of God, posed for Christians the relation between that Kingdom and the institutions of the world (1931). A full range of possible answers are to be found in the history of Christianity including Paul's belief that 'the powers that be are ordained by God' to order human life in a fallen and sinful world through to recurrent revolutionary notions that the institutions of the World are to be overthrown and replaced by those of God's Kingdom. Between these, however, there are also many other alternatives such as that offered by Aquinas who envisaged a relative natural law which would serve as a stage on the way back to man's recovered vision of God or that of the Calvinists, who, assuming that God alone could bring about his Kingdom, sought to make themselves into finely tuned instruments through whom God could achieve his purposes.

These distinctions which Troeltsch developed in his study *The Social Teachings of the Christian Churches* are in principle also applicable to other world religions and I have suggested in another essay that they might be applied to the differentiating of Islamic sects with their differing attitudes to the Islamic State (Rex, 1988: 206, 218).

Ethnicity, Ethnic Groups and Religion

Religious beliefs of these kinds provide a basis for group formation and for the mobilisation of these groups for social and political conflict and co-operation. Yet even prior to the emergence of such religiously based grouping men are united by the simple bonds of ethnicity as such. Geertz, for example, sees religion as one amongst a number of commonalities which are primordial in the human condition and which lead to consciousness of kind and group formation. He speaks of 'the assumed givens of social existence: immediate continuity and live connection mainly, but beyond them the givenness that stems from being born into a particular religious community, speaking a particular language, or even a dialect of a particular language and following particular social practices'. Such ties he argues, exist independently of 'personal attraction, tactical necessity, common interest or incurred moral obligation' (Geertz, 1963).

Other theorists of ethnicity, following Frederick Barth, have suggested that in practice ethnicity is not simply primordial or given in this way but that it is a resource which is used in situations of 'tactical necessity' (Barth, 1969). Nonetheless even this theory assumes that there is a resource available and ethnicity must to some extent be regarded as a given.

What is given, that is the world in which, say a five year old child, finds himself or herself placed, leads, however, by itself to the formation of only small and fairly localised groups. It is the task of political, cultural and intellectual leaders to extend these bonds more widely by developing symbols to which members of many localised groups may respond as representing them and their kind. Quite commonly such symbolic appeals are attached not merely to people but to a territory. As a result there emerge ethnic nations. On the other hand it may the case that those united by the symbols share not so much a common territory as common economic or political interests in a situation of conflict. In this case what emerges is not an ethnic nation but an ethnic class.

Ethnic leaders, however, may also seek to appeal to religious ideas which exist amongst their clientele, while religious leaders, concerned with the whole question of the disparity between the world as it is and the world as God would have it be, may well address themselves specifically to the aspirations and felt injustices of ethnic nations and classes. Religion and ethnicity thus compete for loyalty and religious and ethnic groups overlap. Generally, however, the world religions appeal to a wider constituency than that of a single ethnic group and religious identity may sometimes have a stronger basis than mere ethnic identity mainly because of its claim to sacredness. The most tightly bound groups, on the other hand, are likely to be those in which ethnic and religious community coincide.

Migration, Ethnicity and Religion

All that has been said above involves an oversimplified model in which religious ideas and concepts of ethnicity and ethnic groups are developed *ab initio* in a specific social, economic, political and geographical situation. Hinduism and Sikhism are seen as emerging in the Indian sub-continent, Islam in the Middle East or Christianity in the Middle East and Europe. The problem of the social function of religious beliefs is then seen as one of its functions in relation to a specific historical and geographical context. But religions survive their original historical context and ethnic and religious groups migrate to wholly different contexts. In these circumstances we have to consider both their continuing debate about the circumstances in their point of origin and their changing ideas as they relate to new contexts. We must expect that there will be religious and ethnic traditionalists continually trying to purify their beliefs and practices to get them back to what was appropriate in the times and places of their origin and new creative forms which seek to adapt to their new situation and handle the new problems which that situation presents. Thus in contemporary European societies today we have a wide range of religious and ethnic groups whom we have to understand as developing their beliefs and practices not merely in relation to the world of the here and now, but in relation to past and distant social and political contexts. To use specific

British examples to illustrate this, West Indians will be addressing not merely the problems of a relatively deprived group of immigrants to Britain but the whole problem of the enslavement and transportation to the Americas, and British Asians will have to resolve not merely their problems as migrant workers and businessmen, but all the old problems of the sub-continent and questions of group relations in the Moghul and British Empires.

The Diversity of Religion and Ethnicity in Contemporary Britain

There is no need here to rehearse the statistical facts of migration to Britain since 1945. All that needs be said is that in post-war Britain there were both labour gaps and business opportunities which were filled and taken up by migrants from Ireland, from the Caribbean, from the Indian sub-continent, and from East Africa. Thus there were inserted into a society already marked by its own class, status, regional and religious divisions, ethnic, religious, national and linguistic groups from the outer parts of empire whose structure, culture and belief systems had been developed in colonial and post-colonial contexts. It is against this background that we have to consider the forms of ethnic and religious groupings to be found among West Indians and Asians in Britain. To be more comprehensive we should also consider other minorities like the Irish who are differentiated from the British both in terms of their ethnic and national history and in terms of their religion, but space and time here demand that we should concentrate on the already rich diversity amongst West Indians and Asians.

West Indian Ethnicity, Culture and Religion in Britain

West Indians in Britain, unlike their Asian fellow immigrants, share much with the British. Their ancestral African culture having been virtually destroyed by slavery and colonialism, the culture which they acquired was a version of British culture. *Prima facie* therefore one would expect that they would be able relatively easily to take their place in British society. Yet any serious look at the society and culture of the West Indies would show them to be sharply differentiated from the British in terms of their colour and their class history and even in their language and religion.

Clearly the experience of slavery has left its mark both on the social structure and culture of the West Indians and their relationship with British people. Slavery destroyed family life amongst the slave population and in the aftermath of slavery, though the two parent nuclear family became an ideal for the respectable emergent middle classes, strong traces of the matricental system which was forced upon the slaves remains. So far as culture is concerned, while again the middle classes might aspire to a British and even ultra British life-style, the culture of the poor majority has been creolised so that even the version of English spoken has some of the characteristics of a distinct language. In class terms too, though West Indian workers have adopted British forms of organisation, there is widespread unemployment, the jobs which exist are insecure, and relations between employers and workers are still marked by a degree of unfreedom which differentiates them as migrants from the established, privileged and incorporated working class.

Inevitably in these terms the immigrant population which confronts the British is at first at least differentiated from it in cultural and class terms. West Indians have tended to become a distinct class-fraction or, as some would say, an underclass in British society. Only a small elite has been able to deploy its Britishness to obtain easier acceptance and even for this elite colour prejudice has stood between them and their white peers.

The social and cultural distinction which exists between the small elite who aspire to Britishness and the society and the culture of the masses is also reflected in religion. Many, and not merely the elite have joined the Anglican Church, thereby accepting the most established version of British culture and the mainstream Non-Conformist denominations with their more working class bias have also attracted West Indians to their congregations. This is true both in the West Indies itself and amongst migrants in Britain. Nonetheless the minority religion which stands out is that of the Pentecostalist Churches, while even West Indian Non-Conformity as practiced in the West Indies, shares some of the features of Pentecostalism.

Pentecostal religion is marked by very regular church attendance, charismatic preaching and responses and by a tight and puritanical control over the behaviour of members. A religious congregation of this kind becomes the focal point in the social life of its members. More than any other group such a congregation defines the identity of its members. Most such congregations are small and localised but some of the longer established churches like the New Testament Church of God are now large national organisations which approach the status of the Non-Conformist denominations.

Looking at these churches in what may be called Troeltschian terms, they tend to be politically quietistic, recognizing that God's Kingdom is not of this world, even though such a Kingdom involves a great reversal of the injustices which its members have to suffer in the here and now. At the same time, because religious ecstasy is coupled with puritanical self-discipline in daily life, these churches may also encourage educational success, hard work and, therefore, relative economic success.

Quite different from the more orthodox forms of Christian religion and from Pentecostalism however, is the Rastafarian movement. Rastafarianism sees the political world of Britain as Babylon and, basing itself on the Book of Exodus, seeks the release of its members, not merely from present Babylons but from all the evil done to African people over four hundred years, by a return to Africa where Halle Sellasie or Rastafarai was able to resist colonialism because he was God Incarnate. In the present Rastas read the Bible, hold reasoning sessions and smoke ganga. Theirs is not a revolutionary movement, even though perforce they find themselves in more or less continual battle with police who harass them, but they look for a reversal not in a Kingdom of God which is not of this world, but in Africa which is the Zion to which they hope to return. Here clearly one has an eclectic religion partially based on Christianity which does not simply seek to adjust people to living in a capitalist metropolis. It offers to its members a chance of opting out. Though there is some evidence that the movement is in decline since its heyday in the seventies it has left its mark and provided a religious basis for the Black struggle against discrimination, exploitation and oppression. Not of least interest is the fact that though it is originally a Jamaican movement it has spread to Blacks in other West Indian islands, to Africa itself and widely amongst the children of Black British immigrants.

Indian Ethnicity and Religion in Britain

Indian ethnicity in Britain is based largely on the culture of Gujarat and the Punjab. Indian religion involves Hinduism, Sikhism, Islam as well as Christianity and several minor sects which emerged from Hinduism. We may leave Islam aside for the moment because it merges with the Islam of the Pakistanis and, so far as the small number of Christians are concerned, they are absorbed into the mainstream churches. The main expressions of Indian religion in Britain are, therefore, Hinduism and Sikhism.

The social function of Hinduism in Britain is not easy to understand for two reasons. One is that Hindu religion is practised as much at home as in specific places of worship. The other is that, unlike the religions of the Middle East which are based upon sacred books laying down some kind of moral and social code, Hinduism is as much concerned with man's relationship with Nature. Nonetheless there are Hindu temples in increasing numbers and these operate as social centres for Indian populations. They may be dedicated to any of the Hindu gods or to human figures like Ram or Krishna and the activity of the temple is devoted to the adoration of these divine, semi-divine and human figures. Within this context, too, temples are visited by learned teachers whose sermons may well reflect what is thought of as Hindu teaching on social issues. Temple committees, moreover, are much concerned with charitable work and with liaison with other communities and with the local council.

Communities and temples are divided on linguistic and caste lines, not so much out of an ideological commitment to the caste system, but because these are, amongst Indians, natural communities. The Gujarati community and Gujarati organisations and temples are wealthier than those based on the Punjab, and, Weber's observations on the Other Worldly Mysticism notwithstanding, Gujarati Hindus have enjoyed or achieved great success in business, in the professions and in education.

Sikhism by contrast includes a strong artisan element amongst its followers, though there are increasing numbers of successful Sikh businessmen and Sikh children are doing well at school and making their way into higher education and the professions. The Sikh presence is more evident than that of the Hindus because Sikhs wear turbans and try to retain the five symbols of Sikhism.

Three important features of Sikh life distinguish it from Hinduism. One is the greater importance of the temple or *gurdwara*; a second is the fact of Sikh Monotheism; and a third is the existence of more explicit social teaching based upon the writings of the Gurus. Services in the temple are based upon readings from the holy books and on a collective kitchen which enables the community to eat together. Nonetheless it is important to recognize that there is considerable overlap between Sikhism and Punjabi Hinduism.

As amongst Hindus, so amongst Sikhs, there are caste divisions reflected in the control of the temples. The most important of these is that between the Jats who come from a landowning group in the Punjab, and the Ramgarias who have come mainly via East Africa and, as a result, despite their inferior position in the Punjab, have greater wealth than Jats from the Punjab. It would be wrong, however, to see these distinctions as rigid or to imagine that Jats would be turned away from Ramgaria temples or vice versa.

More than any other immigrant religious groups, Sikhs are concerned with politics. They move easily into working class and Labour politics and the Marxist Indian Workers Associations which have largely Sikh memberships provide a bridge with indigenous labour. Even more significantly, however, they continue to be involved in the politics of the Punjab and Sikhism has also become a religion of nationalism. The struggle for control of the temples is therefore often fought out between rival groups with differing attitudes to an independent state of Khalistan. The more militant pro-Khalistani groups, moreover, see Britain and Canada as bases from which their national struggle can be pursued. In the Sikh case clearly religion, ethnicity and nationalist politics are deeply intertwined.

Before leaving the discussion of Indian religion, we should also note that it is by no means static. New eclectic cults arise drawing upon Hinduism, Sikhism, Buddhism and Christianity and some of these achieve large followings. Amongst the most important of these is the Ravi Dass sect which appeals especially to outcaste and lower caste Indians seeking to upgrade themselves and to strengthen their identity and morale by adopting religious practices from the other religions and building their own temples. A sociology of religion amongst immigrant groups in Britain would not be complete without an exploration of these new creative developments.

Ethnicity and Religion amongst Muslim Immigrants

Islam has far more in common with the Judaeo-Christian tradition than does Hinduism. Literally the term Islam means submission to God; there is one God, Allah; his prophet is Mohammed and the messages which God conveyed to him are contained in a holy book, the Koran. To a greater extent than any other religion Islam claims to be not merely a religion but a whole way of life. Yet, because the duties of a Muslim include prayer five times a day, mosques and other places of prayer and the congregations who pray there are an evident feature of life amongst Muslim immigrants wherever they are.

The principle groups of Muslim immigrants to Britain are, of course from Pakistan and Bangladesh, though there are also many Indian Gujarati Muslims as well as others from East Africa and the Middle East. Amongst Pakistanis many come from the Pakistani Punjab, from the district of Mirpur in what Pakistanis call Azad Kashmir, from the North West Frontier province and from the Sylhet district of Bangladesh. The main forms of Islam in Britain reflect the sectarian divisions to be found in these areas of origin. It should be added also that, given these points of origin, Pakistanis are poorer than Indians and that Bangladeshis are the poorest of all South Asian immigrants.

There are relatively few Shias amongst Muslims in Britain though there are mosques based upon the wealthy Ismaili "Sevener" community who follow the Aga Khan and many of whom come via East Africa, as well as a smaller number of Pakistani Shias. The great bulk of Muslims in Britain, however, are Sunnis who follow the teachings of the Hanafi law schools. Amongst these Hanafi Muslims the principle divisions are between the traditionalist groups who are the overwhelming majority and the small but tightly organised religious and political organisation, Jamaat-i-Islami, which seeks to claim the modern world for Islam, and, amongst the traditionalists, between the Deobandis who are concerned to eliminate Hindu and pagan elements from South Asian Islam and the Barelwis who are led by Sufis and who incorporate into their teachings the ideas of the international Sufi orders.

The Deobandis are complete traditionalists in that they seek to justify their teachings by reference to the Koran, the Hadith and the teachings of the Hanafi law school. They strongly reject the Barelwi belief in intercession with God through living and dead saints. Even more traditionalist is the sect Jamiat Ahl E Hadith based originally on the Wahabi movement in Saudi Arabia which seeks to go back beyond the teachings of the Law Schools and to base itself solely on the Koran and the Hadith. The Deobandis are not at all concerned with political questions in Britain but solely with the purity of Islam. Jamiat Ahl E Hadith on the other hand is often concerned with immediate moral and social connections in the diaspora and, so far as its British members many of whom come from Mirpur are concerned, has a circumstantial commitment of an ethnic nationalist kind to the liberation of Kashmir from India parallelling the Sikh commitment to Khalistan.

The Barelwis are actually the largest single group in Britain. They add to ordinary Islamic teaching the teachings of the Sufis, placing great emphasis upon a discipline which liberates the spirit from the flesh. British Sufi leaders recognize the leadership of so-called *pirs* or holy men in Pakistan and although Pakistan is their main point of reference, they and their *pirs* are usually members of the Naqshbandi Sufi order which extends into the Middle East and the Soviet Union. Sufi teaching and practices range from quite sophisticated philosophic doctrines to simple popular magical practices.

Amongst the Deobandis there is a revivalist movement known as the Tabligh Jammat, which, although originating in India is to be found throughout Europe and Africa. Its British headquarters are in Dewsbury, where imams are trained, and from where missionaries go out to all parts of the country as well as abroad, not to convert non-Muslims, but to urge those who are Muslims to practice their Islam more fully. Tabligh's teaching is entirely non-political.

In contrast to these traditionalist movements is the political and religious movement known as Jamaat-i-Islami. Far from being based upon a return to a traditionalist reading of the scriptures, the Jamaat-i-Islami, represented in Britain by the U.K. Islamic Mission places great emphasis upon 'ijtihad' or interpretation, and particularly the interpretation of the scriptures by its founder the Maulana Maududi. Maududi believed in turning Pakistan into an Islamic state and in the creation of a tight-knit (one might say, Leninist) type of organisation for the achievement of its aim. The U.K. Islamic Mission has yet to make clear the relevance of the doctrine of the Islamic state to Muslims who live as minorities in non-Muslim countries.

It is not helpful to describe any of these organisations as 'fundamentalist'. It would be better in fact to distinguish simply between traditionalists, who are primarily concerned with adherence to the scriptures, and Islamicists, seeking to claim the modern world for Islam. There is no way in which the traditionalists would seek the political transformation of society, whereas such a goal is projected by the Islamicists, under slogans like `Capitalism has failed, so has Communism. Islam is the answer', even though they are not concerned with textual literalism.

It is by no means easy to understand the various Islamic groups in Britain in terms of simple Weberian and Troeltschian, or indeed Geertzian or Barthian categories. Something should be said, however, about the way in which such sects relate to society. Overwhelmingly they tend towards political quietism and the most common response to questions about their social teaching is that they want their members to be good citizens. Nonetheless there are several ways in which they find themselves at odds with British society.

The first of these perhaps is that most forms of Islam insist that their teachings offer a fairly rigid blueprint for social conduct and do not recognize, as Christianity has come to do over the past three centuries, a non-religious secular world of economics and politics, though this is less true of the Islamicist type of group. The second is that Islamicist groups do aspire to an Islamic state. The third is that all Muslims feel the need to defend their religion against what they see as the cynical and blasphemous type of attack represented by Rushdie's *Satanic Verses*. The fourth is that Muslims are concerned, however much they may value educational opportunities such as Britain provides, that such education should not undermine the Islamic way of life of their children. While I do not believe that any of these problems are not resolvable by dialogue, it does seem that such dialogue is prevented at the moment by the insecurity felt by poor Muslims on the one hand and by the kind of racist xenophobia which is evidenced by British people when they regard Muslims indiscriminately as 'fundamentalists'. Nor can it be replaced by the writings of rich middle-class Muslims who have adapted themselves easily to living in a capitalist society by abandoning much that is distinctive about Islam.

Conclusion

From all that I have said it should be clear that we have in Britain today a wide variety of ethnic and religious groups, who in their cultural and religious thinking and practice still have to work out their relationship both with their pre-migration colonial situation and with the position of their members in British society. What British social and cultural policy will have to do is threefold and this may apply to policy in other European states: firstly to leave space for the working out of these problems by the various groups; secondly to promote dialogue to find common values between immigrant and indigenous belief systems; and, thirdly, to allow within the framework of a multi-cultural society for a private and communal sphere within which different religious beliefs and customs may be tolerated and fostered. It goes without saying that such policies can only be expected to work in a society where there is perceived equality of opportunity for all and in which religion and ethnicity have ceased to be markers of inequality, oppression and exploitation.

References

Barth, F. (1969) *Ethnic Groups and Boundaries*, London: George Allen and Unwin Ltd.
Geertz, C. (1963) *Old Societies and New States - The Quest for Modernity in Asia and Africa*, Glencoe: Free Press, Illinois.
Rex, J. (1988) The Urban Sociology of Religion and Islam in Britain in Gerholm Tomas and Lithman Yngve (eds.) *The New Islamic Presence in Western Europe*, London: Mansell Publishing Limited, pp. 206-218.
Troeltsch, E. (1931), *The Social Teaching of the Christian Churches*, London: George Allen and Unwin Ltd.
Weber, M. (1963) *The Sociology of Religion*. Boston: Beacon Press.
Weber, M. (1968), *Economy and Society*, Vol 1, Chapter 6, New York: Bedmister Press.

3

The Political Articulation of Community and the Islamisation of Space in London

John Eade

This chapter examines the ways in which community identities are articulated in local debates about the use of urban space. The debates which I discuss were carried out in local newspapers and were part of political conflicts which heightened a sense of social and cultural difference between Muslims and non-Muslims. The use of Muslim religious and community centres or the possible construction of those centres encouraged protest from local white residents and political activists which focused on religious difference rather than secular sources of community affiliation such as class which cut across religious boundaries.

Around public buildings in two areas of London (Tower Hamlets and Ealing) there developed a discourse of community belonging which proposed a sharp cultural divide between white residents - the 'real' locals - and Muslim outsiders. This discourse formed an intimate part of local political conflicts where notions of an alien Islamic invasion could be exploited in contests between major political parties for the support of white voters. Bangladeshi secular activists in Tower Hamlets, for example, were forced onto the defensive by debates which directed attention away from the need for such resources as housing, education and jobs to the rights of Muslims to use public space, no matter what their country or origin or class position.

The focus on Islam in London has been strengthened during the last five years by national and international events such as *The Satanic Verses* controversy and the recent Gulf war. The appearance of mosques and community centres has visibly reminded white residents of the expansion of Muslim settlers and the demands made on public space as locales change socially and culturally. Muslim representations of their Islamic needs have now locked into white debates about a visible and audible Muslim presence. Although the debates concentrated on religion as a basis of community identity and suggested an increasing polarisation between Muslims and non-Muslims the concepts used by non-Muslims also referred to other notions of belonging which were sometimes racist i.e. to a British or English nation whose cultural heritage was threatened by Muslim outsiders.

The aim of this chapter is to shed light on issues which have attracted scant interest, viz. political debates and conflicts concerned with the physical representation of communities in urban space. Recent post-structuralist accounts of the complex heterogeneous ways in which space is politically and ideologically constructed suggest paths which I hope to explore in a subsequent paper - see, for example, Game (1991) Shields (1991) and Short (1991).

Tower Hamlets and the Establishment of Mosques

This borough adjoins the city of London, the famous 'square mile' of international high finance. Tower Hamlets has until recently been a predominantly working class area depending upon employment in the docks, the garment trade, brewing, paper manufacture, furniture and other specialised crafts. The area has been intimately associated with the settlement of Protestant (Calvinist) Huguenot silk-weavers during the seventeenth century to Irish Catholics in the eighteenth and the first half of the nineteenth century, Russian and Polish Jews at the end of the nineteenth century, Chinese, and more recently, settlers from Malta, Cyprus, the Caribbean, Somalia and Bangladesh. Bangladeshis are now the largest ethnic minority in the borough (over 20 per cent of the population or around 25,000) and in some of the western wards the proportion of Bangladeshis ranges from 30 per cent to over 50 per cent.

The establishment of mosques in the area has been deeply influenced by Bangladeshi settlement since the overwhelming majority are *Sunni* Muslims of the *Hanafi* persuasion. Not surprisingly the well established mosques are based in the western and central wards which form the heartland of the 'Muslim community'. The first building to be used for congregational worship, the East London Mosque, was on the Commercial Road near the docks and served the Bengali *lascars* who jumped ship and stayed on in Britain to work in the Midlands manufacturing industry, to travel the country as pedlars, to set up the first 'Indian restaurants' and work in London's major hotels (Adams, 1987).

The East London Mosque was initially based in private accommodation but in 1985 it moved to purpose-built accommodation on the nearby Whitechapel Road. The new centre provided facilities for a large congregation as well as a bookshop, administrative offices, living accommodation, shops and a funeral service. During the last five years the prominent location and the diverse activities associated with this mosque enabled its leaders to gain a high profile at least amongst white outsiders, especially local and central government officials, politicians, teachers and welfare workers.

During the early 1970s the East London Mosque's management committee studied the possibilities of taking over a building on Brick Lane, Spitalfields, which symbolised the area's intimate association with overseas settlers. It was built by the Huguenots in 1742 and after a period when it was used as a Methodist chapel it was leased in 1895 to an ultra Orthodox Jewish society, the *Machkizei Hadtha*, which worked among the rapidly expanding population of Polish and Russian Jews. The building was adapted for congregational worship and for teaching (supplementing the work of the adjoining *Talmud Torah* school).

In the event the former synagogue was bought by a group of Bangladeshi businessmen and became known rather grandly as the London Great Mosque (*Jamme Masjid*). The building was once again used for religious teaching with the establishment of a *madrassah* and the link with Bangladeshi entrepreneurs form the locality and further afield was cemented by the use of an adjoining building on Fournier Street by the oldest Bengali community organisation, the Bangladesh Welfare Association (BWA).

The two mosques developed contrasting and competing styles. In terms of religious emphasis the Brick Lane Great Mosque recruited *mullahs* associated with the *barelvi* tradition while the East London Mosque was *deobandi*. The Brick Lane mosque was closely linked from the beginning to the Bangladesh government and the Bangladesh High Commission in London - an association which was celebrated by official visits to the mosque by President Ershad. The East London Mosque, on the other hand, relied more heavily on its contacts with Arab states in the Middle East. King Fahd of Saudi Arabia had contributed £1,100,000 of the £2,000,000 total cost and the ambassadors from Saudi Arabia and Egypt were members of the mosque's management committee.

Religious leaders at the Brick Lane Great Mosque had not established many ties with Bangladeshi community organisations and non-Muslim outsiders largely because of the prominent role played by the neighbouring BWA. The leaders of the East London Mosque, on the other hand, were eager to widen their connections with local community organisations and non-Muslims in order to challenge the role played by the BWA. Their building was used by the *Da'wat ul Islam*, a missionary organisation based in Bangladesh and Pakistan whose youth wing, the Young Muslim Organisation, held meetings in the mosque and rented offices in the adjoining street. The funeral director at the East London Mosque was active in another missionary organisation, the *Tabligh Jama'at*, which also occupied a former synagogue in the nearby St. Katharine's ward, while the secretary of the management committee was a leading member of the Council of Mosques U.K. and Eire, a national pressure group supported by Saudi Arabia and located in Central London.

The organisations and individuals associated with the East London Mosque gave the new centre a range of contacts at local and more global levels which were more cosmopolitan than the predominantly Bangladeshi ties established by the Brick Lane mosque through its links with the leaders of the BWA. The East London Mosque welcomed visits from local schools and colleges and its bookshop stocked well prepared English publications on Islam which were produced mainly by groups associated with the *Da'wat ul Islam*.

Although other mosques had emerged during the settlement of Bangladeshis in Tower Hamlets, the Brick Lane, Great Mosque and the East London Mosque played the most important roles in public debates about the presence of Islam in the borough.   Since most Muslims in Tower Hamlets were Bangladeshis those debates reflected factional struggles between Bangladeshi community leaders and organisations as well as the pressure of outsiders such as local government planners, politicians, non-Muslim businessmen and residents.

Disputes over the Use of Mosques in Tower Hamlets: The Brick Lane Great Mosque and Spitalfields redevelopment

A number of public debates developed during the 1980s concerning the use of the buildings occupied by the Brick Lane and East London mosques.   These disputes revealed the different ways in which buildings could be perceived and the impact of political and economic pressures on the operation of the mosques and on the strategies which mosque leader pursued.   The Brick Lane Mosque occupied an eighteenth century site which was 'listed as a building of architectural and historical interest'[1].   It was located in a conservation area which began to be 'gentrified' during the 1980s with Bangladeshi garment shops and tenants moving out to be replaced by affluent white owner-occupiers, City offices and up-market shops. Although Brick Lane had become widely known as the centre of the Bangladeshi ethnic business enclave, the changes taking place to the west of Brick Lane were rapidly changing the character of Spitalfields.   To white outsiders the mosque occupied a building which was both a physical expression of a non-Muslim local heritage and a gentrified, Georgian present.   For the Muslim congregation the mosque was a building close to their council estate homes and in need of considerable adaptation to their Islamic requirements.

External little has been done to Islamise the building.   The only clear indication of its Islamic use is a list of prayer times on its main door and a large notice board in Bengali, English and Arabic on the building which adjoins the former Huguenot chapel and which was used by the *Talmud Torah*. The building to the outsider appears to be what it was originally - a plainly decorated eighteenth century chapel occupying a cramped site.

Internally, however, the chapel has been modified in a way which offended local conservationists and highlighted the different approaches towards the building. After the 1985 visit of President Ershad, the Bangladesh government gave a grant to install a new floor which would enable the mosque to accommodate another 600 worshippers.   The refurbishment entailed the destruction of the old chapel.

No planning permission was required from the local authority but local conservationists protested at the way in which the refurbishment was undertaken. Dan Cruickshank, who was an architectural historian, the features editor of the national weekly, *Architects Journal*, and a leading member of the local conservation movement, was reported in a local newspaper as claiming that:

'What is so terrible is the way in which it was done. A lot of people are renovating houses in that area and they saw panelling being smashed. It was carried out brutally.'[2]

Against this portrayal of brutal pillage by insensitive owners the president of the mosque management committee expressed a concern for the historical character of the building:

'We are taking out a gallery, but the historical things are not being touched, they are being preserved.'[3]

On a more functional note he also noted that the extra space provided by the refurbishment would alleviate a situation where 'people are praying in the streets outside now.'[4]

Both sides in this exchange appeared to agree on the importance of conservation and the historical but they differed as to the way in which modifications were to be made to the internal fabric of the building. Dan Cruickshank's protest expressed the concern of the locally influential Spitalfields Historic Buildings Trust, of which he was 'an indefatigable committee member'[5], about changes which previously caused little public comment - internal modifications of the Brick Lane building by its Jewish occupants during the late 1890s[6]. A Huguenot refugees' chapel was now defined by the conservationist lobby as a vital expression of an indigenous urban culture and landscape - its exterior **and** interior were the concern of more than just its current users.

Yet despite the growing power of the conservationist lobby, the mosque's management committee was able legally to change the interior of the building to accommodate more worshippers. In so doing they were able to get Muslims off the surrounding streets during religious festivals and thereby avoid drawing further attention to the building's Islamic use. The outside could be left relatively free from Islamic insignia: any attempt to project a more public Islamic message by altering the outside of the building through the use of Arabic calligraphic designs, for example, would presumably create an even stronger reaction from non-Muslims.

As I mentioned earlier, the leaders of the Brick Lane Great Mosque pursued a low key strategy which was reflected in the few external reminders of the building's Islamic use. Yet the changes taking place within Spitalfields raised a number of questions about the continuing effectiveness of this strategy. The movement of City businesses and wealthy owner-occupiers into the ward had been accompanied by the migration of Bangladeshi firms and residents away from West Spitalfields as the garment trade shifted its centre to the south and east of Brick Lane. Bangladeshis still dominated council estates in the central and eastern areas of the ward but they began to look in greater numbers to workplaces outside of Spitalfields. The industrial and commercial character of the ward was being radically changed by forces beyond Bangladeshi control (Foreman, 1989; Samuel, 1989).

One commentator even speaks of 'a holocaust which is about to wipe out their (Bangladeshi) tracks': a process of transformation which conservation unwittingly encouraged and which now 'threatens to engulf Spitalfields in a sea of neo-Georgian fakes' (Samuel in Girouard *et al*, 1989: 170).

The leaders of the mosque management committee may well believe that they could use this process to their material advantage by selling out and moving to an imposing, purpose-built centre which could rival the East London Mosque. Through such a move they would be able to escape from both the limitations of the present site and the debate about urban conservation and national heritage. Yet, in the process they could easily exchange one set of problems for another as the later example of the East London Mosque suggests.

Behind the formal Georgian exterior of the Brick Lane Great Mosque changes were taking place inside the building which expressed the changing needs of its users and which were interpreted in terms of wider debates about the historical character of the building. The Islamisation of the building was a largely internal process which was explained with reference to what might be considered another sacred context - a conservationist valuation of local history and urban heritage. The internal changes were designed to increase the mosque's capacity and enhance its reputation as the main centre of Bangladeshi religious expression in the area.

The modifications were made at a time of radical changes in the economic and social structure of Spitalfields created by the wider economic and political system - changes which threatened to undermine the importance of Spitalfields as a Bangladeshi stronghold. The developments posed a challenge to the Brick Lane Great Mosque which was made even more formidable by the opening of a rival mosque in the neighbourhood - the East London Mosque - whose leaders adopted a strikingly different strategy towards representing their Islamic presence in Tower Hamlets.

The East London Mosque and the Call to Prayer

For a start, the purpose-built mosque looks strikingly different from its Brick Lane counterpart, since it was designed by a London firm of architects with Middle Eastern models in mind. Its tall minaret is similar to the minarets which overlook the 'holy of holies', the black rock or *kaaba*, in Mecca while its golden dome and high main entrance accords with popular concepts of what a mosque should look like. The mosque committee was determined from the beginning to remind local people of the building's religious function as loudly as possible. The minaret was used for broadcasting the calls to prayer (*azzan*) thereby raising public debate about 'noise pollution' as local non-Muslim residents began to protest. The issue was eagerly taken up by the media at a national level with reports in the *Daily Mail* (4/3/1986) and the *Daily Star* (14/4/1986). The controversy over *azzan* was fuelled locally by an item in the weekly *East London Advertiser* which claimed that the mosque's leaders wanted to increase both the volume of calls to prayer and their frequency from two to five, including 'one in the early morning' (2/5/1986). The mosque request was supported by local Muslims according to the report - a 'devout Muslim' in a neighbouring street, for example, contended that he could not hear the *azzan* and that the call should be made five times' 'like in other Muslim countries'.

The reference to 'other Muslim countries' indicated that some local Muslims did not see the issue as revolving solely around noise pollution. The *azzan* was seen by some local Muslims at least as a marker of their Islamic presence in the locality and of their links with the Muslim world at a more global level. White hostility to *azzan* also raised the issue of racism according to a mosque representative and some of the letters from local non-Muslim residents appearing in the *East London Advertiser* (25/4/1986) certainly expressed an intolerance associated with racial prejudice. When the mosque representative, for example, mentioned that noise was made by local church bells too the *East London Advertiser* printed a letter which declared:

'What bells? You hardly ever hear them these days. I'm sure I would sooner listen to the tolling of church bells than someone screaming out words I cannot understand and don't want to.'

The reference to 'screaming' supported derogatory images of Muslim fanaticism while a clear distinction was made between acceptable and unacceptable noise. Church bells were preferable because they were an expression of 'our' cultural tradition - a tradition which was audibly challenged by the broadcasting of alien formulae. Yet this highly exclusive presentation was rejected by those whose churches were the symbols of the English national heritage. A group of local Church of England clerics wrote to the *East London Advertiser* (25/4/1986) in support of *azzan*:

'We have no complaint against their 'calls to prayer' and given all the other sounds of traffic, sirens, bells, people, trains and life in general (we) think that two short periods each day . . . are entirely reasonable.'

The letter moved the discussion away from different types of noise to noise in general. Since the East London Mosque was located on a busy main road linking the City of London to the vast metropolitan eastern sprawl the *azzan* made only a brief, if novel, contribution to the buzz of inner city life. Of course, what the clergy considered 'reasonable' - two calls to prayer during the working day - fell far short of the demand by the Muslim correspondent for the complete cycle of *azzan* both day and night like in other Muslim countries.

The East London Mosque had been given permission to broadcast the *azzan* by the borough council - a right which none of the other mosques in Tower Hamlets enjoyed. In response to the public furore over the broadcasts the borough council quickly dashed any hopes that the full sequence could be implemented by the East London Mosque while the local Neighbourhood Committee firmly shut the door on other mosques in the area claiming the right to broadcast the *azzan*.

The opening of the highly visible and unmistakably Islamic East London Mosque resulted very quickly therefore, in a dispute which, on one level, centred around 'noise pollution' in a crowded inner city neighbourhood. Local government officials referred to the 'objective' criteria which could resolve the issue such as an agreed level of acceptable noise which could be measured. However, the boundary between acceptable noise and noise pollution was negotiated in the context of local debates which extended beyond 'objective' measurements of noise levels.

The letter which appeared in the *East London Advertiser* criticising the broadcasting of *azzan* reflected on the cultural significance of the calls to prayer and the virtual disappearance of an indigenous cultural representation, the tolling of church bells. The letter expressed a cultural exclusivism which was ironic given the foreign origins of so many Tower Hamlets residents. The establishment of the church bell as a symbol of indigenous culture in this area was also ironic since this predominantly working class area had been occupied by people who were largely indifferent to religion. Local religious devotion had been confined mainly to Nonconformist chapels, Roman Catholic churches and synagogues - the centres of a dissenting population of newcomers whose contribution to a local pluralistic culture could be easily ignored in a public debate where the only non-Muslim religious defenders of *azzan* to find a voice in the local press were Anglican clerics.

The controversy about 'noise pollution' had widened, therefore, into a discussion about what was culturally acceptable and unacceptable. The leaders of the East London Mosque wanted to establish the importance of *azzan* in Islamic culture and the contribution which Muslim settlers were making to local society. In order to achieve their objective they were far more willing to engage openly in local politics and media controversy than their co-religionists at the Brick Lane mosque. Yet once again their interests were largely ignored as local politicians moved quickly to reassure critics of *azzan* by strictly limiting its use - further evidence of the powerful external constraints on Muslim self-expression which operated in Spitalfields and other neighbourhoods within the borough.

The controversy over the use of the new East London Mosque directed attention away from another debate about the design of the building itself. Although some white residents may have reacted to the new building with a highly exclusive definition of local culture, a few British Muslims were also critical of such buildings for presenting an alien and exotic image of Islam. K. Manzoor, the Features Editor of a new journal, *MuslimWise*, argued that the new mosques 'show little respect for the time-honoured Muslim tradition of appreciating indigenous art forms in the attempt to "Islamise" them'. In the December 1989 edition he claimed that:

'. . . when the consummation of the "Islamic" and the "regional vernacular styles" took place it gave birth to new and exciting art forms which practically reflected the beauty of both.'

He proceeded to exonerate

'indigenous non-Muslims who look in horror at the dome-capped buildings
we are erecting as they are as alien to them as they are to Islam. A good
example of such monstrosity is the East London Mosque in Whitechapel.
It is a cold, characterless and impractical "word-processor" which is
neither aesthetically nor spiritually attractive.'

Nor was the most imposing and celebrated Islamic centre in London - the
Regent's Park Mosque - exempted from this charge.

The emergence of mosques in London's 'East End' had clearly generated a
wide ranging debate which involved Muslim and non-Muslim residents, politicians
and local government officials and raised questions about the symbolic significance
of Islamic buildings in a predominantly non-Muslim country. When it came to
Islamising an historic building or using a purpose-built centre, Muslims found
themselves constrained by forces which operated within the local and economic
arena and which were largely beyond their control. Yet at least in Tower Hamlets
the settlement of such a large number of people who were prepared to identify
themselves as Muslims had provided the basis for substantial mosque congregations
and an East London Mosque which physically and audibly asserted an Islamic
presence. Muslim issues had become an important factor in local politics especially
in the wake of *The Satanic Verses* controversy (see Eade, 1990). Outside the core
areas of Muslim settlement the forces arrayed against the establishment of an
Islamic presence were sometimes far more formidable.

Ealing and the Dawoodi Bohra Community

In Tower Hamlets white hostility towards Muslim centres had not prevented their
expansion across the borough, although the 1986 *azzan* controversy had
repercussions for subsequent proposals by Muslim centres in the borough. In
another London borough, opposition by white residents, workers and businesses to
the establishment of one particular Muslim centre was so strong that its emergence
was seriously hampered. This particular example, therefore, provides an instructive
contrast to developments in Tower Hamlets.

The borough of Ealing possessed a much smaller Muslim population than its
East End counterpart[7]. Most Muslim settlers resided in the Southall area and had
origins in the Indian states of Punjab and Gujarat, Pakistan and East Africa. Two
mosques had been established during the late 1960s and early 1970s in Old Southall
by the Sunni majority while, more recently, the small business community of
Dawoodi Bohras (a Shi'a sect whose heartland lay in Gujarat) had taken over a
former Jewish youth club in neighbouring Boston Manor for its religious and
cultural activities during the early 1980s. The arrival of the Bohras triggered off a
series of events which exposed the racist nature of some white residents' opposition
to Muslim centres.

The Bohras' use of the former youth club (now called Mohammedi Park) soon
led to protests from white neighbours concerning noise and parking. The dispute

involved local councillors and planning officers as white residents challenged the Bohras' right to use the buildings for the religious celebrations which were the main bone of contention concerning noise.   At informal meetings between senior Conservative and Labour councillors and planning officials it was agreed that the Bohras could use the site for social and religious functions but this consensus was destroyed by pressure from white residents who were supported by their local councillor (the Chief Whip of the Conservative Majority Group).

A new Labour administration took over the case after the 1986 elections and offered to buy the Boston Manor site in exchange for a more appropriate location. The Dawoodi Bohras eventually chose a disused industrial site in Northolt, several miles north of the Southall area.   The site had been derelict for over five years and was spacious enough to suggest that any objections about noise and parking could be easily allayed.   (It was proposed to build a centre for religious, educational and social functions, as well as a number of houses).

However, the plan again met with fierce opposition from white residents as well as from local businesses using the industrial estate, their employees and at least one estate agent.   The Bohras were given planning permission to develop the site in December 1988 despite vigorous protests from white people at public meetings where some councillors, officials and Bohra representatives felt physically intimated.

Racist assumptions were evident in local press coverage of the Northolt development dispute.   In the *Ealing Gazette* a garbled report titled 'Islamic ghetto worries' (25/11/1988: 27) referred to a Planning Committee report which described local objections 'to the "alien" nature of the plan'.   The report referred to local claims that:

> 'Northolt is a "garden suburb" and should not become another Southall. This is an alien development - an Islamic ghetto - and will lead to racial imbalance. Integration, not separation is required'.

Here a sharp line was drawn between a green and pleasant Northolt and a Southall which was implicitly associated with a ghetto.   Northolt was purportedly threatened by the development of an alien, 'Islamic ghetto'; opposition to such a threat was, therefore, not racist but based on the desire for a racially balanced, integrated society.

Yet local residential hostility appeared to be really based on a strategy of maintaining a racial imbalance in Northolt which kept the area exclusively or at least predominantly white.   A local estate agency colluded in fears that non-white settlement in Northolt would lead to a fall in property values by displaying a poster which exhorted people to sign a local petition against the plan.   White hostility to 'alien' settlers were also encouraged by the National Front which had long been active in Northolt and whose supporters attended the public meetings which bordered on serious violence.

White protesters rejected charges that they were being racist. They made the familiar claim that they were the ones suffering discrimination. As one protester put it:

'They have called us racist but we are the ones being discriminated against. The council has treated us as second class citizens'. (*Ealing Gazette*, 2/12/1988: 7)

The sense of betrayal extended to the local Labour councillor, Len Turner, who became the Leader of the Majority Group after the 1986 election. A letter from a local resident published in the *Ealing Gazette* (18/11/1988: 14), for example, claimed that the councillor:

'appeared to care nothing about the people of Northolt who elected him to represent them and not the Muslim community who do not even reside in Ealing'.

Len Turner replied to his critics by reminding them that:

'Public opinion is not in itself enough to refuse an application. Unless there are abiding reasons in planning law why an application should be turned down the committee cannot do so'. (*Ibid*, 25/11/1988: 27)

While the Labour leader located the Bohra proposal within the context of bureaucratic and legal procedures another white representative appealed to moral principles. The Anglican minister of the church, which overlooked the industrial site and provided a glimpse of the area's former rural character, distanced himself from local opponents to the Bohra scheme by arguing that:

'the proper Christian response is to make welcome those from different cultural and religious backgrounds coming into the area'. (*Ibid*)

Although the residential association fighting the proposal had used a view of the church in its logo, the minister refused to identify his church with the exclusivism of his neighbours (some of whom presumably belonged to his congregation).

Many local white residents ignored this liberal plea for tolerance and have continued to fight the redevelopment of the Northolt site through letters of protest to politicians and the *Ealing Gazette* and public demonstration after the Conservatives regained control of the borough council in 1990. The reasonableness of their objections was steadfastly asserted by the local Conservative MP, Harry Greenway in the *Ealing Gazette* where he contributed a regular column on local affairs. In November 1990 he provided a summary of the High Court decision to let the planning permission given by the previous Labour council stand and described how 'Northolt people wrote in their thousands to object' not to `the right of the sect to worship freely but to the construction of a mosque on a job site in an area of high unemployment' (*Ealing Gazette* 2/11/1990). He called on the Conservative council to honour its election pledge to find the Bohras an alternative site claiming that the 'eyes of Northolt are upon a council which has inherited a planning permission which it voted unanimously to oppose' (*Ibid*).

The image of a united Northolt community resisting the unreasonable and economically destructive intrusion of an alien religious sect was portrayed once again in a more recent letter to the newspaper. A resident of Northolt Village thanked Harry Greenway for 'supporting us in our fight to stop the building of a national mosque' and after describing the mayhem which the centre would cause the writer claimed that 'very few (Dawoodi Bohras) live locally and have made it clear that they do not wish to be part of our close and friendly community' (*Ealing Gazette*, 24/4/91). Although they had been offered alternative sites in the borough the Bohras had turned them down - further evidence of their unreasonable behaviour, perhaps, to the general reader.

Given the controversy surrounding the Bohras' plan, activists in other localities would probably be just as opposed to their arrival. Indeed a correspondent, who criticised Harry Greenway's November 1990 account of the dispute and referred to the racist tone of the public meetings chaired by the MP appeared to be concerned that the Bohras might return to the Boston Manor site in his neighbourhood. He claimed that the Northolt estate was 'better than Mohammedi Park when it was in Boston Manor and the disruption to nearby residents and businesses would be minimal' (*Ealing Gazette*, 9/11/90). In an attempt to put the ball back into Harry Greenway's court the correspondent suggested that the MP 'should use his contacts in the Church of England' to find a disused church for the Bohras or any other 'large redundant place of worship of another religion'.

Since I live very close to the Burhani Centre in Fulham, I have been able to observe local reactions to the Bohra presence. The Centre is close to a private housing estate in a predominantly white neighbourhood and judging by the odd broken window it has not escaped some antagonism in a relatively quiet locality. However in the summer of 1989 when the Bohras used a nearby secondary school for the kind of lengthy and lively celebration which caused so much hostility in Boston Manor the event passed by without adverse local comment. Their presence in the Labour controlled borough of Hammersmith and Fulham did not play a significant role in local politics, although it may well have done had they envisaged the kind of major redevelopment proposed in Northolt.

The position by early 1992 is that the Northolt site is at last being developed for the Dawoodi Bohras. The High Court decision in November 1989 appears to have been decisive and the Bohras' strategy of working through the planning and legal process has been successful. The public protests, the ministrations of Harry Greenway and local Conservative councillors and legal action by Gallaghers who used an adjacent site on Rowdell Road, delayed the scheme for several years but the sect has eventually been allowed to go ahead with building what was advertised as an 'Arabic Academy Campus Project' which incorporated an imposing *masjid iwan* and *madrassah* with 22 two and three storey houses. Using the site may well prove difficult, at least initially, given the opposition generated by local activists who threatened to challenge their Conservative representative over the issue in any future elections. The final section of this paper attempts to analyse the complexity of these cases to illustrate those social and political issues which have significant bearing on the position of Muslims in British society

Discussion : Islam and Definitions of Community in Local Political Arenas

In my introduction I claimed that the disputes described above revealed a shift in the local politics of Tower Hamlets and Ealing - a shift which involved 'white' as well as 'black and Asian' political activists. During the early 1980s the overwhelming majority of Bangladeshi community representatives in Tower Hamlets claimed to reflect the needs of 'their community' which were defined as secular terms (see Eade, 1989; 1990; 1991). They campaigned over the provision of housing, education, jobs and amenities and made alliances with white activists using the language of class frequently expressed in socialist political discourse.

The defeat of the Labour Party in the 1986 borough election and the abolition of the GLC and ILEA dealt massive hammer blows to the alliance between secular Bangladeshi activists and white radicals, although the devolution of council services to Neighbourhood Committees by the new Liberal Democrat regime enabled the alliance to continue in some localities up to the 1990 election. The weakening influence of secular activists strengthened the position of those Bangladeshis who wished to emphasise the Islamic needs of local residents both in white-controlled institutions such as local state schools and, even more importantly, in the area's mosques, prayer halls and *madrassahs*. Community identity was to be defined in terms of a universal Islam and the buildings where Muslim solidarity could be publicly celebrated rather than in terms of nationality (Bangladesh, Britain or both countries), family, village or class.

The greater prominence of Muslim representatives locally during the late 1980s excited an antagonism among white residents which secular Bangladeshis had wished to avert through their emphasis on issues which could unite Bangladeshi and non-Bangladeshi residents. When Bangladeshi activists had criticised certain local white residents over racial prejudice and personal attacks on Bangladeshis, for example, they had attempted to maintain their alliance with white radicals and to appeal to the values of tolerance, fairplay, justice and class solidarity to which, they claimed, most local residents subscribed. Disputes surrounding the Brick Lane or East London mosques enabled white residents to make claims which were implicitly racist but about which secular Bangladeshi and white activists had nothing publicly to say. These conflicts opened up an alien terrain for secular representatives and it was left to the Anglican clergy to appeal for toleration and reason in the case of *azzan*, for example.

However, I do not wish to over-emphasize the significance of religious constructions of identity in Tower Hamlets politics.   Despite the heightened awareness of Islam among local Bangladeshis and the expansion of mosques and prayer halls across the borough, Bangladeshi activists in the Labour and Liberal Democratic parties concentrated on trying to represent the material needs of their supporters and defined themselves in terms of secular discourses about nationality, class or locality.   White councillors did not get publicly involved in the two controversies discussed above - they left the issues to be dealt with by Muslim representatives and planning officials within the council administration.

Nevertheless, what the debates in the local newspaper did highlight was the greater visibility of Islam in the borough and the reaction of at least certain white residents to the Islamic presence.   Media attention strengthened a particular theme about community and identity while the disputes over the use of mosques brought into the public arena certain issues which secular representatives had, for a time, been able to keep at bay.   The debates strengthened the position of Bangladeshi activists who, during the 1986 borough elections had criticised Bangladeshi Labour Party candidates for ignoring Islamic issues.   Those claiming to represent the 'Bangladeshi community' were under increasing pressure to declare at least a formal concern for the provision of Islamic facilities as well as the championing of the rights of Bangladeshis in the areas of public houses, state education, jobs and amenities.

In Ealing, the public debate about the use of space for Islamic purposes did not involve substantial numbers of local Muslim residents.   The borough's South Asian settlers had mainly come from the Punjab and Gujarat and were predominantly Hindus and Sikhs.   The Dawoodi Bohras, a minute Shi'a sect, were scattered over the metropolis and possessed no local political power base.   Throughout the controversy they refused to be drawn into making any public statements and relied on the operation of legal and bureaucratic structures and their informal links with powerful local councillors.   Islam was used by white activists rather than Muslims, therefore, to describe an alien invasion of local space and to put pressure on Labour and Conservative political leaders to respond to what the activists claimed were the interests of local (white) residents.

Despite the differences between the social and political dynamics in two London boroughs the media debates revealed a common theme - Islam as an alien threat to an indigenous, non-Muslim urban community and culture.   The theme could be defined in terms of architectural heritage, the design of a building, the call to prayer and could engage well healed gentrifiers and working class `Cockneys' in a defence of tradition.   Interestingly, the only white defenders of the Islamic presence in the two boroughs who did not use bureaucratic planning procedures to justify their position in the media were Anglican clergymen; they appealed to the values of toleration and ethnic pluralism in a debate where opposition to Muslims sometimes masked a racist exclusion of 'immigrants' defined in terms of their country of origin rather than their religion.

With the appearance of more purpose-built mosques and the articulation of 'Islamic' needs in London and other urban areas the kinds of issues described in this paper could well become more common and 'Islam as alien threat' may well play a more significant role in local urban politics. The Islamisation of local urban space is only one element in a public debate about Islam in Britain's media which *The Satanic Verses* controversy raised to a national level. Yet as the intensity of the feelings raised by the publication of Salman Rushdie's book fades and Iran tentatively approaches Western powers the public, physical manifestation of Islam at a local level continues to remind the non-Muslim majority in London and elsewhere of the Muslims presence and to provoke among some members of that majority at least a conscious reflection on local community and culture - a reflection which is linked with the articulation of identity, community and culture at other levels, i.e. what it means to be 'English' or 'British' at a national level.

Footnotes

1   When the future of the Brick Lane building as a mosque was being discussed in 1970 the *East London Advertiser* ran a story which claimed that the 'Pakistanis wanted to pull down the three inner galleries and Tuscan columns to provide the open space needed for their services'. The article proceeded to note that the GLC was 'unlikely to favour this alteration to such an historic building' (*East London Advertiser* 27/11/1970). Significantly, perhaps, the refurbishment took place after the demise of the GLC.
2   *Ibid*, 17/10/1986
3   *Ibid.*
4   *Ibid.*
5   Girouard *et. al.* (1989).
6   See *Jewish Chronicle*, 7/3/1975.
7   Local estimates claimed that of approximately 40,000 South Asian/East African settlers in a borough of over a quarter of a million residents only about 5,000 were Muslims. Two mosques had been established in Old Southall, one of which has been recently refurbished and expanded in a more demonstrably Islamic mode.

References

Adams, C. (1987) *Across Seven Seas and Thirteen Rivers*, London: THAP Books.
Eade, J. (1989) *The Politics of Community: The Bangladeshi Community in East London*, Aldershot: Gower.
Eade, J. (1990) 'Nationalism and the quest for authenticity', *New Community* 16(4), pp.493-503.
Eade, J. (1991) 'The Political Construction of Class and community' in Pnina Werbner and Muhammad Anwar (eds.) *Black and Ethnic Leaderships: The Cultural Dimensions of Political Action*, London: Routledge, pp.84-109.
Foreman, C. (1989) *Spitalfields: A battle for land*, London: Hilary Shipman.
Game, A. (1991) *Undoing The Social: Towards a Deconstructive Sociology*, Milton Keynes: Open University Press

Girouard, M. (ed.) (1989) *The Saving of Spitalfields*, London: The Spitalfields Historic Buildings Trust.

Samuel, R. (1989) 'The Pathos of Conservation' in Girouard M (ed.) *The Saving of Spitalfields*, London: The Spitalfields Historic Buildings Trust.

Shields, R. (1991) *Places on the Margin: Alternative Geographies of Modernity*, London: Routledge.

Short, J. R. (1991) *Imagined Country*, London: Routledge.

4

A Mosque of our own?
Turkish immigrants in Gothenburg
facing the effects of a changing World

Kirsti Kuusela

One Sunday at the beginning of May 1991 large police reserves had been summoned to one of the squares in central Gothenburg. On the following day the newspaper columnists were relieved to note that the encounter between racist and anti-racist groups had passed without any violence. This event was about a debate among Swedish people in relation to building of a mosque in Gothenburg, the second biggest city in Sweden with a population of about 440,000 inhabitants and a largest concentration of immigrants.

On this Sunday morning not more than 17 people from the anti-immigrant organisation *Sverigedemokraterna* (The Sweden Demokrates) had gathered. This was not the first incident of the kind. A year earlier Muslim immigrants had gathered in the same square to hold collective prayer in open. Over 200 Muslims attended and prayed in front of the media and journalists. They demonstrated that the authorities had refused to allow them to build their own mosque. The controversy generated interviews, debates, articles and public hearings in the media. However, much of the coverage was negative. A Swedish priest claimed that Muslims should not be allowed to build this mosque, as Islam was dangerous for young Swedes, and specially for young Swedish women. Many Swedish organisations gave the same message. Islam was a danger to basic Christian Swedish norms and values and especially in its attitudes towards women and children.

The opposition to the building of a mosque in Gothenburg contradicts the results of an official investigation by the Swedish authorities as shown in a discrimination investigation (*Diskrimineringsutredningen*) (Westin, 1984). According to this report the tolerance among Swedish people for immigrants and immigration was said to have increased between 1969-1981. A later study showed that the relationship between Swedes and immigrants was free from conflict (Westin, 1987).   But the 'mosque issue' showed that the relationship between Swedes and foreigners is more complex and fraught with tension.   My own investigation and other findings indicate that the Swedish attitude to immigrants like the Muslims has changed.   An investigation conducted by TEMO for a major Swedish newspaper (*Dagens Nyheter*, June 1992) shows that six out of ten Swedes are dissatisfied with the Swedish immigrant policy and eight out of ten responded negatively about receiving more immigrants and refugees like Kurds, Turks and Iranians from the Middle East.

It should be noted that Swedes are very split and highly ambivalent on this issue.   The old Swedish tradition of universal humanity and solidarity can not be taken for granted any longer.   Racism, discrimination and negative attitudes against immigrants can be interpreted in two different ways.   It can be argued that Swedish belief in universal human values of welfare and justice have declined.   On the other hand, it can be argued that class differences have increased in Sweden and created a social tension familiar in other societies with similar socio-economic problems. The decline of welfare and justice is evident in recent political and economic changes introduced by Social Democratic, Liberal and Conservative governments. They have begun to dismantle the welfare state.   These changes undermine collective solidarity and allow expression of prejudice more than before. Intolerance towards different groups is now more legitimate and it can help racism to gain root more widely.   Racist organisations have appeared in media and public places more than before and cases of abuse and violence against the immigrants have occurred.

Increasing intolerance may explain the success of the newly established *Ny demokrati* (New Democracy) which no longer subscribes to the traditional vision of the old parties.   This party is against refugees and immigrants and uses negative generalisations about them.   The leaders have exploited dissatisfaction with the immigration policy to express hardened attitudes towards immigrants who have been stereotyped.

Although there are many Swedes who are positive about immigrants and willing to receive more refugees, they do not want to live in areas densely populated by immigrants and desire no social interaction with them in private life.   Many immigrants have lived in Sweden for twenty years without ever visiting a Swedish home.   Most Swedes still expect immigrants to assimilate and accept the Swedish norms and way of living.   They tacitly assume that the Swedish way of living is the most modern one.   They see immigrants' own cultures as old fashioned and incapable of fitting into the Swedish society.   Therefore they consider it natural for immigrants to 'become Swedish'.

It is now sixty years since Sweden became a land of immigrants from its earlier profile as a land of migrants.   9% of Sweden's total population (760,000 out of 8.5 million) are born abroad.   The immigrants number 1.3 million if both first and second generations are included.   Sweden is today unquestionably a multicultural society with an international population.   The largest foreign born groups come from Nordic neighbours (42%). By far the largest immigrant group are the Finnish (200,000). Norwegians are the second largest group followed by the Danes in the third place. After these Nordic immigrant groups follow Yugoslavians, West Germans and Iranians. Both European and non-European immigrants in Sweden constitute approximately 30% of the population each. Immigration from outside Scandinavia has doubled during last five years. Most of the newcomers have been refugees and dependents of immigrants already settled in Sweden. Some of them are even related to Swedes (*Tema Invandrare*, 1991).

Migration to Sweden has changed both the migrants as well as the Swedish society. Immigrants have contributed greatly in industry, health-care and other service jobs. They have also made many positive cultural contributions. However, their settlement has also created problems of cultural conflicts. Unemployment has led many to criminal activities. Although immigrants experience discrimination and disadvantage in housing and jobs, Swedes still feel threatened by them. They believe that the immigrants will increasingly undermine their life chances and pose a potential for conflict in their harmonious society. They express this concern through political channels available to them as my research shows in the following narrative, especially in response to housing issues.

Ethnic residential segregation

Immigrants live segregated in Gothenburg. Most of them live in public sector rented flats built during the so-called 'Miljon Dwelling Program' which occurred between 1965-1975 when one million flats were built in Sweden. While foreigners comprise 8.7 per cent of population, in 9 out of 93 primary statistical areas of the city the proportion of foreigners is more than 22 per cent. These areas are, as a rule, in the north eastern part of the city and on the island of Hisingen. In 31 of the primary statistical areas, the proportion of foreigners is less than 3 per cent. In general these areas are located in the southern and south western part of the city. There are, however, large differences in the residential pattern of different immigrant groups.

The ethnic residential segregation in Gothenburg coincides with the socio-economic segregation. Discrimination against immigrants by private landlords and their unwillingness to accept newcomers as tenants force immigrants to move to the least attractive areas. In Gothenburg immigrants were directed into vacant public sector housing. Immigrants and Swedes with social problems were allocated to these vacant flats. Politicians, bureaucrats and the local housing officials have explained in interviews that it was an economic question in regard to filling these vacant flats. The empty public sector flats had cost millions every year for the local government in Gothenburg in the form of lost rent. The decision to fill these flats with immigrants and refugees found support both amongst politicians and bureaucrats. As a result immigrants were steered into housing that was unattractive for Swedish citizens. This allocation was not difficult. The flats were modern and the areas had good connections to the industries where many immigrants worked.

Many immigrants were willing to live where their countrymen had settled. As long as there were many empty flats, neither politicians nor bureaucrats were concerned with ethnic residential segregation in the municipality. The situation changed in the latter 1980s, when a housing shortage occurred in areas where immigrants lived. This changed the political debate. Then ethnic residential segregation began to be regarded negatively. Ethnic conflicts in these areas were discussed and the unwillingness of the immigrants to adapt and integrate within Swedish society became an issue. Today there are still empty flats in these areas. Sweden is experiencing an increasing ethnic residential segregation elsewhere in the country. In the three major cities - Stockholm, Gothenburg and Malmö - the percentage of immigrants living in suburban areas built under the 'Miljon Dwelling Program' has dramatically increased.

Turkish Muslims in Biskopsgården

Turkish Muslims living in Gothenburg and the Western parts of Sweden have struggled to have a mosque of their own for more than ten years. They had expressed a preference for a mosque in Biskopsgården where most immigrants live. When they voiced their demand the local politicians and bureaucrats opposed this project from the start. This happened in 1988 after the Muslims had acquired a vacant plot of land where construction could begin. The local media and residents mobilised a strong collective opposition to this project. Not only was opposition expressed towards the building of the mosque, but also towards the Islamic culture and the right of Muslims to practice their own religion.

The suburb of Biskopsgården was constructed towards the end of the 1950's to meet the needs of the expanding economy of Sweden's largest industrial centre. Housing was required for workers at Volvo and the shipbuilder Götaverken, companies which were expanding at that time. Initially the area was regarded as quite attractive. But the picture began to change from as early as 1960s. The area soon became a site for alcohol and drug abuse with the rise of local gangs and vandalism. In short, the area acquired a bad reputation.

At first mainly Swedish families from mixed background lived there. During the 1970s the housing began to show signs of deterioration. The area was densely populated and in poor condition through mismanagement. Gradually, middle class families moved to more attractive residential areas. When the number of workers coming from countries like Turkey increased during the 1970's, the immigrant families were advised to rent and to occupy empty flats in this location. Turkish immigrants wanted to live close to each other and began to apply for flats in Biskopsgården. While Swedish citizens increasingly left the area, ethnic groups, such as those from Turkey, Yugoslavia, Portugal, as well as poor Swedish citizens moved in.

Norra Biskopsgården - one of the areas I have studied - is densely populated by immigrants in Gothenburg and is an area of low socio-economic status. Over 30 per cent of the people are immigrants of different nationalities. Amongst school children over 60 per cent have an immigrant background. As a consequence, in some schools there are few or no Swedish children in the classrooms. There is also a large population of Swedish workers and Swedes with social problems. Population in this area has fewer resources than in other areas of Gothenburg in regard to employment education and social services. Unemployed local residents take little or no interest in local politics and elections. The number of single parent household is two times greater than in general in Gothenburg. The number of social service clients is over 20 per cent of the population, while in Gothenburg in general the average is approximately 5 per cent. The people living here have a lower average income than the general population in town.

Norra Biskopsgården includes only tenant housing. Housing here has been for long time shabby and mismanaged, but the area is now being renovated. Social stability in the area has been influenced by the high frequency of tenant change and vacant apartments. The most houses are owned by the local government through the housing companies like 'Poseidon' and 'Bostadsbolaget'. As these flats were rapidly built, the quality had suffered. Many of these flats were impossible to repair and improve. Hence some of them are now being demolished.

Turkish Muslims are the largest immigrant group in the area. In 1989 4,192 people were living in Norra (North) Biskopsgården of which 1599 were foreign citizens and of these 449 were Turkish Citizens. 365 Turkish citizen live closely in Södra (South) Biskopsgården. They are the most isolated group and, according to Swedish teachers in the area, the Turkish children have more Swedish language problems than other immigrant children. Some Swedes such as teachers and bureaucrats, feel the Turkish Muslims are dominant in the area. The school faces special problems. The Turkish children isolate themselves from Swedish children. Authorities also say that there are no conflicts between Turkish and Swedish youth in the area.

The Turkish immigrants in Biskopsgården are from villages in Kulu and Konya in Anatolia. They migrated to Sweden during the 1960s and 1970s during economic depression in their own country. First the men would come on their own and bring their families after they had jobs and accommodation. Initially they only wanted to stay in Sweden for a short period during which to save enough to make return to Turkey as soon as possible. They saw themselves as temporary workers and were also perceived as such by the Swedish people.

They soon found out that money they had saved was not enough to set up a new business or was sufficient to use as a personal pension. As the years passed the temporary workers became more permanent members of the Swedish society. The children played an important part in their long term settlement as they did not want to return to Turkey as strongly as their parents. They discovered that they were more at home in Sweden than in Turkey.

The result of this change was that they had become a settled minority group. At the same time, the Turkish immigrants became more concerned about their own cultural identity. When the prospect of returning to Turkey began to disappear, the concern for passing Turkish cultural values to the children became stronger. They turned to Islam as it constitutes a very basic framework for the Turkish cultural identity. This is especially relevant for people with close connections to village life.

The pattern of integration described here is based on a paradox. As the immigrants are exposed to forces of assimilation, the need to sustain their own cultural identity grows stronger. This paradox clearly highlights the distinction between integration based on ethnic identity as being different from assimilation. The Swedish government policy is as follows: ethnic minorities with cultures different from the majority shall be given the right to maintain central characteristics of their own cultures, language, basic norms and values, religion and customs. At the same time they shall have equal opportunity to participate in Swedish society and social life in general and obtain equal reward for this participation. This is what is normally referred to as a policy of integration as distinguished from assimilation. The local politicians, bureaucrats and local Swedes do not share this perspective. Instead of supporting the building of the mosque, the local politicians and functionaries have led the opposition. On their part, the Turks argue that the local politicians' actions have created a negative public image of Muslims in Biskopsgården saying that they will become dominant in the area. All Turks want is to preserve their cultural identity and religion.

The Swedish policy of integration worked relatively well up to mid-1980's, when most of the refugees and immigrants came from countries dominated by thought and life patterns similar to those in Sweden. Thus the likelihood of real ethnic conflicts were limited. When new immigrant groups like Muslims arrived with different cultural traditions, the situation changed. The state ideology of Swedish multiculturalism centred on the ideological policy objectives of 'equality' 'freedom' and 'partnership' has met a new realism of political and institutional practices in a Sweden making advances towards Europe. More and more Swedes speak about limits to freedom of religion and freedom of choice. The ideological climate has changed in ways that seems to bring Sweden to European community where policies towards Third World refugees are getting more brutal and where frontiers are policed more than before. Even a wall between Muslims and European Christian world is reconstructed and the idea of Turkish peril is being revived. Today the emphasis is more on assimilation, unity and homogeneity than integration based on heterogeneity and multiculturalism.

The Turkish immigrants have realized and come to accept that they will remain in Sweden. Therefore it is important for them to build their own institutions and they give the building of a mosque a high priority. Those Turks who were not actively religious previously are becoming so now. Others are increasing their religious activities and involvement in Islam. Many are making pilgrimages to the holy city of Mecca, thereby becoming Hajji, a religious title which gives a higher status within the Muslim immigrant group. (Turunc, 1990).

When Turkish immigrants get involved in Islam in Sweden, changes in their homeland also affects them. The process of modernization, which brings with it the opening up of the country towards the west and the rest of the world, is a formidable process of cultural confrontation. This is true regarding Turkey in relation to the external world, village life in relation to urban life, and different regional cultural patterns in relation to each other within Turkey itself. It can therefore be said that the increased interest in questions of cultural identity is something that the Turkish immigrants in Sweden share with their fellow countrymen and women. In this way the process of cultural articulation among the immigrant groups has been supported by a parallel process in Turkey.

Turkish immigrants wish to live in Biskopsgården in accordance with their own culture. They wish to eat ritually butchered sheep, save for a trip to Mecca, and live in peace and well-being. They often express a wish that their children will remain true to their old traditions and the Islamic way of life.

The Turkish immigrants have networks and contacts based on kinship and extended family traditions. The networks provide the Turkish immigrants with protection and increased security, but they imply at the same time that the contacts are naturally directed inwardly toward their own group and culture. Within these networks one becomes independent of outward contacts, but it does not exclude outward contacts altogether. Most Turkish immigrants in the area live in nuclear families, but they have an intensive social intercourse with other Turkish families in the area. The families are often intact and relatives are close by.

Most Turkish women in northern Biskopsgården work outside the home. They work as cleaners or manual labourers in factories during mornings and evenings as there is always a relative to take care of the children. In their spare time the women meet in each other's homes and have the benefit of companionship and mutual support. But living in northern Biskopsgården does not only mean security nourished within the ethnic fold. It also means that Turkish women have a very limited contact with Swedish women and men. There is a sense in which the security of their own network increases their isolation from the surrounding society.

Some of the girls are married early, often with men from Kulu. Sometimes they acquire high status in the matrimonial market in their homeland. In Sweden they exercise greater control over their own incomes, which results in greater prestige in the home. Some of the girls protest against the traditional Turkish women's role. They are often torn between the Swedish role they are confronted with at school and the Turkish role they encounter at home. They question the older generation without totally rejecting the customs of their parents and their communities.

Many Turkish families have little contact with Swedes and other immigrant groups in the area. Cultural differences prevent contact with Swedes to any greater extent. They keep away from Swedish culture and norms and regard Swedes as immoral in their sexual behaviour and drug abuse. Their picture of the Swedish culture is highly influenced by both media and their own experiences. They know it is difficult to make Swedish friends. Turkish immigrants, who are employed at Volvo claim their Swedish co-workers never invite them to their homes; they only invite other Swedes. Isolation from the Swedes in the area is compensated by the fact that one lives in one's own community. In the networks which the Turkish immigrant women build, there is regular expression of solidarity through kinship, friendship and the neighbourhood which make them feel secure in new environment. This is especially important for Turkish women who are often illiterate and who would otherwise become isolated. The Turkish immigrant women experience problems in Sweden because of their adverse location in the Swedish economic, political and cultural power relations in which culture has become an idiom for social ranking structured along the segregationist lines of gender and ethnicity. Their unfavourable position is perhaps most evident in the labour market in which there is high overall participation by immigrant women. Through their poor and deteriorating health, they pay a high price for working in physically taxing, stressful, dirty or monotonous jobs with anti-social working hours, poor work environments and high risk of occupational injury. Debates on immigrant women's problems, however, contain ideological undertones which do not benefit the women themselves. They are gradually being lulled into picturing themselves as vulnerable, in need of help, as undermined by their inferior position in the labour market, by their tradition, cultural heritage, husbands, large families, life-styles and values. All this helps them to develop a negative self image (Ålund, 1991). The immigrant women, the Swedish society and the Swedish social workers see problems of immigrant women very differently. The Muslim women can see childcare, unemployment, or housing as their main difficulties when the Swedish social workers see the husbands of the immigrant women or their family structure or the Islamic value system as a problem for the women.

The Mosque project in Gothenburg

There are around 100,000 Muslims in Sweden today. The largest number have come from Iran, Turkey, Yugoslavia and Iraq. In 1960 there were only few hundred Muslims in Sweden. In 1970 the number has increased to approximately 10,000 and 1985 to around 50,000. The Turkish Muslims were the first Muslim group to come. Up to 1985 they were the largest Muslim group, which gave them a special position. Their opinion was heard and for many Swedes they were the 'real' Muslims. Up to the early 1960s there were no organized religious activities in the group. In the later 1960s the Turkish Cultural Association (*Turkiska Kulturföreningen*) acquired its own facilities in the centre of the town. The Muslims rented the second floor in the premises as a prayer hall. The plans for a real Mosque began to take shape when the number of people visiting the prayer hall (*Musalla*) had grown around a thousand. In 1977 a formal religious 'congregation' The Islamic Centre was also founded in Gothenburg (Sander, 1991).

In 1973 the first Swedish national Muslim organisation or federation was created. Today there are three national federations, organizing over forty local congregations. There are one hundred and fifty places in Sweden, where 70,000 Muslims meet for prayer on a relatively regular basis. Of these congregations only three have mosques built especially for this purpose. Ahmadiya mosque in Gothenburg, a Sunni mosque in Malmö and a Shia mosque in Trollhättan. The rest of the congregations have facilities in dwellings which are more or less reconstructed for the purpose of prayer. Many of them are in basements in a poor condition and ill-suited for the religious activities (Sander, 1991).

In early 1986 the city offered a larger building in Biskopsgården to The Islamic Centre for conversion to a mosque for a reasonable price and architects were soon engaged on the project. In October the same year a local newspaper published an article about the plans on building a mosque with a picture of the proposed building. A flow of protests started. People arranged protest meetings and signed petitions against building of a mosque in the area. In early 1987 a deed was set up and accepted by both the Islamic Centre and the representatives of the owner of the building. At this time the project also was economically secure. However, before the next board meeting when the Islamic Centre was about to sign the deed, some members of the board went to Turkey. Åke Sander writes in his book *The Road from Musalla to Mosque* (1991), that while they were there, a 'revolution' occurred in the Islamic Centre and the chairman and his supporters were removed from the board. The new board claimed they could only buy the site on the condition that they did not have to pay any interest on borrowed money as it was against Islam to do so, and the deal was shelved.

In 1988 the Islamic Centre was sent a new proposal for a building site for a Mosque in Biskopsgården, which they accepted and submitted an application for a building permit to the local housing and building committee. Their first application was rejected on the grounds that the proposed area was not planned for that kind of building. At the end of the 1989 they submitted a new application. With the help of a retired Swedish politician as a chairman of a joint building committee, who could help them to cope with the Swedish bureaucratic system. In February 1990 the city building authority told the city housing and building committee to consider the application for a planning permission.

The question was a little later submitted to the district council (*Stadsdelsnämnden*) in Biskopsgården. This council suggested an investigation to find more suitable sites for the Mosque and proposed six alternatives which were all rejected by the Muslims. Biskopsgården District Council offered their opinion on the proposed site which dealt with the question of limited space with a long tirade against Islam and Muslims.

The local politicians and bureaucrats in Biskopsgården rejected the proposal on the basis of traffic, environmental and segregation problems. The local council argued that a mosque will make immigrants dominant in the area; intensify the ethnic segregation in the city as a whole; stigmatise Biskopsgården as an area of immigrants; increase the problems faced by teachers and educational officials and create 'fundamentalist' forms of Islam.

The association of tenants (*Hyresgästföreningen*), a very large tenants association, organizing hundreds of thousands of Swedes living in rented flats supported the dismissal of this application. The issue was very controversial. Many people were not convinced by the arguments put forward by the local authority. Some people saw their unwillingness to grant permission for the building of a mosque as a sign of the beginning of racism in Swedish society. Public debate brought out contradictory opinions. Some people defended the right of Muslims to practice their religion. Many Swedes protested against the building of a mosque in the area. Politicians from the city's central administration took a stand against the district council's rejection and defended the right of the immigrants to build a mosque. The Bishop and the politicians declared that neither the church nor the political parties could accept discrimination and racism.

The local opinion was strongly against the mosque. Some argued that educational problems could be seen as related to the density of immigrants in the area. The discussion amongst politicians, bureaucrats, teachers, as well as Swedes living in the area was critical of any measures which would increase the density of Turks living locally. Swedes living in the area felt powerless in the face of the developments towards segregation. For the Muslims, the construction of the mosque therefore generated a feeling that their voice was not heard. Their demand for a mosque had been turned down.

After the negative decision in Biskopsgården, the building commission in Gothenburg came to an unanimous decision on August 20th, 1991 to submit a detailed plan for the construction of a Sunni mosque in Brämaregården, another part of Hisingen. The opponents of the proposal claimed that the building site was an ancient Viking cult site and therefore unsuitable for the location of a Muslim mosque. The opposition to the mosque in Brämaregården was organized by a city association in the area. In a letter to the offices of the Bishop of Gothenburg, association leaders have demanded a referendum to determine whether a mosque should be built at all.

The city association (kommunalföreningen) has clearly stated that they are strongly opposed to the construction of a mosque on the proposed site. In the letter the association does not mince words when they describe the horrors awaiting the parish if the mosque is built. Speaking in the name of all inhabitants in Brämaregården, the association claims that everyone in the area is strongly opposed. They argue that a religion which looks down upon women is not worthy of any support. They give references from the Koran, which they claim, judge a woman, guilty of adultery, to be buried to her breast and stoned to death. The new Bishop in Gothenburg, as well as the parish pastor dissociate themselves from the idea of a referendum.

The building commission claims that their decision was simply based on the question of construction site suitability, but that it goes without saying that they fully support the freedom of religion. On the day the building commission decided not to grant permission to Muslims to build their mosque, all of the seven political parties in Gothenburg signed a common declaration assuring the freedom of opinion, the freedom of assembly, and the freedom of religion for all of the inhabitants in the city of Gothenburg. In their declaration, citizens were reminded that it was the immigrants who had built the city and that immigrants through the centuries had made their contributions to developing it.

The politicians hope that with the support of the declaration people will begin to discuss immigrant and refugee questions at their places of work and begin to understand the standpoints of all the parties involved. The declaration is expected to put a stop to the quasi-official statements on the part of some politicians in the city active in the opposition to the mosque. Today it seems that the mosque is going to be built in Brämaregården even if the city association complains about it to the European Court of Justice.

Why was the building of the Mosque so controversial?

The fact that Christian Assyrians in another typical immigrant district of the same city had been able to build their own church without any resistance from the Swedish population highlights the facts that hostility towards foreigners might be more easily bred where such cultural differences as religion emerge. As a matter of fact it seems that there exists a sense of fear (implicit or explicit) towards Islam which is not directly related to immediate confrontation with the immigrants as such, but which is nourished by the developments in the world at large.

When the Ahmadiya mosque was built in Gothenburg ten years ago, the event passed without any noticeable debate in public. However now the immigrants face more hostility than before. Images of Muslims as fundamentalist in the Western world have influenced the Swedes' fear of Muslims. It has even influenced the Swedish attitude towards the Turkish workers who have lived peacefully in Gothenburg. The Swedish mass media has often portrayed Islam from a negative point of view as an ethnocentric, one-sided, sensational and as a confrontational belief system.

In particular, the Khomeini-Rushdie affair and Saddam Hussein have had the greatest significance. Today Betty Mahmoody's book *Not without My Daughter* about her forced confinement in Iran and her and her daughter's flight from Iran has further influenced Swedish public opinion. The book paints a racist picture of the Muslim culture. It has sold hundreds of thousands of copies in Sweden and the publicity around the book, and now the movie, has not gone without notice.

Åke Sander, who has studied the Muslims in Gothenburg, argues that we, Nordic people, are quite naturally influenced by our own Lutheran religion which permeates our culture and way of thinking, even if we regard our contemporary Swedish culture as secular. A part of our fear for Islam is probably due to our difficulties in understanding the Muslim manifestation of their own religion in their everyday life. Consequently it is not surprising that we regard those Muslims who pray at their place of work or who dress in a special way as fanatical. In contrast, the Swedes have a more private relationship to their religion.

Åke Sander argues that the discrimination of Muslims cannot be exclusively regarded as a witch hunt based on negative stereotypes and attitudes which many Muslims tend to believe. Rather discrimination must be seen in the light of the Swedish society and its bureaucratic attempt to minimize disputes and conflicts. The protection and maintenance of (traditional) agreement and homogeneity is regarded as a precondition for a 'good' and 'just' society. Sweden has been, until the last few decades, an unusually ethnically, culturally, socially and religiously homogeneous society, which has consciously tried to protect itself from foreign influences with the aid of highly restricted legislation particularly in the sphere of religion. Sweden was not formally granted a freedom of religion act until 1951. Sweden was built from the formula: one nation, one people and one religion. Notions of a common cultural heritage and language still influence Swedes and their attitudes to immigrants. Evangelical Lutheran Christianity has influenced the Swedish culture and its norms and value system for almost five hundred years. Christianity is still viewed as central to the national identity, even if Sweden today is a highly secularized society (Sander, 1991).

I will argue, though, that one must even interpret the local opposition against the Mosque in Biskopsgården as an expression of a general dissatisfaction with the pronounced residential segregation in Gothenburg and with neglect and mismanagement in this area. Behind the opposition to the mosque one can find fear. Many Swedes believe that a mosque in the area will be a visible symbol of a suburb on its way to decay, populated by workers, Swedes with social problems and immigrants, people who have a low status in society.

The Swedes have little understanding of adaptation of Turks to their social surroundings in Sweden and the way Turkish immigrants want to preserve parts of their own culture. The Turkish way of life and certain norms within the Turkish culture are regarded as improper in Swedish society. Turkish integration is regarded as a problem, not only by people living in the area, but by bureaucrats, teachers, and local politicians as well. They argue that Turkish immigrants have isolated themselves and have not assimilated Swedish norms sufficiently.

Alexandra Ålund and Carl-Ulrik Schierup argue in their book *Paradox of Multiculturalism* (1991) that the prescribed multiculturalism of the Swedish state is running a risk of generating new, more sophisticated and subtle forms of racism in term of commonsense cultural racism. The authors say that one of the primary sources of this disjuncture is the culturalization of ethnicity by the state. Immigrants and in particular immigrant youth and women have become a social problem in political and institutional practices. Rather than attempting to rectify the imbalance of power or attending to discriminatory practices in housing, employment or education, social problems are conveniently located within the cultures of immigrants themselves. Their cultural baggage is described as orthodox and backward and being on a collision course with the Swedish culture. Problems of the immigrants are explained on the basis of their immigrant culture.

Immigrants must be taught to adapt to the prevailing social order. The objective for state institutional practices becomes one of ethnic integration. For control and monitoring, the Swedish state has constructed an immigrant 'industry' and a massive institutional apparatus. Even the academic researchers from the community of immigrants in Sweden often assume that problems they study lie within the culture of immigrants themselves. This shows the that the intellectual culture about immigrants has a powerful influence on all sections of the Swedish society. Immigrant research has reinforced the mechanism of control by lending an ideological support which can lead to new forms of racism legitimated in cultural terms.

Although the immigrants have formed their own associations, they are not allowed to develop political channels for their ethnic groups. Integrated into the corporate state, the immigrant organizations are marginalised in nation's political life. The real challenge to the established system of prescribed multiculturalism out of which a new genuinely trans-ethnic society may develop is to be found within new forms of spontaneous ethnic grassroots activities (Ålund and Schierup, 1991). These kind of grassroots activities are already started by the Finnish immigrants in Gothenburg and it might also be a way for the Turkish and other Muslim immigrants to follow.

References

Ålund, A. and Schierup, C-U. (1991) *Paradoxes of Multiculturalism*. Aldershot, England: Avebury.

Kuusela, K. (1988) *Etnisk Bostadssegregation i Göteborg, Del I Lägesbeskrivning*, Gothenburg: Department of Sociology, University of Gothenburg.

Kuusela, K. (1991) *Att bo i invandrartäta områden, Etnisk bostadssegregation i Göteborg Byggforskningsrådet*, (Swedish Council for Building Research), Rapport R 60.

Sander, Å. (1991) *The road from Musalla to Mosque. Reflections on the process of integration and institutionalisation of Islam in Sweden*, Gothenburg: Department of Philosophy, University of Gothenburg.

Tema Invandrare (1991) Statistiska centralbyran Rapport 69.

Turunc, C. (1990) *Framtidsbild för en etnisk grupp i Day, D. och Kos-Dienes, D.: Kulturkontakt och internationell migration - Möjliga framtidsbilder*, Papers in Antropological Linguistics 23, KIM-rapport Nr 12.

Westin, C. (1984) *Majoritet om minoritet*, Liber Förlag, Stockholm

Westin, C. (1987) *Den toleranta oppinionen*. Deifo. Stockholm

5

Schools and Muslim Girls:
Gateway to a Prosperous Future or
Quagmire of Racism?

Some Experiences from West Yorkshire

Haleh Afshar

This three generation study in West Yorkshire shows some contradictions between the lived experiences of school girls and their mothers' and grandmothers' concept of education as a process which improves their life[1]. Interest in Islam and Islamic identity among the young stems from this contradiction which this chapter attempts to explain. The women interviewed for this study assume that through schooling, their daughters and grand daughters will gain access to knowledge and find the gateway to success in the host society; a view shared by immigrants[2]. Educational qualifications would enable the new generation to rise to a better economic position than their parents and to gain the recognition and status they deserve. Education is seen as the best investment for the future.

The Muslim women that I talked to and those interviewed by Khaldeh Sheikh for this project, were committed to educating their male and female children. Even those who did not qualify for state schools were prepared to pay exorbitant school fees to keep their children within the system. The research revealed that the families were prepared to bear enormous financial burden to ensure that their children received best education.

Those women who are lucky enough to qualify for free education for their children are all to aware of what a boon it is. In addition, the mothers are keen to ensure that their children would be 'good' students. Many come from an Islamic culture and expect their children to revere education and respect teachers. The mothers are concerned about anything that would undermine confidence of a teacher in their children's ability and performance, given the influence teachers have on the futures of their pupils[3]. This conscious attempt at retaining the teacher's approval is a valid strategy for mothers to adopt. But in practice this belief is more than mere strategy. It is almost an article of faith that teachers hold the key of knowledge, which opens the door to success.   Approval at school is assumed to ascribe immense status not only on the pupils concerned, but also on the whole family who can bask in its reflected glory.   Thus, not surprisingly, for mothers and grandmothers, often 'the best thing that their daughter had ever done' was their scholastic success and the 'worst' was reprimands by teachers.   A child being 'rude' or 'answering back' was a source of anguish.   By contrast those children who gain their teacher's commendation, are praised to high heaven.   A number of mothers confirmed this trend and asserted how good behaviour and educational success raised the honour of their *biradari*.

The Curriculum: Dreams and Realities

Despite the deep commitment of Muslim parents to schooling, in practice the curriculum falls far short of their needs and expectations.   Far from being a haven of peace, our temples of learning are jungles of racism where immigrant children have to carve a corner for themselves.   Seni Seneviratne's poem *Just Jealous* provides a vivid illustration of this experience.

> Just Jealous
> They're just jealous
> My mum used to say to me
> when I came crying
> Home from school
> Saying they'd called me "nigger"
> And it made sense then
> Because I liked my brown skin.
> But it didn't make sense
> In later years
> And when my own daughter
> Comes home from school
> Asking why they call her "Paki"
> Shall I say "just jealous"
> Or try to explain
> The centuries of racism
> That are heaped behind that word?
> And will it make more sense
> Than what my mother said to me?[4]

The younger generation walks a psychological tight rope, coping with the school, its racism and the alien curriculum, while at the same time protecting the older generation, respecting their needs and their dreams.   The curriculum is that of the erstwhile colonisers.   The millennial history of the Asian sub-continent is totally ignored and the history of imperialism is couched entirely within the imperious perspective of the colonial rulers. Nor is there much emphasis on geography, language or religion of immigrant communities. Mrs. C. is a second generation immigrant whose memories of her school days are bitter sweet. Nevertheless her conviction in the importance of a good education for her daughter is firm. This even though she knows that:

> the education system treats black people as non-existent and says nothing about their culture and history.

Like most immigrants, the Pakistani community preserves an idealised vision of what 'back home' is like and mothers are instrumental in conveying this view to their children. This barely counteracts the thinly veiled and sometimes blatantly stated racists views of teachers and heads. Some like Ray Honeyford, the notorious head of Drummond School in Bradford, are convinced that Pakistan is a land of despots and dictators, riddled with corruption, 'the heroin capital of the world' and a thoroughly undesirable place for his pupils to visit[5].

Though Honeyford is most notorious, such ideas about where immigrants come from are in no way rare. The inherent racism of the educational system, which posits a world view that commences with capitalism in the West and equates modernisation with civilisation, is echoed by the media and the everyday experiences of immigrants. In Bradford the situation was exacerbated with the Rushdie Affair which was portrayed by the media as a typical backlash by the uneducated immigrant against the forces of liberalism. What the host community observed on television, in the newspaper and in talks and lectures on the radio and elsewhere, was the confirmation of their worse fears; a book burning, threatening minority on the rampage.

For the immigrant community this once more posed the problem of divided identities. As Shabbir Akhtar noted at the time what we saw festooned across the press was the image of Islam as an anti-intellectual creed, which he describes as:

> 'one of the many ironies and paradoxes generated by the Rushdie episode. [Since] Islam is, in fact, a literary faith par excellences based as it is on a document revered as an "intellectual miracle" of reason and speech. The Koran can claim the unique privilege of being the direct inspiration for a major world civilisation founded on a religiously sanctioned respect for literacy and scholarship' [6].

The gulf between self perception and host perception could hardly have been wider, we thought in 1989, but then we had the Gulf war and its repercussions in 1990. Throughout this period the Muslim community saw itself as the defender of its faith, engaged in the unequal struggle for justice and righteousness against blasphemy, against uncontrolled western might. While the media poured out the prejudices of the host society and argued for its right to abuse Islam and the Muslims.

For immigrant women, as for the men, these events have turned the last years of the 1980s and the early 90s into a period of polarisation and identity crisis. Those women who had held critical views about some of the Islamic dictum concerning their duties and obligations, or had held their peace during the Rushdie affair, could not do the same while watching hundreds of women and children die under the 'surgical' attacks of the Western forces. The divisiveness increased and many returned to Islam and fundamentalism as a unifying force that would make of this immigrant minority a world power and a large one at that; the concept of *umma*, the people of Islam everywhere, provides a powerful base to retreat to.

But the retreat to revivalism carries its own elements of unreality. For many it is a matter of returning to the sources of Islam; but for the young women that I talked to, this philosophical return required some kind of physical existence; what was Islam? Where was its home? And was the home the same as the religion?

A few of the better off families, who can afford to, do occasionally go back home. Some even take their children with them. But on the whole the English educational system takes a dim view of such travels. The Honeyford episode in Bradford merely highlighted a prevailing view among headmasters. Trips to Europe are generally perceived as educational and desirable (though not for Honeyford himself whose proud boast is that he has never left the British shores in his life). By contrast, visits back home to Pakistan are viewed as a retrograde step and, in the case of Honeyford, virtually forbidden by the head. At the same time, whereas the school curriculum enables pupils to form some idea of what life in Europe or north America may be like, there is no teaching about Asia and the pupils have little or no perception of what their 'homeland' is really like. What they have seen on the television screens does little to help as a young visitor to Pakistan explained to me:

'You know like you see on the telly. Well it was completely different. There were nice houses and really done up. My mother had her own house and she had some relatives. There was a river there and we used to play in there. You see houses and you see cars and in the country its really nice and green . . . We went to Kerachi and we went to Ruapindi and it was really interesting. We did a lot of sight seeing.'

Language

Even though many of our respondents were born and raised in West Yorkshire, the problem of language was perceived as paramount by those who had come to England not knowing the English language well and by those whose children did not speak Urdu well. For the mothers and grandmothers their own language with its rich literature and cultural connotations was a source of strength, identity and pride, which they valued and wished to preserve. But for the youngest generation, who had grown up in Britain and who used the English language as a matter of course there was a dilemma. They prefer to speak English. The combination of television and schooling soon makes English their first language as a respondent noted:

'We ended up speaking English all the time . . . Now we speak to each other in English. But when my aunt come to speak we must speak Penjabi because it would seem rude to speak English. Sometime we speak Penjabi, but most of the time we speak in English to my mum and everyone. I mean I can speak Punjabi, but when we want to say something we say it in English.'

But though they spoke English fluently, they were well aware that their use of words and the attitudes that their speech conveyed was quite different from that of their English contemporaries. D. said:

'They speak a different language, theirs is completely different. The way they talk to their parents calling them by their first name and that. We just think that's awful.'

C.'s family had come over to England without a working knowledge of English. The adaptation to English schooling had been easier for the younger sisters. But the eldest F. who was twelve was kept at home:

'We went to school before she did. She couldn't go not knowing what they said and that. We used to bring English words to the house and you start picking it up as you go. S. (the youngest sister who was five years old at the time) learned English faster than any of us.'

But whereas the Urdu speaking sister gradually learned English, the younger sister's efforts to learn their mother tongue was less successful. The young do not see much need for it, and they find it hard to make the time to 'study' their own language; it is difficult to fit it in. If taught outside school hours, there is the problem of time. All the young women interviewed described these sessions as 'boring'; a sad epitaph for those of us who fought long and hard to introduce mother tongue teaching into school. Our findings supports much research elsewhere that mother tongue teaching has not on the whole been very successful[7].

Often it is mothers or grandmothers who take on the responsibility of teaching their children their mother tongue and their religious rituals. Mothers who are first generation migrants, and do not speak English, find this easier. Confined to *chardivari*, 'four wallls of the house' they manage to teach their children to speak Urdu and to read the Koran. But for many mothers doing so is far from easy. Invariably when the various strategies to teach the younger generation about their language and religion fails, it is the mothers who blame themselves and feel they have failed in one of their paramount responsibilities. Mrs. P. tried all the options:

'We should teach them our own language and our own culture. I was more concerned for them to learn the Koran first and then to learn Urdu. Little did I realise that the older they get the more home work they are going to get and the work load would get heavier and they'd have little time left. I am very concerned about their reading and writing in Urdu. I began by

sending mine to classes. There they could have learned the language and
met with other children of the same age and background. But I had a lot of
trouble getting them there on time and so I decided that I could easily
teach them at home. I used to teach Urdu myself at the community centre.
I taught it for four or five months yet I couldn't make time to teach my
own children. We never seem to put time aside. I keep on pestering my
children about this, because if you leave it too late . . . We speak Urdu at
home, but not as much as we should be doing. We slip up and use English
and then they get a mixture. You see my father said "no Urdu at home" so
that we learn English. So we never used mother tongue. When we were
young it was a lot easier because we already knew the language whereas
my children have to learn from scratch and its a lot more teaching than my
parents had to do. I've been a bit slow in getting going and a bit too soft.
My niece is 14 and she has got her Urdu O level already.'

Teaching children about religion, prayers and rituals is even more difficult than
language teaching and once more it is the women who see it as their duty to
inculcate religious values and practices in the family. As a respondent said:

'I knew the Nemaz and had started reading the Koran before we came over
and so it was a continuation. A friend of my mother who lived locally
taught me. With my mother working, she didn't have the time to do it
herself. The trouble is that I go in patches with Nemaz. Once you get
going it is very easy, but once there is a gap then you forget. My mother
prays regularly. but I am aware that I don't practice what I teach and then
you are setting a bad example.'

The only third generation child who knew how to say the *Nemaz* was the
daughter of a white English woman married to a Muslim. She was scrupulous in
following most of the traditional customs, though she did not say the *Nemaz*, but
her nine years old daughter could say *Nemaz* and read the Koran. Though her
grandmother was insistent on the practice, even this child did not always say her
five *Nemaz* each day.

In practice the most effective means of learning the language for the youngest
generation was through watching Indian videos and the home use of Urdu. The
young speak a mixture of Urdu-English sufficiently useful as a basis for learning
the language fully if they ever returned to Pakistan.

Peer groups

The young women recognise the idealised conception of 'return' to their 'home'.
Yet at school they have to negotiate very different realities and ideals, and so they
have become adept at juggling two identities and coping with two very different
perceptions of realities. As Verity Saifullah Khan explains:

'The secondary socialisation of the school . . . introduces a different
presentation of reality. It does not reinforce the values and skills of the
home, and the child's move to school presents him/her with a disjunction

between two meaning systems. The education system presents a new set of relations and references, some of which have already been absorbed by the child through the media or local neighbourhood contacts. It is through the schools' lack of contact with community aspirations and systems of support and education, and the lack of recognition of the child's existing social and linguistic skills that children of ethnic minorities assess the relative values placed upon their identity and affiliation . . .   The children of ethnic minority families belong to both systems . . . But the second generation child and adolescent is 'of' two systems and creating a new one.'[8]

For young women the tensions become impossible at the time of adolescence. A marked change occurs at adolescence in parental attitude towards their daughters' schooling, peer group pressure and outdoor activities.   These tensions vary according to class position; as we move up the social ladder, there is a less strict approach to daughter's activities. The middle class parents send their daughters to brownies, swimming classes, ballet and gymnastics etc.   But generally such participation comes to an abrupt halt after primary school. As Mrs. P. explained:

'I like my daughter to do things for education and interest so that they know what these things are. I am not too bothered about whether they go on with it or not. She occasionally also goes to play and stay for tea with a friend. But when she grows up I'd be concerned about where my daughter goes and would not expect her to have boy friends or go to discos or anything that is not acceptable by our community. On that I'll be very firm. I am sure that it will not be too difficult given firm guidance and good examples set by her cousins.'

Her daughter O. loves school Brownies and outings they arrange. At ten she is still too young to have developed the barriers that Muslim girls learn to put up against their white contemporaries later in life. O.'s best friend at primary school was an English boy and in the middle school it is an English girl; they sit together, play together and visit each other after school.

But, although schools are perceived as a means of upward social mobility, mothers see them as a threat to pubescent daughters; particularly mixed schools which have the most undesired 'liberalising' impact that peer groups have. The problem for young women is either to operate a double standard, conforming to the West during school hours and to the East at home[9] or to exercise a self imposed separatism. Women I talked to also told of girls who had 'defected' to adopt western styles and values and had in the process 'lost face' and 'dishonoured their families' as a young respondent explained.

'The worse thing is, if a girl is about my age and she runs away from home and goes out with boys, that's the worse thing because that really hurts mum and dad then. One day some girls cut their hair and everything and they all wore westernised clothes and bunked off and didn't come back again. Their parents were really strict, you know, because their father used to pick them up from school and they used to put scarves on their heads and they used to have long plaits and they used to wear *shelvar kemiz*. But seeing that their English friends were wearing all these westernised clothes and things, they wanted to be like that as well. Well, their parents beat them up and all and even threatened them with the police. But in the end they couldn't do much about it. Now the girls live in flats and things like that and have English boy friends. You have bad rumours and everybody is talking about them and really it has put their mum and dad's name through the muck and everything. I mean they can't show their face in the Asian community because they are right ashamed of what their daughter have done.'

The problem for those Muslim girls who decided to 'keep themselves for marriage' is that their views fit ill within the prevailing school ethos. As a result they have to keep themselves apart from their white contemporaries, from the boys because of 'shame' and from the girls to avoid peer pressure. C., one of our respondents explained:

'I have lots of school friends, but friends I hang around with are all Asians. We feel a lot closer to the Asian people because what their parents want for them our parents want for us. So we feel close to them than we do to the English.'

For older girls, English friends are seen as a source of temptation. C. recalls with shame that the 'naughtiest thing' she ever did was to give in and go to a disco:

'I was about nine then . . . well I went, it was just like a youth club and you know had a disco. I had some English friends and they used to go a lot so I met them there. It got quite late and me brothers were looking for me. They didn't know I was there . . . But it was only once. I got told off but me mum knew that it was my first time. You know them friends, me mum knew some people who mixed with white people, they said 'well that's what they want to do and they tell your children to do it too' . . . so I got told off, I expected that. But I did it only once.'

It is obvious that young Muslim girls establish friendship with other Asians whom they meet in the school. However, even Asian friends are strictly speaking 'just school friends' and as C. explained, parents do not expect any close contact between them and their daughters as they deeply feel concerned about the preservation of honour or *izzat*. If a young daughter has her *izzat* tainted in the local community, she may be stigmatised and may have to carry bad reputation for a long time to come.

'We hang around only when we are at school, that's the only time. When you come home . . . like I've had holidays and I haven't seen them for a bit. We don't go to the cinema or swimming or anything. We watch videos at home. You see there are lots of films in the video shop and we just walk down there and get two or three films and watch them. Its more comfortable at home, I don't really like cinemas anyway its dark and scary.'

Education: hopes, constraints and achievements

The extent to which the educational system provides a channel for social mobility is debatable. However, the Muslim mothers definite views on the issue. A surprising number of them saw education as a necessary liberalising force. A traditional mother who claimed she had never been involved with white people had faith in British education and wanted her daughters properly educated against her husband's wishes as she had done so with regard to a working daughter.

'My daughter E. works and this goes against our family's tradition. My husband asked me to ask her not to work, to stay home and he would give her the same amount of money that she gets by doing her job. I had to persuade him to allow her to work.'

This willingness to accept change is also a marked characteristic of many of the women interviewed especially in view of their *chardivari* 'four walls of the house' domestic confinement. The mother in question was prepared to act on the basis of her faith in education and was prepared to allow her daughter to learn to drive so that she would not have to wait at bus stops in the cold like her mother. What is of interest is that as a first generation migrant, she is an agent of social change in her family. It is the mother, who knows little of the language and virtually nothing of the people of this country who insists on her daughter using every available means to be more liberated than she had been able to be.

By contrast women educated in England may hesitate to give their daughters opportunities for personal and educational advancement as the following case shows:

'I did my A levels and was accepted at a teachers training college at Southall school of chiropodists. Friends of my father warned him against allowing his unmarried daughter to leave home as this was something that the community did not accept. My father was such a considerate person that I couldn't bear to see him under pressure and I dropped out . . . I did a diploma in chiropody by correspondence and did my placement with a friend in Barnsley. That meant that I could travel daily and be back home at night.'

This mother, however, had internalised the values of constraints and was unwilling to allow her daughter to be away from home. Her own experience of giving up work under family pressure was a significant factor in influencing her own responses to her daughter. After giving up her employment as a computer operator, she and her husband opened a newsagent shop and she worked and raised her children, helping them with their homework and preparing them for grammar school entrance exams. Although her son was shy and not a high achiever like her daughter, she put him in a private preparatory school, at a great cost to the family. Eventually, he did very well and got an assisted place. It was not without some feeling of hesitation that she sent her daughter to an all-girls school as she had managed to pass the entrance examination, unlike her son.

As for her own children, the mother is convinced that her son will continue his education and have a profession. She is however less certain about her daughter, she does not want to stop her education but does want her to be 'sensible'.

This concern for the moral welfare of young women by their family may affect their educational and employment opportunities. Besides this fear, there is much evidence to show that the better qualified and educated the immigrants, the more intense is the degree of discrimination that they experience. As early as 1967 The Institute of Race Relations had noted that:

(i)   As immigrants become more accustomed to the English way of life, as they acquire higher expectations and higher qualifications, so they experience more personal direct discrimination. This . . . is reflected in the experience of school leavers who are the children of immigrants . . .

(ii) Awareness of discrimination, prejudice and hostility tends to make immigrants withdraw into their own closed communities[10].

This conclusion is supported by much subsequent work and our interviews[11]. Of the women I talked to, it was always the youngest generation, who were usually the best educated, with the highest aspiration, who experienced the most intense degree of racism and disillusionment and desire to become self-employed so as not to incur discrimination and exclusion. In some cases, family elders were extremely pleased about their daughter's decision to open a shop, and supplied capital for this venture.   This result, though satisfactory to all concerned, does highlight the obvious conclusion that the third generation migrants as a whole and women in particular have come to reject education as a viable means of upward social mobility and have retreated to the traditional bastion of immigrants: small business, trade and hard work.

Conclusion

There is little that research on education of immigrants can say that was not said two decades ago. What hope there is, exists amongst the older generation, and much disillusionment amongst the young.   For young women the situation is considerably worse. They are the public face of their community and it is they who are burdened with guarding the honour of the family by their behaviour, their garments and their attitudes[12]. It is a responsibility that they have shouldered and, which as mothers and grandmothers, they will transmit to their daughters and grand daughters. It is a burden that changes over time. Some have already shed the duty of learning and transferring the mother tongue while others have begun to view

view religion as more of a general code of moral behaviour than a strict set of daily rituals and activities. Nevertheless, all the women interviewed saw themselves as the moral and cultural anchor of the family. All saw marriage and child bearing as an unavoidable and desirable stage in their lives. Even educated divorcees expected their daughters to marry and raise children.

The combination of racial discrimination at school and at work, the obligation to uphold the public face of family morality and the impending duty of motherhood play a powerful part in curtailing the education and career ambition of third generation women. With the advent of the Honeyford and the Rushdie Affair and the Gulf war, even those women who had been more optimistic about their future in the host society have revised their opinion. The last years of the 1980s and the early 1990s may well prove to have been a watershed for many third generation immigrant women. The rampant racism that echoed throughout the country threatened the delicate balance of conflicting values and identities that they had maintained over the years. With the racial lines drawn and the Muslims as a community threatened, many amongst the youngest generation found that they had no choice other than returning to the fold and suspending all criticism of the *biradari*. They have chosen to return to Islam, the religion that offers them a sense of identity, of belonging not only to a small immigrant minority, but to a vast, vibrant and vocal community, an *umma* that is prepared to defend the cause against all odds. There is a real sense of pride in belonging to the righteous group and defending the cause, the morality and the honour of Islam. What this means in terms of the personal lives of the youngest generation is a question that needs a more long term analysis in the future.

Footnotes:

1   An earlier version of this paper entitled 'Education: hopes, expectations and achievement of Muslim Women in West Yorkshire' was published in *Gender and Education*, 1989, 1(3), pp.261-271.
2   See Catherine Ballard in Verity Saifullah Khan (ed.) 1974, Taylor, F., 1974 and Pryce, K., 1974.
3   See for example Ryrie, A. C., Furst, A. and Lauder, M. and Smith, I. and Woodhouse, P. (eds.) 1984.
4   In Shabnam Grewal, Jackie Kay, Lilian Landor, Gail Lewis and Pratibha Parmar (eds) 1988.
5   For further details see Honeyford, R., 1983, 1984a and 1984b. For more detailed discussions, see Olivia Foster-Carter 1984 and 1987 and for the views of a white observer see Murphy, Dervala, 1989.
6   *The Guardian* 27th February 1989.
7   See Logan, Penny 1989
8   Saifullah Khan, Verity, 1982.
9   See Saifullah Khan, *op. cit.*, p.211.
10   Institute of Race Relations *Supplement to Newsletter* April 1967.
11   See for example Bhatnagar, Jyoti (1970) among many others.
12   For further discussion see Afshar, H. 1984

References

Afshar, H. (1984) 'Muslim women and the burden of ideology, *Women Studies International Forum*, 1984, Vol.7, No.4.

Ballard, C. (1979) 'Conflict, Continuity and Change: Second Generation South Asians' in Saifullah Khan Verity (ed.), *Minority Families in Britain*, London: The Macmillan Press Ltd., pp.109-129.

Bhatnagar, J. (1970) *Immigrants at School*, London: Cornmarket Press, pp.35-39.

Foster-Carter, O. (1984), 'The Struggle at Drummond Middle School, Bradford', *Critical Social Policy*, 12, pp.74-78.

Foster-Carter, O. (1987) 'The Honeyford Affair: Political and Policy implications' in Troyna, B. (ed), *Racial Inequality in Education*, London: Tavistock Publications, pp.44-58.

Honeyford, R. (1983) 'Multi-ethnic intolerance', *The Salisbury Review*, Summer, pp.12-13.

Honeyford, R. (1984a) 'Diary of a Week at Drummond Middle School' *The Times Educational Supplement*, 4 May, pp.20-21.

Honeyford, R. (1984b) 'Education and race - an alternative view', *Salisbury Review*, Winter, p.20.

Murphy, D. (1989) *Tales from Two Cities*, Harmondsworth: Penguin Books Ltd., pp.103-142.

Taylor, F. (1974) *Race and Community in Berkshire,* Windsor: National Foundation for Educational Research.

Pryce, K. (1979) *Endless Pressure*, 1979 Harmondsworth: Penguin Books

Ryrie, A. C., Furst, A., and Lauder, M. (eds.) (1974) *Choices and Chances*, Seven Oaks: Hodder and Stoughton

Shabnam, G., Kay, J., Landor, L., Lewis, G., and Parmar, P. (eds.) (1988) *Charting the Journey: Writings by Black and Third World Women*, London: Sheba Feminist Publications.

Saifullah, K. V. (1982) 'The role of the culture of dominance in structuring the experience of ethnic minorities' in Husband, C. (ed.). *Race in Britain: Continuity and Change*, London: Hutchinson University Library.

Smith, I. and Woodhouse, P. (1984) 'Learning your place' *ESRC Newsletter* 52, pp.16-19.

6

Sociological Analysis of Jamaat-i-Islami in the United Kingdom.

Ahmed Y. Andrews

This essay examines the position of Jamaat-i-Islami among British Muslims[1]. Studies of British Muslims have mostly seen Muslim political activity as being associated with politics of the Indian sub-continent, related to the British party political system, or to struggles over internal Muslim organisations such as the control of local Mosque committees and community organisations. Dahya (1973: 273-5), Anwar (1973: 418-23) and Shaw (1988: 147-53) provide examples of this pattern. As yet, Islamic political ideologies rooted in overseas Islamic movements, but which have been brought to Britain have received insufficient attention, although it has been recognised that some British Muslim organisations are funded by overseas governments[2]. Joly has identified the Pakistani political party 'Jamaat-i-Islami', claiming that it is '. . . represented by the U.K. Islamic Mission.' (Joly, 1987: 20); this view is supported by Robinson (1988: 20). Modood (1990: 15) also identifies the presence of the Jamaat in the U.K., seeing it as being, '. . . represented in Britain by the Islamic Foundation in Leicester . . .', as well as by the U.K. Islamic Mission.

This chapter argues that the Jamaat has moved from party political activity, which Roberts sees as seeking, '. . . success through the electoral system . . .' (Roberts, 1970: 7-8), to pressure group politics. It also considers the effect such organisations have on the future of Islam in Britain.

The data presented here is based on research done between 1987-88 at the Islamic Foundation while I was a member of the U.K. Islamic Mission (Leicester Branch). In addition, it includes work undertaken during the summer of 1990 at Leicester University. The study examines the social network existing between Jamaat-i-Islami, the Islamic Foundation and the U.K. Islamic Mission, and also seeks to incorporate the Young Muslims U.K. and Dawat-ul-Islam. These last two groups are included due to my own observations, and because 'members of Dawat-ul-Islam are suspected by others of sympathy with the Jamaat-i-Islami . . .' (Barton, 1981: 70-71). Part of a survey to assess how these groups are perceived by both the

Muslim community, and some of the non-Muslims with whom they come into contact, is included in the discussion.

The method employed in the survey was that of a structured questionnaire sent to sixty Muslim religious leaders in Bradford, Leeds, Nottingham and Manchester. This was followed by in depth interviews with ten community leaders. These cities were surveyed as they all have substantial Muslim communities representing the mainstream *Sunni* divisions from the Indian subcontinent. The sample group was made up of two thirds *Barelwi* and one third *Deobandi*, with the non-Muslim sample being drawn from members of the clergy involved in inter-faith dialogue, and academics involved in either the study of community religions or ethnic relations.

The first part of this chapter gives an account of Jamaat-i-Islami in Pakistan, providing a background for the rest of the paper, while the second discusses the links between the Jamaat and the groups previously mentioned. An explanation is also offered as to the functions of these organisations within the U.K. The third section gives an overview of the survey findings, while the final part considers how representative Jamaat-i-Islami is of Muslims in Britain.

The Jamaat-i-Islami in Pakistan

Jamaat-i-Islami was founded by the Muslim journalist Abul Ala Maududi (1903-1979) in 1941. By 1944, membership had risen to 750 (Bahadur, 1977: 19). A self taught theologian, Jameelah says that Maududi was influenced by, '. . . above all, the Arabian puritan, Shaikh Muhammad bin Wahab (1703-87)', and was opposed to the traditional *Ulama*, the religious experts. In particular it is claimed that he denied the Ulama's concept of the Islamic legal principle of *Taqlid*, declaring that a modern reaction was needed to questions posed by the situation of Muslims in the modern world (Jameelah, 1987: 117).

In founding Jamaat-i-Islami, Maududi stressed the need for a party different from other Muslim parties, claiming that Islam was superior to both Capitalism and Socialism and that the right ideology needed a righteous party (Maududi, 1942: 158). Although opposed to the Muslim League and the formation of the state of Pakistan, civil unrest in East Punjab forced Maududi and his companions to seek asylum in the newly formed Muslim State. Once in Pakistan, Maududi campaigned for the replacement of the Pakistan Penal Code, and other British based statutes, with Islamic Law. He refused to endorse Pakistan's fight for the control of Kashmir. As a consequence, the West Punjab Government detained him in October 1948 under the Punjab Public Safety Act (Bahadur, 1977: 58-59).

Jamaat-i-Islami has never had a mass following in the Indian subcontinent[3] except from the petty bourgeoisie and Muslim immigrants to Pakistan from India. According to Aziz (1976: 141), it has been strong in its organisation, while Hussain (1983: 52) observes that most followers were migrants into Pakistan and not, '. . . people of the soil . . .', claiming this as a reason for the Jamaat's limited success in the Pakistani political structure. According to his analysis, this structure consists of traditional feudal landlords and religious leaders, and the British trained army and civil service.

The leader of the Jamaat is the *Amir*, a post which Maududi held from 1941-72, who in turn is supported by council of fifty people, called the *Shura*, the ruling committee directly elected from the membership for a period of three years. There is also a smaller group of twelve members, appointed by the *Amir*, who undertake all the policy decisions of the *Shura* when it is not in session. Until the Bangladeshi war of independence, the Jamaat was divided into two provincial organisations, each divided into circles, and each circle having its own *Amir* and *Shura*.

The party has seen Maududi's writing as a vehicle for propagating its views through the Islamic Publications Ltd. in Lahore, and the Islamic Research Institute in Karachi. The organisations which support the Jamaat are the Islami Jami'at Tulaba Pakistan, which recruits from among students, and the Labour Welfare Committee which influences the workers (Bahadur, 1977: 154-5).

Jamaat-i-Islami has played a prominent role in the political life of Pakistan despite its small membership. For example, in the Punjabi Provincial Assembly elections in 1951, only one Jamaat candidate was elected. The party featured prominently in 1953, when a court of inquiry implicated it as being involved in civil unrest targeted against the Ahmadiyas in the Punjab (Munir, 1954: 132). Consequently Maududi was sentenced to death, a sentence later reduced to two years imprisonment.

Political parties in Pakistan were banned between 1958-1962. The Jamaat re-emerged as a party in 1962, opposing the regime of Ayub Khan and his new constitution. In 1964 Maududi was again arrested and the Jamaat-i-Islami banned. However, on this occasion a High Court in Dacca ruled that the ban on the Jamaat was invalid and Maududi was released from prison. Having previously declared that a woman could not be head of an Islamic State, Maududi and the party supported Fatima Jinnah's candidature in the 1963 Presidential elections. This failed however to stop Ayub Khan from being elected President with support from the traditional *Ulama* and *Pirs*.

In 1968 Jamaat-i-Islami associated itself with Ayub Khan on the basis that his government was right wing, and that Jamaat was a right wing party (Bahadur, 1977: 119). However, the Jammat soon distanced itself from Ayub Khan, helping to force him out of power in cooperation with workers and the urban middle class. Ayub Khan fell from power in May 1969. In the 1970s, the Jammat attacked Zulfikar Ali Bhutto's Pakistan Peoples Party (PPP) and its policy of 'Islamic' Socialism. However, in elections in 1970, the PPP had come to power and the Jamaat had gained only 6 per cent of the votes with four seats in the National Assembly (Ahmed 1976: 79). Bahadur claims that during the Bangladesh war, Jamaat-i-Islami came to the support of the West Pakistan army, and that K. J. Murad, then a *Shura* member in Dacca, was sent to Europe to counteract propaganda from a variety of sources which was in favour of Bangladesh (Bahadur,

1977: 133). The Jamaat again came to prominence in 1978, when General Zia revealed plans to introduce an Islamic Penal code and co-opted the Jamaat-i-Islami to work in his cabinet.

In this overview of the Jamaat in Pakistan, a number of points emerge. Firstly the Jamaat was formed as a religious/political party at the time when the call for Indian independence was at its height, and when the Muslims of India were hard pressed. According to Barber (1968: 178), the feeling of '. . . "deprivation" - the despair caused by inability to obtain what the culture has defined as the ordinary satisfaction of life', precipitates a call for a return to a golden age. This call can be seen in Maududi's demands for the formation of an Islamic State.

Secondly, Maududi, never underwent a traditional Islamic education, and was in fact opposed to the traditional *Ulama*. This meant that he did not have a base in the traditional Islam as practised in the Indian subcontinent, and his party was therefore divorced from the rural masses of Pakistan. This is important as Nairn (1981: 100-101) has pointed out the intellectual middle class '. . . is always compelled to turn to the people', and this implies speaking their language and taking a '. . . kindlier view of their culture', including their religious culture. Maududi's early followers did not speak the regional languages of the newly formed Pakistan, being Urdu speakers from India, nor did they respect the traditional religious culture of the rural masses. As a result, although the Jamaat has attempted to attract a following in Pakistan by offering changes in its policy, it has not succeeded in drawing support away from the traditional leaders.

Jamaat-i-Islami in Britain

In considering Jamaat-i-Islami in Britain, I turn first to the organisation and work of The Islamic Foundation in Leicester, which has been described as '. . . a research and *Dawah* organisation'[4]. It is widely known through its publication of books and other material on Islam, and has as its chairman Khurshid Ahmed. At the time I was in the Foundation, he was a Senator in Pakistan representing Jamaat-i-Islami. Furthermore, Khurram Murad, was the first director general of the Islamic Foundation, holding office from 1978-1986.

A breakdown of titles by author of the Islamic Foundation's 1990-91 publications list showed Khurshid Ahmed as having written, or co-authored nine books published by the Foundation, while Khurram Murad had written or co-authored eighteen publications. Zafar Ishaq Ansari has three publications listed. Ansari has also co-authored two publications with Khurshid Ahmed. All three authors have been identified by Bahadur as having been inducted into the *Shura* of Jamaat-i-Islami in Pakistan during the 1950's. (1977: 145).

Of other works on the list, Maududi has ten books featured, while other known supporters of Maududi's views have contributed nine titles. These include members of the U.K. Islamic Mission Leicester Branch involved in the Foundation's work, one of whom edits a journal called *Focus* which monitors

Muslim/Christian relations. One of them, who has been an author of five books, was also acting director-general of the Islamic Foundation. He has admitted having been involved in Jamaat-i-Islami activities in the Indian sub-continent and also being a member of Dawat-ul-Islam.

What is most significant is what the publication list does not contain. The Islamic Foundation is regarded as a research institute, and if this is so, one might expect it to publish works on a wide spectrum of Islamic subjects, written by a wide range of scholars. There are, however, no publications on Shia theology, and only one on Sufism. Likewise there are no books written by traditional theologians of the Indian sub-continent such as Ali Thanvi of the Deoband, or Sheik Ahmad Riza Khan of the Barelwis these being the principle divisions to which the majority of South Asian Muslims in the U.K. and the Indian sub-continent belong. The absence of such works gives the impression that the only Maududi's Islamic view is propagated.

Furthermore, unlike other Islamic centres of learning in the U.K. such as Darul-al-Um in Berry, apart from two Maulanas from the Saudi Arabian Daral-Ifta organisation, there were no traditionally educated religious leaders in the Foundation. All senior staff had European higher educational qualifications with Khurram Murad being a qualified engineer, while Khurshid Ahmad is on record as having been a postgraduate student in Economics at Leicester University. This absence of traditionally qualified Islamic scholars appears odd for an Islamic Research Institution, but is consistent with the educated middle class profile identified by Bahadur as making up the Jamaat-i-Islami membership. Also, all the senior staff were from families who had migrated to Pakistan from India, which is consistent with Bahadur's view that the Jamaat appeals mainly to Muslims who have migrated to Pakistan.

That a link existed between the Islamic Foundation and Saudi Arabia was evident during my time of observation. The Foundation's public relations director was a regular visitor to Saudi Arabia, and the acting director-general who regularly attended conferences held by the Saudi Arabian backed Muslim World League. In addition, the Islamic Foundation relied heavily on donations from the Gulf States, and in 1987 its senior staff were expressing concern over the detrimental effects of Iran-Iraq war on the flow of donations into the organisation.

From the available evidence, it seems as if the primary function of the Islamic Foundation is to disseminate one form of Islamic ideology in the U.K.; that propagated by Maududi, free from the traditions of *Pirs* and Sufism which they regard as innovation, but which features widely in the Islamic practices of the Muslims of the Indian subcontinent. These practices, such as the recitation of *Zikr*, a form of ritual chanting, and the veneration of the tombs of Muslim 'Saints', were constantly criticised by members of the Foundation as being signs of ignorance, and the result of a subcontinental legacy regarded as a 'Hindu infected past'.

During the time observations were made, the Islamic Foundation was hosting weekend training courses for both the U.K. Islamic Mission and the Young Muslims U.K., and it is to the first of these groups I will now turn.

The U.K. Islamic Mission (UK) came into being in 1962 to, '. . . convey the true spirit of Islam to the Western world' (Faruqi, 1986). Its structure resembles that of Jamaat-i-Islami, in that it is made up of members, probationers and sympathisers, and has a national *Shura* and *Amir* which oversee local branches. At branch level the local *Amir* oversees the activities of the branch, and monitors the work of members who are expected to read the 'approved' Islamic works of Maududi, Khurshid Ahmed and Khurram Murad. Members are also instructed to develop relationships with other Muslim organisations, and to identify Muslims who may be sympathetic to U.K. Islamic Mission's objectives. These objectives are the spreading of Islam free from innovation, and to work towards the ideal of an Islamic State. The concept of the Islamic State propagated within U.K. Islamic Mission is that outlined by Maududi (Maududi, 1955).

Local branches of the organisation take part in community affairs such as pressuring local councillors on issues affecting Muslims, and in Leicester the local branch has been criticised for acting independently of the Leicestershire Federation of Muslim Organisations, to which it is affiliated, regarding community issues such as the appointment of Muslim governors to local schools.

Members of U.K. Islamic Mission were also active in forming relations with non-Muslim academic institutions. For example two of its members were involved in the production of the research paper *Resources for Teaching Islam* (Nielson *et.al.*, 1985). One of them was elected *Amir* of U.K. Islamic Mission's Leicester branch in 1987, and is public relations director of the Islamic Foundation; another member is now employed as a lecturer in Islamic studies in a British University. In addition, a member is now involved in post-graduate study at Selly Oak Colleges, and a former employee of the Islamic Foundation is now on the staff of the same institution.

At the time of my contact with U.K. Islamic Mission, its activities appeared to be mainly directed towards the Muslims of the Indian subcontinent resident in the U.K., especially those from Pakistan. This view is not, however, supported by the survey presented below, which shows that their activities extend into contact with certain sections of non-Muslim society.

My observations have identified an overlap between the membership of the Islamic Foundation and U.K. Islamic Mission, and when one takes into account that members of the former are on the national *Shura* of the latter, the link between the two organisations appears to be well established. Furthermore, this link is seen to extend to Jamaat-i-Islami owing to the involvement of both Khurshid Ahmed and Khurram Murad.

The Islamic Foundation has regularly hosted courses and meetings for the Young Muslims U.K. which has branches throughout the United Kingdom, and this group is particularly active within University Islamic societies. Besides holding weekly meetings, the Young Muslims organise one day and weekend conferences, as well as summer camps; and reports of these activities show them to constantly feature speakers who are members of both the UK Islamic Mission and the Islamic Foundation. For, example both Khurshid Ahmad and Khurram Murad are regular speakers at these events. The structure and organisation of the Young Muslims is similar to that of the UK Islamic Mission, and its membership seems to be drawn mainly from students. I have little evidence of it recruiting among working class Muslim youth; in this respect it appears to resemble Islami Jami'at Tulaba Pakistan. There is also a Young Muslim Women's section.

The impression one gets of the Young Muslims U.K. is that it is a recruiting and training body for the UK Islamic Mission, seeking to identify potential members with the 'right ideas'. That is, ideas which are not bound by the traditions of the mainstream of the Muslim community in the United Kingdom, and which are idealistic in that they seek a return to a 'pure' form of Islam free from the 'innovation' of their elders. Although there appears to be clear links between the Young Muslims and the UK Islamic Mission, they have had their differences. One criticism by the youth has been that the Mission is ethnocentric, failing to make adequate room in its ranks for non-Asian Muslims. Recent informants have told me that there is now a move within the Islamic Foundation to launch a new organisation aimed at forming links with Muslims in other European countries.

The links between the foregoing organisations and Dawat-ul-Islam appear to be the most tenuous, although two members of the Islamic Foundation are closely identified with it. In addition, a number of ex-members of the Young Muslims known to me are now members of Dawat-ul-Islam. Furthermore, both Khurram Murad and his son regularly appear at Dawat-ul-Islam gatherings. Finally, when invited to speak to an audience at a Mosque in London district of Seven Sisters, I found that a number of them had not only been active in Islami Jamaat-i Tulaba in Bangladesh, but were now members of Dawat-ul-Islam. I was also given to understand that Dawat-ul-Islam had split from the U.K. Islamic Mission because, the unspecified '. . . special needs of the Bangladeshi community means that they need a separate organisation'. On the basis of this evidence, I am left with the impression that Dawat-ul-Islam may well have as its function the dissemination of Maududi's ideas among the Bengali community in the United Kingdom.

Although the above shows that links exist between Jamaat-i-Islami and groups such as the Islamic Foundation, little indication is given as to how close these are. I used social network analysis using a programme developed at the University of California, 'UCINET' to ascertain the strength of the network. According to Scott (1988: 55), 'Social network analysis depicts agents - individuals or collective - as embedded in webs of connections and the task of the sociologist is to describe and explain the patterns exhibited in these connections'. In particular it was decided to use a Clique analysis. Scott (1988: 58) defines a Clique as '. . . an area in which all points are connected to one another by paths of a specified maximum length'.

While a Cluster, '. . . can be seen as relatively densely connected points within a larger and less dense graph' (1988: 58).

The findings based on this network analysis suggests that a close relationship exists between Jamaati-i-Islami, The Islamic Foundation, The UK Islamic Mission, and The Young Muslims, but the case of Dawat-ul-Islam is more problematic. The Jamaat has many direct links, especially at a personal level, but fewer indirect ones. This is to be expected if, for example, the Jamaat is directly controlling the activities of the other groups. Weaker links were found to be important in bringing Dawat-ul-Islam more fully into the network, and this is consistent with the views of Granovetter who has pointed to the importance of weaker links in network analysis. (Scott, 1988). The question then arises 'Is Dawat-ul-Islam an independent organisation?' I suggest that although there is some evidence to link this organisation with the Jamaat, the presence of only a few strong links leads me to conclude that more investigation is necessary to confirm the fears expressed by such groups as the Bengalis of Bradford mentioned by Barton (1981).

Whether Jamaat-i-Islami, the Islamic Foundation, the UK Islamic Mission and the Young Muslims are the same is perhaps less debatable, being more a question of definition. If to be seen as one organisation they need to share funding, the same constitution, name and leadership; then it might be argued that they are separate organisations. On the other hand, if sharing the same ideology as witnessed by an overlapping membership and leadership is considered a bases for regarding them as one organisation, I would argue that there is sufficient justification to consider these seemingly different groups as stemming from the same system of ideas about Islam. It is also important to reflect on their influence on both Muslims and non-Muslims. The nature of this influence clearly indicates the effect they have on Muslims and non-Muslim awareness of Islam.

Muslim and Non-Muslim Perceptions

In a survey of Muslim community leaders, sixty were asked whether they considered Jamaat-i-Islami to be present in the United Kingdom. 55 per cent of respondents saw the Jamaat present in the form of the Islamic Foundation. When the same question was put to a group of non-Muslim clergy and academics, 80 percent identified the Islamic Foundation as being a front for Jamaat-i-Islami in the United Kingdom. That the figure was higher among non-Muslims, may be accounted for by the fact that being in English, the Islamic Foundation's publications are less accessible to many Muslim leaders, who tend to read books in community languages. Even where community leaders can read English, however, they appear to resist Islamic Foundation publications. Indeed, in a number of mosques such books are banned as they do not follow the traditional teachings of the community.

Of the other organisations featured in the study:- 95 per cent of community leaders perceived the UK Islamic Mission as being associated with Jamaat-i-Islami, while all of the non-Muslims perceived it as such; 75 per cent of community leaders identified the Young Muslims, as against 65 per cent of the non-Muslims; while 45 per cent of community leaders and 50 per cent of non-Muslims identified Dawat-ul-Islam as being a Jamaat-i-Islami related organisation.

The questionnaire also sought to establish whether respondents had contact with any of the groups under study, and if so which. Respondents giving a positive reply were also asked as to which groups they had been in contact with and why, and whether such contacts had been beneficial.

It was discovered that 20 per cent of Muslim respondents had been in contact with at least one of the groups under study, and all of the non-Muslim respondents had been in contact with one or more groups. Of Muslims, 5 per cent had been in contact with the Islamic Foundation, compared with 30 per cent of the non-Muslims. In relation to the UK Islamic Mission, 15 per cent of Muslims had been in contact with the group as opposed to 40 per cent of non-Muslims. None of the Muslim respondents had any contact with the Young Muslims, but 83 per cent of them knew of its existence. Among non-Muslim, 30 per cent had been in contact with the Young Muslims. Only 5 per cent of Muslims, and none of the non-Muslims, had contact with Dawat-ul-Islam. In all cases, except with Dawat-ul-Islam, there was a greater degree of contact between non-Muslims and the subject groups, than between these groups and Muslims. Furthermore, only 6 per cent of Muslims had felt that contact with the groups had been beneficial, as opposed to 60 per cent of non-Muslims.

When interviewing respondents the following comments emerged regarding the benefits of contact with the subject groups.

Among the non-Muslims who had thought contact had been beneficial, most felt that the contact had helped them to better understand the Muslim community. Three respondents felt that Muslims had also benefited. Among Muslims, only one had felt that they or their community had benefited. The most common complaint among Muslims was against the UK Islamic Mission, and was to the effect that this organisation had attempted to 'take over' the respondents' community or mosque.

When Muslim respondents were asked their opinions on Jamaat-i-Islami, a constant criticism was the Jamaat's failure to observe *Taqlid*, and to uphold the teachings of the traditional *Ulama*. The Jamaat was also condemned by Barelwi leaders because of its attack on Sufi practices, and its identification with Wahabi thought. Nine Muslims thought that the Jamaat was capable of creating an Islamic State in Pakistan, while 48 felt that it could not attract a significant enough following in that country.

In relation to the United Kingdom, both Muslims and non-Muslims thought that the UK groups were incapable of integrating Muslims into British society, although one non-Muslim felt that organisations such as the Islamic Foundation, UK Islamic Mission and Dawat-ul-Islam, '. . . act in a helpful and constructive way in all community issues'. He continued by saying that, 'these bodies, although linked to the Jamaat-i-Islami, pursue activities that enhance the public image of Muslims';

and added, '. . . the UK Islamic Mission supports the principle and practise of dialogue with non-Muslims'. An academic having personal knowledge of the Jamaat-i-Islami in the Indian sub-continent seemed to be less favourably disposed towards them, however. He said, '. . . when in a position of weakness, or in a minority situation, one would expect Jamaat-i-Islami, and groups identified with it, to be pragmatic. However, once in a position of strength, they might show their real nature and revert to the tactics which they have employed in Pakistan'. Both these respondents saw Jamaat-i-Islami as existing in the U.K., '. . . not technically but under the guise of related organisations'. Both named the Islamic Foundation and the U.K. Islamic Mission as being related to Jamaat-i-Islami. Another academic, said of her contact with the UK Islamic Mission, 'hopefully my research enables people to understand better the situation of Muslims in Britain'. If, as I believe the survey of Muslims suggests, there is little support among Muslims in the UK for organisations such as the Islamic Foundation and the UK Islamic Mission, one may be prompted to ask how these organisations can help further understanding of Islam among non-Muslims.

Conclusion

I suggest that the data produced seems to support the view that Jamaat-i-Islami is indeed active in the United Kingdom, not as a political party, but rather as a series of pressure groups, organised so as, '. . . to influence policy (towards Muslims) in a relatively limited number of areas . . .' (Roberts, 1970: 7-8). It is clear that links exist between all the organisations under study, and that at least in the case of Jamaat-i-Islami, the Islamic Foundation, UK Islamic Mission and Young Muslims, there is an attachment to the ideas of Maulana Maududi.

The reason that the Jamaat works through a series of pressure groups relates to the fact that political conditions in the UK are different from those in Pakistan. In the Indian subcontinent Islamic symbols have been used to mobilise political support, and like Bhutto and Zia, Maududi also attempted to use Islam through his concept of the Islamic State. Maududi's failure however was that he had no following among rural Pakistanis as his Islam did not relate to theirs.

If the Jamaat's version of Islam could not gain influence among the majority in Pakistan, it is even more unlikely to do so in the U.K. where Muslims follow traditional Islam. U.K. Jamaat-i-Islami organisations have failed to mobilise Muslim support as they have not done anything to improve socio-economic conditions of ordinary Muslims, nor have they moved towards traditional symbolism.

It would appear, therefore, that to avoid the resistance Jamaat-i-Islami encounters from most sections of the Muslim community, it has decided to propagate its ideology within the host community by targeting religious and educational establishments in order to affect the host communities perception of Islam, and to establish its version of teaching within religious studies. If this analysis is correct, it can be said that the Islamic Foundation is acting as a propaganda, publishing and research resource for the U.K. Islamic Mission, and as a publisher of ideologically biased material for non-Muslims. The U.K. Islamic Mission can be seen to be conducting its activities at two levels. It attempts to maintain contact with Muslim groups and also tries to influence the perception of Islam held by non-Muslims. Given what has been said about the Muslim community, this latter objective, which is achieved by representing its view through inter-faith dialogue, and through contact with educational establishments and local government bodies, is likely to be the most effective, and has the potential to influence the perceptions of Muslim Youth within the school system. The Young Muslims can be regarded as attempting to propagate the Jamaat's ideology among young Muslim intellectuals, while Dawat-ul-Islam may be seen to be involved in propagating the same ideology among the Bangladeshi community.

Although these organizations may have some influence with the host community, they will not, I believe, affect the future of Islam in the United Kingdom. For, as I have pointed out, they lack any grass root support. Where Islam has raised its voice in Britain, for example over the Rushdie Affair, it has been the voice of the traditional Islam of working class Muslims and their Ulama, not the voice of organisations such as those associated with the Jamaat-i-Islami.

Footnotes:

1   My thanks are due to Professor John Scott of the Department of Sociology, Leicester University, for his assistance with the social network analysis, and for allowing me access to the draft of his book *Social Network Analysis*. Also my thanks to Paul Henderson, again of Leicester University, for his supervision of the fieldwork report on which this paper is based.
2   See *The Times*, 17th August 1987.
3   According to its own estimates, membership of the Jamaat was only 2,500 in 1971. *Tarjuman al-Quran*: vol. 74, no. 6 p.30.
4   See *Impact*, 24 October 1986, p.14.

References

Ahmed, I. (1976) *Pakistan General Election 1970*, Lahore: South Asia Institute, Punjab University.
Anwar, M. (1973) 'Pakistani participation in the 1972 Rochdale by-election' *New Community*, 2.
Aziz, K. (1976) *Party Politics in Pakistan*, Islamabad: National Commission on Historical and Cultural Research.
Bahadur K. (1977) *The Jamaat-i-Islami of Pakistan*, New Delhi: Chetana Publications.
Barber, B. (1968) 'Acculturation and Messianic Movements' in Eisenstadt, S. N. (ed), *Comparative Perspectives on Social Change*, Boston: Little, Brown & Company.
Barton, S. W. (1981) *The Bengali Muslims of Bradford*, University of Leeds: Department of Theology and Community Religion.

Criterion (1969), 4(3)

Dahya, B. (1973) 'Pakistani's in Britain: Transient or Settlers?', *Race* 14(3): 273-75.

Faruqi, I. (1986) *The Path of Dawah in The West*, London: UK Islamic Mission.

Hussain, A. (1983) *Islamic Movements in Egypt, Pakistan and Iran*, London: Mansell.

Impact 24th October - 13th November 1986.

Jameelah, M. (1987) 'An Appraisal of Some of the Aspects of Maulana Sayyid Ala Maududi's Life and Thought', *The Islamic Quarterly* 31(2): 117.

Joly, D. (1987) *Making a Place for Islam in British Society: Muslims in Birmingham*, University of Warwick: Centre For Research in Ethnic Relations.

Maududi, A. (1955) *Islamic Law and Constitution*. Lahore: Islamic Publications Ltd.

Modood, T. (1990) 'British Asian Muslims and the Rushdie Affair', *Political Quarterly* (April-June): 152.

Munir, M. (1954) *Report of the Court of Inquiry Constituted Under the Punjab Act 11 of 1954 to Enquire into the Punjab Disturbances of 1953*, Pakistan: Lahore.

Nairn, T. (1981) *The Breakup of Britain*, London: Verso.

Nielson, J. *et al* (1985) *Resources for Teaching Islam A Discussion of Problems of Production and Use*, Birmingham: Selly Oak Colleges.

Roberts, G. K. (1970) *Political Parties and Pressure Groups*, London: Weidenfield and Nicholson.

Robinson, F. (1988) *Varieties of South Asian Islam*, University of Warwick: Centre For Research in Ethnic Relations.

Scott, J. (1988) 'Social Network Analysis and Intercorporate Relations', *Hitotsubashi Journal of Commerce and Management*, 23(1).

Scott, J. (1991) *Social Network Analysis: A Handbook*, London: Sage Publications.

Shaw, A. (1988) *A Pakistani Community in Britain*, Oxford: Blackwell.

7

The Politicisation of Religion in Punjab:
1849 - 1991

Roger Ballard

Religious and ethnic polarization is one of the most salient sources of social and political instability in the contemporary world. This chapter outlines the complex process of politicisation of religion in Punjab in both the colonial and the post-colonial periods, exploring in particular the history of the Sikhs' relationship with Muslims and Islam, with Hindus and Hinduism and with the British and the Christian missionaries in order to explain the complex forces which led the Sikhs to transform themselves into a steadily more distinctive ethnic and religious community. More broadly, it seeks to understand just how and why such vigorous processes of ethnic polarisation have erupted in contemporary Punjab.

Polarization and Partition in Punjab

When the Punjab was divided between India and Pakistan in 1947, the processes of ethnic polarisation which had pitted Muslims on the one hand and Hindus and Sikhs on the other did not come to an end; instead deep divisions have subsequently erupted between Punjabi Hindus and Sikhs, such that their mutual hostility is now almost as great as that which they had jointly felt against the Muslims back in 1947. As those tensions built up, the Punjab was subjected to a further administrative division in 1966, which separated the nominally Hindi speaking (and Hindu dominated) state of Haryana in the south-east, leaving a heavily truncated state of Punjab with small Sikh majority to the north-west. But although Punjab has since made the most of the potentialities of the Green Revolution, such that its people have the highest standard of living of any state in India, the local social order has been far from tension-free. Major conflicts have erupted both internally, as between differing sections of the local population, as well as between the Punjab as a whole and the central administration in Delhi.

Centre/Periphery Tensions in the Indian Union

At an all-India level, regional autonomy has always been greatly constrained by central rule, for even though the Indian federation devolves much day-to-day administrative responsibility to state governments, all the most decisive powers and especially the power to overrule have remained firmly concentrated in the hands of the central government in Delhi. Pandit Nehru and Sardar Patel, the original architects of Indian Union, believed that such a structure was essential as a means of ensuring stability in the midst of the massive diversity of Indian society. Right from the outset, however, Punjabis chafed against Delhi's overweening powers. As they see it (and there is considerable justice in their arguments) central government policies have always been heavily biased in favour of the central Hindi-speaking areas, with the result that all the more peripheral regions - from Kashmir to Tamilnad, and from Assam to Kerala - have been systematically disadvantaged.

In the Punjab case, arguments against central control have been particularly vigorously articulated around the issues of language and religion. Very soon after Independence, Punjabi-speaking Sikhs began to grow increasingly alarmed about the central government's tendency to offer special privileges to the Hindi language, to the Devanagari script, as well as to their own preferred version of Hinduism. At the same time they also began to feel that their material interests were also being overlooked. Their complaints included the diminishing scale of Sikh recruitment into the central services and especially the Army; the absence of large-scale state-financed infrastructural projects within Punjab; low procurement prices for wheat and rice; the escalating price of essential agricultural inputs such as diesel and fertiliser; inequities in the inter-state distribution of irrigation water; lack of progress on border disputes with the neighbouring state of Haryana; and not last but certainly not least, lack of progress over the final transfer of Chandigarh, which is the shared administrative capital of both Punjab and Haryana, to Punjab's sole control.

The absence of any serious response to these demands for greater autonomy, together with the tensions thrown up by the differential distribution of wealth in the Green Revolution made space for the emergence of a charismatic Sikh preacher Jarnail Singh Bhindranwale, whose rawly xenophobic anti-Hindu chauvinism began to catch the imagination of many not-so-well-off Sikh peasant farmers in the late nineteen seventies and early eighties. However his death (some would say martyrdom) in the chaos of Operation Bluestar, when the Indian Army found itself fighting a very hot war right within the sacred precincts of the Golden Temple, had even more disastrous implications. It led to a widening of the gulf between Punjabi Hindus and Sikhs, as well as further reinforcing the contradictions between Punjab and Delhi. Emergent Punjabi nationalism then found itself confronted by an equally chauvinistic form of Hindu nationalism, which now seems to be sweeping all before it right across the Hindi-speaking heartland of central north India.

The Rise (and Fall) of Sant Jarnail Singh Bhindranwale

As Mark Tully and Satish Jacob (1985) have shown, Bhindranwale's rise from obscurity was greatly facilitated by the covert support of Indira Gandhi and Gyani Zail Singh, who were then respectively serving as Prime Minister and President of India. Their reasons differed slightly, but both were equally machiavellian. On the one hand Mrs. Gandhi was adept at making friends with her enemies' enemies as a means of keeping potentially errant state governments in check, while Gyani Zail Singh, a former Chief Minister of Punjab, was keen to cause as much embarrassment as possible to his own long-standing rivals and erstwhile colleagues. So both seem to have concluded for their own reasons that Sant Jarnail Singh Bhindranwale was their man.

Blessed with much personal charisma, Jarnail Singh, a Sikh revivalist preacher had succeeded to the leadership of the Damdama Taksal (a shrine-cum-seminary) at the early age of thirty in 1977. The core theme of Bhindranwale's teaching was that Sikhs should return to the behavioural rules of the *khalsa*, as laid down by Guru Gobind Singh in 1699, if they wished to avoid the danger of sliding back into Hinduism once again - a position which he shared with many other preachers of Sikh revivalism.

Other aspects of Bhindranwale's arguments directly represented the interests of Punjab's smaller peasant farmers, and especially those who were finding it hard to keep their heads above water in the increasingly commercialised context of the Green Revolution (Ballard, 1984). Indeed a major part of Bhindranwale's appeal arose from his vigorous criticisms of Punjab's political elite, whom he accused of overlooking the interests of small but good-hearted and honest peasants, a charge which was once again not without some substance. Jarnail Singh also articulated his criticisms in particularly graphic terms, insisting not only that the elite was corrupt, but that they had sold out to the faithless, money-grubbing Brahmins of Delhi.

Even though it may have brought them short-term benefits, both Indira Gandhi and Zail Singh clearly made a grave mistake in facilitating the rise of Bhindranwale, not least because they grossly underestimated the potential appeal of his anti-Hindu, anti-Brahmin, anti-shopkeeper, and anti-Hindu-chauvinist rhetoric to large sections of rural Sikh society, as well as to educated but unemployed Sikh youth. Not only did his message seem to offer swift salvation, but also clear solutions. Amongst the reasons for Bhindranwale's popularity was his justification of the use of force, on the grounds that Guru Gobind Singh had taught that Sikhs should act as *sant sipahi*, as saint-soldiers prepared to take whatever action was necessary to advance righteousness. Not only did his followers begin to arm themselves - they preferred Kalashnikovs - but they carried their weapons with great confidence, secure in the belief that they were warriors for justice. So it was that they began to unleash a reign of terror across Punjab which the police were powerless contain, at least at the outset because of the combined machinations of the President and the Prime Minister of India.

Having based himself within the sacred precincts of the Golden Temple in Amritsar, Bhindranwale also began to organise an alternative system of justice. Villagers could petition him freely, and offenders were summoned - on pain of death - to answer for their misdeeds. Bhindranwale's judgements were instant, and summary; and while the outcome was very often in keeping with popular moral assumptions, there was also scope for all manner of mayhem. One notorious example was the assassination of the second in command of the Punjab Police, who was himself a Sikh, on the steps of the Golden Temple itself; to Bhindranwale's opponents this was an outrage, but to his supporters it simply represented the just will of Sikhism's new saviour.

Operation Bluestar and its Consequences

As Bhindranwale became an uncontrollable threat to the established order, it became clear that some kind of action would have to be taken to contain him. However the Government of India's chosen course of military action, code-named Operation Bluestar, turned out to be a disaster, and yet further worsened the relationship between Sikhs and Hindus. Even so, by the time the authorities chose to act, the problem was formidable, since Bhindranwale and his men had fortified positions in and around the Akal Takht - the second most sacred Sikh shrine after the Har Mandir Sahib itself - right in the midst of Golden Temple complex in Amritsar. Taking him out was not going to be easy. However by no means all Sikhs favoured Bhindranwale's military occupation of their most sacred shrine, and those with a commitment to the more spiritual dimensions of the Gurus' teachings for the most part regarded his actions with horror. While a siege aimed at starving him out might well have succeeded without alienating the majority, the crass brutality of the Indian government's preferred strategy of military action closed all such options.

Strategically guided by Major-General Shubeg Singh, a guerilla warfare expert, Bhindranwale's men put up a far stiffer resistance than the Army had been expected. Within minutes of the assault, as many as a hundred soldiers had lost their lives in a murderously constructed killing field just inside the entrance to the *parikrama*. Command and control collapsed, and the normally well disciplined Indian army simply ran amok, and vented its anger on the softest target available, innocent Sikh pilgrims who had taken shelter in two Dharamshalas at the opposite end of the compound from the Akal Takht. Only then did they turn, once again, to the elimination of Bhindranwale and his two hundred or so armed followers. It took over 48 hours before they were all dead, during which a number of light tanks were driven right onto the sacred *parikrama* in order to shell the Akal Takht itself, virtually demolishing it (Ballard, 1985; Nayar and Singh, 1984; Tully and Jacob, 1985).

Though conducting a siege rather than mounting an outright assault would undoubtedly have been a tricky exercise, it would at least have offered the prospect of securing Bhindranwale's surrender while leaving the temple itself undamaged.

But such was the destruction wrought by Bluestar's execution that all Sikhs - including those who had previously been deeply hostile to Bhindranwale's antics - were horrified and outraged by what they inevitably viewed as an act of sacrilege. However critical some may have been of Bhindranwale beforehand, the circumstances of his death were such that he was instantly transformed into a *shaheed*, a martyr who could by definition do no wrong.

Nor did the Government take any sensible steps to assuage Sikh feelings in the aftermath of these horrors. Instead of promoting reconciliation, central government spokesmen argued that Sant Jarnail Singh Bhindranwale was a Pakistani agent hellbent on destroying the unity of India, while a flurry of stories suggesting that his followers were drug addicts and sexual perverts appeared in the newspapers. Worse was to follow, however. After two of Indira Gandhi's Sikh bodyguards avenged the insult by turning their guns on their mistress six months later, large numbers of Hindu thugs were trucked in from the suburbs, and let loose on Delhi's generally prosperous Sikh population. For forty-eight hours, the police stood by - perhaps following official orders - and did nothing; in the carnage that followed more than 2,000 Sikhs lost their lives, while many more saw their property looted and destroyed. Yet although this happened on the streets of the capital, not a single charge was brought against the perpetrators. Government inaction was far from unpopular, however. Amongst North Indian Hindus there was a widespread feeling that the Sikhs needed to be 'taught a lesson', and it soon became apparent that these ideas were but a component of a huge wave of chauvinism which identified all non-Hindus - be they Sikh or Muslim - as being the source of all of India's many ills. So powerful were these currents that the Government was loath to ignore them. Indeed it was on the back of just these chauvinistic feelings that a new Congress Government was swept into power, under the leadership of Mrs. Gandhi's son, Rajiv.

At the outset, Rajiv's policies were much more positive than those of his mother. He made a point of visiting Amritsar, to make at least partial amends for the atrocities of Bluestar. He also struck a deal with Sant Harcharan Singh Longowal which met almost all the Sikhs' demands, including the transfer of Chandigarh wholly to Punjab, a review of the distribution of irrigation water, more sympathetic treatment for the Army's 'Sikh mutineers', and the convening of an independent inquiry into the causes of the Delhi riots. But this window of opportunity did not stay open for long. Soon after he had signed the accord, Longowal was assassinated by some of Bhindranwale's impossibilist followers, who argued that Longowal was nothing more than a sell-out. But the authorities were far from blame-free either. Had the accord been fulfilled, the extremist argument that in no circumstances could Hindus or the authorities in Delhi be trusted would have been discredited. But their refusal to implement the accord - largely because they feared that if they did so Congress might lose an election in the neighbouring Hindu-dominated state of Haryana - simply reinforced all the militants' arguments.

Sikh fears were confirmed, and inter-ethic tensions between Sikhs and Hindus intensified yet further.

Since then the security situation in Punjab has deteriorated alarmingly: in an ever-increasing spiral of violence, the death toll - whether from 'terrorist' assaults, or from 'police encounters' of one kind or another - has risen to more than 3,000 a year.   But no solution is in sight.   Having pulled the plug on processes of democratic representation for fear that it would bring 'extremists' to power, all normal and judicial procedures have been put into abeyance as the authorities have sought to suppress terrorism by force.   But in doing so they have lost out on all fronts: while violence continues unabated, the Government has lost all semblance of credibility, especially in the countryside.   It is here that most 'terrorists' have their base, and here, too, that the Police and the Army have used every available means to track them down.   Villagers have therefore found themselves in a most unenviable position.   Though they would much prefer to avoid harassment by *goondas* (bandits) altogether, when faced with the stark choice between submitting to the demands of an alien and oppressive police force or to those of local lads with guns, most villagers prefer to do a deal with the latter.   They can at least be regarded as 'our boys'; and if the worst comes to the worst, their deaths can be legitimated by identifying them as martyrs for the sacred cause of local autonomy - Khalistan.

But if the Punjabi countryside has consequently become a hotbed of 'Sikh militancy' from which the Hindu population - most of whom made their living as shopkeepers - has fled in fear, Punjab's towns, which in any case have always been dominated by Hindu merchants, have begun to look like Hindu islands set in a Sikh sea.   Not that population transfer offers any kind of solution.   For Sikh peasants, the villages remain as dangerous as ever; and even after their retreat to the towns, Punjabi Hindus still feel anything but secure.   As hit and run attacks - directed at least as much at persons as at property - have grown ever more frequent, Punjabi Hindus have demanded ever more vigorous police and para-military intervention to suppress Sikh 'terrorism'.   By and large the authorities have indeed responded by applying yet more violence - as needs they must, given the weight of popular demands to 'save Hinduism' emanating from the Hindi-speaking areas further to the east; but in doing so the ever-deteriorating process of religious and ethnic polarisation between Punjabi Sikhs and Punjabi Hindus has been given yet another vicious twist.   The process seems unstoppable.

Against this background two crucial questions are worth asking.   First of all, was ethnic polarisation of this particular kind a feature of pre-colonial Punjab?   And secondly, how far did the imposition of British rule fuel to antagonism and conflict between Hindus and Sikhs?

Ranjit Singh and the Kingdom of Lahore

The eighteenth century was one of the most chaotic periods in the development of Sikhism (Khushwant Singh, 1966; McLeod, 1976). The line of hereditary Gurus had come to an end, and despite Gobind Singh's creation of the *khalsa*, by no means all Sikhs accepted his reforms; many preferred to remain faithful to Nanak's original teachings. The virtual collapse of Mughal authority following the Emperor Aurangzeb's death in 1709 also added to the chaos. Not only did this open up the possibility for local revolts against central authority, but also left Punjab extremely vulnerable to external attack from the Afghan highlands. Amongst the groups who took advantage of the growing chaos were the *misls*, guerilla bands whose members used Gobind Singh's notion of the *khalsa* as a justification of their military activities. While many recent nationalists have perceived the *misls* as heroic exemplars of Sikh ideals, we should, I believe, be much more sceptical. Closer examination suggests that the *misls* put very little energy into defending the collective interests of the Sikh community: at that time no such entity existed. Rather the primary concern of each *misl* was to maximise the territory which it controlled, and from which tribute could be extracted. Far from cooperating, inter-*misl* competition for political influence was intense.

All this was transformed, however, as a result of the immense strategic success of Ranjit Singh (1780-1839). Having taken control of Lahore as the last of the Afghan invasions finally petered out in 1799, the young leader of the Sukherchakia *misl* gradually consolidated his hold over the greater part of the Punjab, which he ruled with great success for the next forty years. Hence after centuries of incorporation into wider imperial structures, Punjab had at long last gained its own Maharajah, and hence comprehensive political autonomy.

What sort of entity had Ranjit Singh constructed? To many latter day Sikh nationalists, the answer seems self-evident: this must have been a Sikh kingdom. Nominally, at least, there is much to support this view. In his personal life Ranjit Singh was very consciously a Sikh, while many of the formal symbols of his rule were explicitly Sikh in character. The coins struck to mark his accession to power bore Nanak's name, and his government was known as *Sirkar Khalsaji*. Yet in other respects the Sikh veneer was very thin. Not only were the majority of people over whom he ruled Muslims, but the Sikhs were predominant in only one sphere: the military. Similarly virtually all the Maharajah's senior administrators were either Muslims or Hindus. It is also worth emphasising that Ranjit Singh's assumption of the status of Maharajah contradicted the egalitarianism of Sikh ideology. As leader of the Sukherchakia *misl*, Ranjit Singh could, and did, claim to be no more than primus inter pares - at least amongst his fellow *misldars*. Yet despite his strategic recourse to the rhetoric of the *khalsa sirkar* wherever it suited his interests, the new Maharaja also employed precisely the same legitimising strategies as those deployed by all previous aspirants to Kshatriya status, paying vast sums to expensively imported Brahmins to persuade them to perform royal rituals.

His death was marked in a similarly classic way: when his eldest son lit the funeral pyre, four ranis and seven concubines went to their deaths in company with their royal master.

Yet although the forty years of Ranjit Singh's rule were one of the most glorious periods in Punjab's history, they were not, paradoxically enough, a glorious period for Sikhism. During this period the Sikh tradition was not revitalised, nor did it attract many new recruits. Indeed all the evidence points in the opposite direction: the initial assessment of Punjab's new British rulers was that Sikhism was on the point of collapse. Thus as Sir Richard Temple reported that

> men joined in thousands, and they now depart in equal numbers. They rejoin the ranks of Hinduism whence they originally came, and they bring up their children as Hindus. The sacred tank at Amritsar is less thronged than formerly, and the attendance at the annual festival is diminishing yearly. The initiatory ceremony for adult persons is now rarely performed. (Quoted in Ibbetson 1884: 140)

The noted Sikh historian Teja Singh confirms this view, and goes on to argue that most Sikhs had become virtually indistinguishable from Hindus. As he puts it,

> Sikhism . . . became a mere fashion of temple and beard . . . but in all other ways the Sikhs showed no life in them. They worshipped the same old gods, indulged in the same old religious practices from which their Gurus had worked so hard to extricate them. Their baptism and five symbols became a mere anomaly. They were Hindus then, and it would have astonished them if anyone had suggested that they were not (Teja Singh, 1944: 118-19).

But if Sikhism underwent a vigorous process of revival during the British Raj, how can its almost terminal decline during the preceding period be accounted for? The answer seems clear enough. Once a small Sikh elite had entrenched itself in a position of power and privilege at the heart of the new kingdom, the militant egalitarianism of the *khalsa* was reduced to little more than window-dressing; and the more the Maharajah began to act as a Hindu *kshatriya* - as *rajniti* (statecraft) demanded that he must - the more symbolic his commitment to Sikhism necessarily became. But even though the *khalsa* consequently fell apart, commitment to other less militant strands of Sikhism - or in other words to the teachings of Guru Nanak - remained very much alive.

In the early days of British rule the Sikhs most certainly did not form a distinct, clearly bounded and self-conscious community: rather they were best viewed as one of Hinduism's many revisionist sects. It was only as a result of the polarising processes set in train by British rule that the Sikhs began to perceive themselves as members of a coherent and socially autonomous ethnic group, and thus as followers of a distinct and a wholly independent religious tradition of their own.

Hinduism in pre-British Punjab

Largely due to the lack of royal patronage prior to the arrival of Ranjit Singh, Punjabi Hinduism can boast of no major temples, no major pilgrimage centres, and no major centres of religious scholarship.   Nor do Punjabi Brahmins enjoy an exalted position. In the absence of royal sponsors, they have long had to rely on the Jat peasantry as their patrons; and given the Jats strong commitment to egalitarianism, and refusal to accept that anyone might be their superiors, Jats have always identified Brahmins as mere 'reciters of mantras', and hence as little more than a superior kind of *kammi*.

Religious and ethnic polarization was not a salient feature - if, indeed, it was a feature at all - of pre-British Punjab, for the different Hindu sectarian traditions (one of which was Sikhism) flowed seamlessly into one another. We are therefore left with a puzzle: why did British rule precipitate such cataclysmic polarization in Punjab, the like of which had never seen before?

The Religious and Cultural Implications of British Rule

The impact of British rule was a good deal more intense in Punjab than elsewhere in India. Since this was the last major province to be incorporated into the Raj, the colonists were in a very self-confident mood by the time they arrived, and their aim was improvement.   A new administrative structure was swiftly established, after which they set about improving and revitalising the Punjab's canal irrigation system, so laying the foundation for the province's future prosperity.   But the British did not restrict themselves to technical improvements, for while maintaining a vast social gulf between themselves and those whom they ruled, they also set about 'improving' Punjab both socially and culturally, by taking steps to abolish *sati*, child marriage and a wide range of other allegedly backward and superstitious practices.   The underlying message was clear: in all possible spheres British ways were regarded as infinitely superior to those of the natives.

How though, did Punjabis react to the imposition of comprehensive Imperial hegemony? Although they did not support the 1857 mutiny - thanks largely to the memory of the role of the Bengal Army in ensuring their subjugation less than a decade before - the uprising provided a clear model of one form which resistance might take: the simultaneous restoration of both *din* and *dharm* as a means by which Indians might free themselves from the morally destructive consequences of alien rule.   So if the British sought to legitimise their Raj in terms of their 'civilizing mission' to introduce 'Christian standards', Indians were equally aware, at least in principle, that religion, and especially inter-religious cooperation, offered a sound moral basis for organising resistance to an alien Raj.

Physical resistance was a dangerous business, however, for the British were prepared to be utterly ruthless in suppressing dissent. Thus in the aftermath of the mutiny their favourite tactic to underline their power was to tie dissidents to the mouth of a cannon and then quite literally to blow them to bits.   Yet precisely because this was a step of last resort, the fact that it was used against the Sikh-revivalist Kuka movement - eighty of whose members were blown away in 1872 - demonstrates that religiously inspired resistance movements were the basis of some very effective challenges to British hegemony.

The Growth of the Arya Samaj

Yet effective though the Kuka movement was - at least in terms of the extent to which it alarmed the British authorities - it proved to be the last of Punjab's wholly traditionalist uprisings, for all subsequent movements were a product of much closer contact with the Raj and its ideas and institutions.   This was particularly true in the case of the Arya Samaj (Jones, 1976).   This was the most important Hindu reformist movement in nineteenth century Punjab, and its impact has been so dramatic that every other ethno-political movement in Punjab has, to this day, to be understood in relationship to it.

The initial growth the Samaj was a direct consequence of exposure of Punjab's Hindu elite to Western-style education, which came about as the British established a network of schools and colleges throughout the province as a means of training up a new cadre of clerks and junior administrators.   The emergence of this rising generation of newly-educated Punjabi graduates, most of whom belonged to Hindu and Sikh trading castes, was to have an immense impact on the politics of the province.   Not only did this small group of graduates soon become a core component of the region's urban elite and nationalists, but many also became enthusiastic supporters of the Arya Samaj.

The reasons why the first generation of western-educated Punjabi Hindus became ardent nationalists are not hard to discern.   Though keen to participate in all the new opportunities which were opening up in the expanding Raj, the very education which was their passport to success had also made them aware of the extent to which the Raj brought with it a full-blooded assault on virtually every aspect of their social, religious and cultural traditions.

In itself conversion was nothing new, for saintly teachers operating in Hindu, Muslim and Sikh religious modes had long attracted devotees through the strength of their mystical commitments and insights.   But the new Christian missionaries adopted very different tactics.   Theirs was a utilitarian and thoroughly unmystical understandings of what religion might be all about, and they sought to achieve conversion primarily through rational persuasion.   Education consequently became a major battle ground, for the new colleges offered a great opportunity for missionary teachers to persuade their students that India's manifest economic, technological and political weakness was an inevitable consequence of the moral and ethical inferiority of its civilization.   Besides this the missionaries also had a penchant for street-preaching, where their favourite tactic was to hurl scurrilous invective against the indigenous faiths in an effort to prove that they were as morally unsound as they were ethically unsustainable.

Since the Arya Samaj developed in response to pressures of this kind, it is hardly surprising that the movement modelled itself closely on the missionaries' own organisational styles. They published tracts to counter those circulated by the missionaries, appointed full-time preachers, and proposed a thoroughgoing reform of Hinduism, with the object of weeding out what they identified as 'irrelevant' and 'erroneous' accretions. Their principal targets were precisely those practices - such as *sati*, the ban on widow-remarriage, the elevated status of hereditary Brahmins, and the worship of physical images of deities - of which the missionaries were most critical. But that was not all. Having established that Hinduism was just as textually-based, and just as firmly grounded in ethical monotheism as was Christianity, they also set out to demonstrate its superiority to the Christian tradition. Not only did they argue that Hinduism was more ancient than its semitic rivals, but also that it was far more compatible with - and perhaps even the precursor of - modern science.

Nor was Arya Samaji resistance solely conducted at an ideological level. A whole network of Dayanada Anglo-Vedic schools and colleges was rapidly established right across Punjab, competing directly with those established by the Government and the missionaries. As a result the education which was a necessary qualification for entry into the Punjab's professional elite could now be achieved without wholesale exposure to Christian thought.

Yet although the Arya Samaj offered a very effective means of resisting the hegemonic impact of the Raj, their reformist arguments, which were deeply critical of most aspects of popular Hindu religious practice, outraged many local Hindus. Hence the growth of the Samaj was countered by the emergence of a whole series of Sanatanist - traditionalist - movements, whose central concern was to ensure that Hinduism was not undermined from within by the Arya Samaj's militant young modernisers. Nor were these reactions confined to Hindus alone. Local Sikhs and Muslims were even more alarmed by the rise of Arya Samaj, especially when its preachers began to borrow the missionaries' most scurrilous arguments and to replay them in spades against their fellow-countrymen. Hence what both Sikhs and Muslims came ever more explicitly to identify as a Hindu 'threat' began to have far reaching effect on politics in Punjab. Not only did this gradually lead to a transformation of Sikh and Muslim political consciousness, but it created the conditions in which both groups began to feel that only by mobilising themselves collectively could they begin to protect their religious and political interests.

The Roots of Sikh Revivalism

Three main factors can be identified as crucial determinants of the revival of Sikhism during the late nineteenth century. Firstly Gobind Singh's ideal of a militant *khalsa* was a very effective vehicle for organising communally specific resistance to the Raj and its institutions.   Secondly, the British Indian Army's recruitment policy, which gave special preference to *khalsa* Sikhs, also contributed to a sharp resurgence in conformity to the external conventions of the *Khalsa*. However it was their reaction to Arya Samaji propaganda which precipitated by far the strongest boost to Sikh distinctiveness.

In their campaign to rid Hinduism of all its alleged accretions, Guru Nanak himself was amongst those who became targets for Arya Samaji criticism.   From their perspective it seemed straightforward.   Nanak knew no Sanskrit and taught in Punjabi.   How, asked the Arya Samajis, could he possibly have anything of philosophical significance to say?   To Sikhs, however, this was outrageous.   Thus while many members of the Sikh elite had joined the Samaj in the early days, most now changed their minds, as the prospect of Hindu hegemony began to look almost as alarming as that offered by the British.

Prompted by these fears, the Sikhs began to organise a rival chain of Singh Sabhas (Kapur, 1986), the better to defend themselves against the encroaching force of Arya Samaji criticism.   In doing so the Singh Sabhas central objective was out to construct a clear categorical boundary between themselves and their Hindus rivals. Before long they, too, became a very actively reformist group, whose perspective was just as revisionist as was that of the Arya Samaj with respect to orthodox Hinduism.

Since their central concern was to distinguish themselves from Hindus, the Singh Sabhas began to put steadily greater emphasis on Gobind Singh's rather than Nanak's teachings, and to insist that conformity to the rules of the *khalsa*, and therefore the wearing of a beard and turban, were absolutely central to being a Sikh. Yet important though this was as a first and very public step, it still did not fully answer the Arya Samaji argument that Sikhs were 'really' Hindus, not least because almost all Sikh families still employed Brahmin *purohits* to conduct domestic rites of passage.

To refute that charge, the Lahore Singh Sabhas began to prepare a comprehensive refutation of the Arya Samaji position.   They argued that Nanak's religious inspiration was wholly independent of Hinduism, and that Nanak's avoidance of Sanskrit was not a matter for regret.   Rejecting celebration of incomprehensible Sanskrit by the Arya Samajis, they praised the Gurus' use of the local Punjabi language and equally local Gurmukhi script, regarding both as positive markers of Sikhism's religious and cultural distinctiveness.   Between 1890 and 1910, the Singh Sabhas also began to create new, and distinctively Sikh rituals with which to cope with the major life-crises of birth, marriage and death, thereby freeing themselves from the necessity to call upon the services of Brahmin priests. But as Oberoi has shown, the way in which the marriage ritual was changed points very directly to the dialectic character of the underlying processes.   Thus if the Arya Samajis made the fire sacrifice, *hawan* a central feature of their worship, the Singh Sabhas used the *Guru Granth Sahib* for exactly the same purpose: it was this, rather than the sacred fire which the young couple were required to circumambulate, while anyone capable of reading the *Granth Sahib*, rather than a hereditary Brahmin, was deemed capable at officiating at the marriage (Oberoi, 1989).

Although only used at first by a small section of the urban elite, the introduction of these new rituals was viewed with great alarm both by the Arya Samaj and by the Sanatanist Brahmins: the former saw this as yet another irrelevant and unnecessary diversion, while the latter were more concerned about their income and privileges. Hence both groups vigorously opposed the new rituals.

While these contradictions arose largely as a result of the imposition of British rule, it now fell to the British, ironically enough, to arbitrate. The question at issue was simple, though crucial: were the new-style marriages legally acceptable, such that they would guarantee paternity and the transmission of property rights? Court rulings indicated that legislative change was required. The Singh Sabhas immediately began to organise large-scale protests demanding change, and in so doing greatly enhanced their authority as collective defenders of Sikh interests. And although they were successful, the fact that the new law was pushed through in the teeth of vigorous Hindu opposition further reinforced the Sabhas' argument that they represented a vital bastion against Hindu hegemony.

The Gurdwara Reform Movement

If the mass protests which eventually led to the passage of the Anand Marriage Act in 1909 were the first stage in the Sikhs' collective politicization, then a much larger movement involving much more violent confrontations, and led by the Akali Dal, finally put the seal on these developments. This time round, the issue at stake could hardly have been more crucial: nothing less than control of the Sikhs' own historic Gurdwaras.

Just as if they were Hindu shrines, the guardians of all Punjab's most important Sikh Gurdwaras were ascetic *mahants*. Though closely akin to Hindu *sannyasis* in status, behaviour and appearance, the *mahants* were members of the *udasi* sect. As such they were in a broad sense Sikhs, for they trace their origin back to Guru Nanak's son, Sri Chand. However the *udasis* differed from the mainstream in that their members remained celibate, while also wholly rejecting Guru Gobind Singh's reforms. To the new reformers, this was anathema, especially since the *mahants* had prospered under British rule. The land holdings attached to their Gurdwaras had increased in value, growing prosperity in rural Punjab had increased the volume of devotees' donations, while the new British legal system enabled the *mahants* to act, not as trustees, but as virtual owners of their temple's assets.

Although *mahants'* role in the Gurdwaras had never before been a cause for great concern, the increasingly influential Tat Khalsa wing of the Singh Sabhas now took the view that all interpretations of Nanak's teachings other than those developed by Guru Gobind Singh were little more than misguided sell-outs to Hinduism. From their perspective the non-*khalsa mahants'* control of the community's most sacred shrines seemed wholly untenable. Hence the *mahants* soon found themselves under intense pressure either to conform to neo-orthodox expectations or to abandon their offices. Not surprisingly, the *mahants* were most unwilling to abandon their offices, and saw no reason why they should change the theological positions to which they and their predecessors had long been committed. Conflict was inevitable, and most especially since this was an issue around which large scale mobilisation of the peasant masses, rather than just a narrow section of the urban elite, could take place.

There was an enormous popular response to the Akali Dal's call for the expulsion of the *mahants* during the early nineteen twenties, to which the *mahants* responded with vigorous appeals for legal protection. This presented the British with a major dilemma. Their immediate instinct was to protect the *mahants'* property rights, and to vigorously suppress all threats to public order, as vocal Hindu opinion, led by the Arya Samaj, was urging them to do. However the popularity of the cause - offering, as it did, an opportunity to challenge both British *and* Hindu hegemony - was so great that local officials were painfully aware of how dangerously provocative a policy of unmitigated oppression might be. In the end the British cracked before the Sikhs: after 400 people had been killed and more than 30,000 arrested, control of all the historic Gurdwaras was handed over to an elected Sikh body, the Shiromani Gurdwara Prabhandak Committee in 1925.

Nationalism and the Logic of Ethnic Polarisation

The protests that led to the establishment of the S.P.G.C. were by far the most substantial challenge to its authority that the British Raj in the Punjab had yet witnessed, for they involved a far larger number of people than did the Kuka revolt half a century earlier. If no resort was made to execution by cannon this time round, it was not so much because the rebellion was less threatening, but because by the early nineteen twenties it would have been most impolitic to use such a self-evidently savage form of repression. But it was not just the British who had changed in the intervening period: so, too, had the character of nationalist resistance itself.

To be effective, a nationalist movement must generate a powerful sense of moral solidarity amongst its members: the greater that sense of solidarity, the more powerfully equipped it will be to achieve its goals. But in India, as in most other culturally and religiously plural societies, national unity has proved elusive. As the Punjab all too clearly demonstrates, the ideas and symbols which appeal to the majority may well alienate minorities, and so could be an exceedingly potent recipe for national disunity.

Whenever ethnic polarisation erupts, it is very often interpreted as an outpouring of 'ancient hatreds'. Yet closer examination is much more likely to reveal the very opposite - as when the very earliest resistance movements, such as the rebellion of 1857, cut across the disjunctions which have subsequently proved so intractable, by pitching their appeal for moral solidarity around a perception of common alienation from their immoral *feringhee* overlords.   But as the Raj matured, so too did the resistant nationalist movements.   Although all acknowledged the need for unity, the possibility of inter-religious and inter-sectarian cooperation grew steadily more remote as nationalist movements became more complex and sophisticated.   Nationalism, democracy and even Independence have brought very mixed benefits: at least as much has been lost as was gained.   Why?

As nationalist movements matured, so inverse definitions of unity (of *din* and *dharm* united against the wholly immoral *feringhee*, for example) exercised a declining appeal, especially amongst the educated elite.   Hence the newly emergent intelligentsia put a great deal of thought and effort into constructing a more positive vision of themselves and their history, the neo-traditional vision of themselves and their history which they constructed was not nearly so 'traditional' as its proponents supposed.   Although the reformers looked to the past as a source of inspiration, this did not mean that they were *actually* returning to the practices of some former golden age.   Rather they were adjusting current practices, and invoking a largely mythical past in order to legitimise their innovations.

Two dimensions are crucial to this process of cultural reinvention.   Firstly the sleight of hand which presents such developments as 'traditional' ensures that new ideas, including some which may have been directly borrowed from their oppressors, can be seamlessly and unthreateningly integrated into the local order. Secondly such ideas also directly facilitate the construction of a powerful sense of corporate unity and common purpose, and ultimately of nationhood itself.   The Arya Samaj is a classic exemplar of both these processes.   Yet however successful the Samaj may have been in generating a sense of unity amongst Punjab's Hindu elite, it carried a large sting in its tail.   Like so many other nationalist movements world-wide, the Arya Samaj signally failed to address the fact that the population which it was trying to draw together in this way was anything but culturally, linguistically and religiously homogeneous.   Precisely because its nationalism was grounded in the ideological assumptions of the upper-caste Hindu elite, it alienated all those who stood outside the mainstream of upper-caste Hindu orthodoxy.

Conclusion

This paper has sought to highlight the extent to which the Sikhs' reactions to this perceived threat closely parallelled the Arya Samaj's reactions to the Raj itself. Like the Samajis, the Sikhs have systematically reinterpreted past history to establish a new orthodoxy, which they have subsequently used to transform themselves into a very active socio-political group whose boundaries are clearly marked, and where those contained within them feel a powerful sense of mutual obligation.   And although the dialectics of Arya/Sikh polarisation has its roots in the colonial context, independence of India has in no way lessened the vigour of that process.   Indeed the arena within which mutual polarisation is being worked out has now been extended to cover the whole of North India, while the gulf between the two sides has become wider than ever before.

References

Ballard, R. (1984) 'The Bitter Drama of the Sikhs' *New Society*, 21st June 1984 pp.464-466.
Ballard, R. (1985) 'Punjab's Uneasy Calm', *New Society*, 20th September, pp405-406.
Ibbetson, D. (1881) *Report on the 1881 Census of the Punjab*, Government Press, Lahore.
Jones, K. (1976) *Arya Dharm: Hindu consciousness in 19th-century Punjab*, Berkeley: University of California Press.
Kapur, R. (1986) *Sikh Separatism: the Politics of Faith*, London: Allen & Unwin.
McLeod, W. H. (1976) *The Evolution of the Sikh Community*, Oxford University Press.
Nayar, K. and Singh, K. (1984) *The Tragedy of Punjab*, Delhi: Vision Books.
Oberoi, H. (1988) 'From Ritual to Counter-ritual' in O'Connell, J. T., Israel, M. and Oxtoby, W. G. (eds) *Sikh History and Religion in the Twentieth Century*, Toronto: University of Toronto Centre for South Asian Studies.
Singh, K. (1966) *A History of the Sikhs* (2 Vols), Oxford: Oxford University Press.
Singh, T. (1944) *Sikhism: Its Ideals and Institutions*, Lahore.
Tully, M. and Jacob, S. (1985) *Amritsar: Mrs. Gandhi's Last Battle*, London: Jonathan Cape.

8

The Punjab Crisis and Sikh Mobilisation
in Britain

Darshan Singh Tatla

The previous chapter has provided a historical sketch of the forces which have formed and determined the relationship between politics and religion in Punjab. This chapter illustrates how the Indian army invasion of the Golden Temple in Amritsar has made a deep impact on Sikhs in Britain and North America and mobilised them for action and transformed their political organisation[1]. An account of Sikh political organisations before and after 1984 clearly shows that the Sikhs have expressed their political demand for an independent homeland through religious symbolism and religious institutions.

Sikh Political Organisations in Britain

Sikhs in Britain retain close religious, cultural, political and economic ties with their Punjab homeland. Their settlement in Britain has reproduced religious and social life which is similar to patterns found in Punjab. There are about 150 active *gurdwaras* and political organisations like the Akali Dal, Communist Party and Congress Party which follow home based politics.

Approximately, half a million Sikhs live in Britain. Their experience of iron foundries and textile mills combined with language difficulties made educated ones among them the *batoos* (interpreters) and leaders. From their experience of harsh working conditions, coupled with discrimination and marginality, the Indian Workers Association emerged as the first political organisation in 1956. In company with leaders of other black organisations, communist members of the IWA gained popularity among the Panjabi workers. In the 1960s, IWA was able to establish a network of branches in every major Sikh locality in Britain and IWAs in Southall and the Midlands became large organisations.

In 1966, Sant Fateh Singh from Punjab visited Britain and established Akali Dal as an extension of the Sikh political party in UK. Thus IWA, Akali Dal and the local *gurdwara* provided a context for political action. From the 1970s, the Akali Dal began to control *gurdwaras* and supported IWAs in their campaigns. While the IWAs campaigned against immigration laws and racial discrimination, Akali Dal showed solidarity with Sikh leaders in the Punjab. IWA also attracted some Panjabi Hindus who became prominent in its activities.

Although Sikhs were greatly concerned with fairness and equality in Britain, what aroused the passion of leaders and followers alike was politics in the Punjab which influenced the local organisation and mobilisation. For example, the splits in the Indian Communist Party also created divisions within the IWA.   With a significance loss of membership in 1990s, separate IWAs have now come together to form a single organisation. Home politics have led to mobilisation and rallies. For instance, IWAs, Akali Dal and Sikh groups demonstrated on 19th October 1969 to demand that Chandigarh, the capital of Haryana, should be returned to Punjab[2]. The demand for autonomy and eventually independence in the establishment of Khalistan (the land of pure ones), a separate Sikh state, was to find expression amongst Sikhs in Britain.   The following section is concerned with tracing two interrelated developments.   It shows that the concern for an independent homeland had developed among Sikhs well before 1980. Secondly it shows that this demand became more fully defined as a wider political issue after 1984.

The Homeland Issue

In 1960s Sikhs organised a number of campaigns to retain their right to wear turban as a symbol of their religious identity.   The Wolverhampton Transport Authority had eventually allowed Sikh drivers to wear turban[3].   Some Sikh leaders had appealed to Indian ambassador to intervene in the dispute. As he was unwilling to do so, Sikhs denounced the Indian government and Mr. D. S. Parmar demanded a Sikh Ambassador who would be sympathetic to Sikh issues.

In his opposition to the Indian High Commission, Charan Singh Panchi formed the Sikh Homeland Front which broke ties with the Akali Dal. When Dr. Jagjit Singh Chohan, an ex-finance minister in the Punjab government, came to Britain, he created a political organisation to propagate the idea of Sikh Homeland.   The majority of the Sikhs in Britain and North America did not share his sentiments. Leeds and Wolverhampton Sikh *gurdwaras* criticised him. There was little if any acceptance of his views in Southall.

Denounced by other Sikh leaders and denied entry into the main *gurdwaras*, Dr. Chohan continued his activities. These included the hoisting of a Khalistani flag in Birmingham, organising meetings and visiting Sikhs in North America. When Zorawar Singh Rai of Sikh Homeland Front became the president of Akali Dal in June 1972, the relationship between Sikhs and Indian High Commission deteriorated. Zorawar Singh Rai asked all *gurdwaras* to boycott the Indian High Commission[4]. Under his leadership, an Akali Dal faction organised a protest rally against the Indian High Commission in August 1973. This was the first overseas Sikh protest against the Indian authorities.

Although the Sikh Homeland Front was in disarray with differences between modest Charan Singh Panchi and more active Dr. Chohan, the latter maintained regular demonstrations outside the Indian High Commission on Republic Day of India, on 26th January each year. In the late 70s and early 80s, the turn of events in the Punjab suited Dr. Chohan's separatist aims. After burning the Indian national flag, for which he was arrested, and after he had received a communication from Sant Bhindranwale[5], he could still barely attract any significant support from *gurdwara* audiences.

Political events in India continued to influence Sikh politics in Britain. Between 1972 and 1977, Akalis launched several protest marches to embarrass the Punjab Congress ministry. When they came to power in 1977, they honoured a number of overseas Sikhs by inviting them to Punjab. In August 1977 Dr. Chohan proposed that Punjab should be renamed as the Sikh homeland. In November 1979, he took up the case of radio transmission from the Golden Temple. An International Golden Temple Corporation was set up by a number of prominent Sikh businessmen. The Corporation invited Sant Jarnail Singh Bhindranwale to the UK, and it also arranged a 'World Sikh Festival' in July 1982 at which a seminar theme was 'Sikhs are a nation.' Ganga Singh Dhillon's, an American Sikh was the main force behind a resolution passed at the Sikh Educational Conference in Chandigarh asserting 'Sikhs are a nation'. The Sikhs began to debate for and against the Sikh state and whether or not Sikhs constituted a nation.

From 1982 onwards, as the Akali campaign for autonomy took a confrontational position against the government of India, under the titular leadership of Sant Bhindranwale, the Akali Dal in Britain was increasingly drawn into the Punjab campaign. Sant Longowal, president of Shiromani Akali Dal sent several letters of appeal to Sikh leaders in Britain, North America and the Far East to draw their attention to repression and suffering of the Sikhs in Punjab.

From 1983 onwards, the Sikh campaign in the Punjab found increasing support among Sikhs in Britain. On 7th February 1983, some five thousand Sikhs held a march in London to show solidarity with the Punjab campaign. This coincided with Punjab Sikh leaders' campaign of *Rasta Roko* (Block the Roads). Giani Amolak Singh, president of Akali Dal (Longowal) toured *gurdwaras* in Britain to collect money for the Indian campaign. When Indira Gandhi arrived at Royal Festival Hall to inaugurate the Festival of India in 1982, Sikh demonstrators including IWA and Hind Mazdoor Lahir members protested against her presence. At a reception for the Indian Prime Minister, only representatives of small sects of Sikhs, the

Namdharis and Ramgarhias were invited to the Grosvenor Hotel.   A major demonstration led by Puran Singh Karichowale, a Sikh saint, on 10th May 1984 in London attracted some 10,000 Sikhs.   On instructions from Amritsar, a section of Akali leaders also burnt a copy of Act 25 of Indian Constitution in front of the Indian High Commission office.   Conscious of sympathy and mobilisation among British Sikhs for the Punjab cause, Akalis in Britain, raised a considerable amount of money and sent it to Sikh leaders in Punjab.   They also proposed that each city should have a branch of Akali Dal and that the national leadership should be elected from these local branches.   However these plans remained unfulfilled as the Sikhs were struck by an overwhelming tragedy in June 1984.

Invasion of the Golden Temple and the Sikh Reaction to it

The Sikh demand for autonomy and resolution of territorial disputes took a more violent turn as the negotiations between the central government and the state of Punjab broke down[6].   On 3rd June 1984 when the Indian armed forces mounted an assault on the Golden Temple under 'Operation Bluestar,' to 'flush out the extremists'.   Sikhs were shocked and angry.   The Golden Temple represents a sacred entity as did no other historic shrine for them.   Many could not believe that their own government could set its armed forces upon its own citizens.   Some who would have disputed Sant Bhindranwale's strategy began to hail him as a martyr. As the shock wave spread in the community, Sikhs held special meetings and passed resolutions condemning Indian government's action.

On Sunday, the 10th June, Sikhs from all walks of life joined in a protest march from Hyde Park to the Indian High Commission.   Over 50,000 Sikhs chanted slogans denouncing the Indian government and shouting 'Khalistan jindabad' (long live independent Sikh State).   The march passed off peacefully.   The Sikhs expressed their anger in several ways.   They called for the 'liberation of the Golden Temple' and volunteers were recruited to go to Punjab.   All *kabbadi* tournaments were cancelled across the country for rest of the year.   A number of video-tapes and books received from Indian High Commission were publicly burnt at many *gurdwaras*.   Some organised local demonstrations, others wrote angry letters to the press and several events within the Sikh community followed in quick succession[7]. Between 3rd June and 31st October, 1984 when her Sikh body guards had assassinated Prime Minister Indira Gandhi in New Delhi, two major Sikh organisations had been formed.   These were the Khalistan Council and International Sikh Youth Federation.   Both were committed to nothing less than an independent Sikh state.   While the Indian state defended the army action in the Golden Temple for unity of India, British Sikhs were outraged over what they thought was the wanton desecration and destruction of their most sacred and historic shrine.   The community saw the events very differently from the version officially presented by the Indian government. Subsequent events leading to the massacre of over three thousand Sikhs in Delhi, and hundreds of Sikhs in other cities, the consequent spiralling and worsening of law and order coupled with increasing militancy among the Sikh youth have embroiled Punjab in an unparalleled scale of violence.

These events changed the organisational pattern and style of leadership among overseas Sikhs. The pictures of Sant Bhindranwale along with Subeg Singh and Amrik Singh and other prominent Sikhs killed in the army action in Amritsar have gone up in British *gurdwaras*. New Sikh martyrs are now revered. Many traditional religious practices within the *gurdwara* have seen radical changes. The practice of inviting Indian politicians to visit the *gurdwara* was scrapped. Even the so-called 'moderate' Sikh leaders visiting Britain in the post 1984 period had to address the Sikh congregation away from the main *gurdwaras*. Those connected with Khalistan movement or those whose relatives were tortured by the Indian authorities have been honoured[8]. Several major *gurdwaras*' management committees changed hands replacing the old Akali leaders with more younger Sikh youth calling for revenge and a sovereign state for the Sikhs. Thousands of Sikh youths have taken *Amrit* - a Sikh ceremony for initiating into the Khalsa tradition. Ragis (religious hymn-singers) and Dhadis (folk-singers) have recorded songs in the memory of Sikh martyrs who have laid down their lives bravely against the Indian army. Videos, tapes and literature celebrating the heroic deeds of those who fought and lost their life for the cause of Sikh nation, preserving *izzat* (honour) and sovereignty, and have been brought out and purchased by eager and ordinary Sikhs[9].

Support for Khalistan among British Sikhs

Sikhs expressed their support for an independent Khalistan by forming the Khalistan Council on 23rd June in Southall. A Sikh business family provided it an office in Central London. An appeal for funds raised £100,000 in months. Khalistan Council held weekly meetings in various *gurdwaras* to discuss news from Punjab by anxious Sikhs amidst the cries of demand for an independent Sikh state. At one stage in 1985, the Khalistan Council claimed that Ecuador authorities were willing to recognise the government of Khalistan in exile.

Since 1984, main activities of the Khalistan Council have been to mobilise Sikh support for Khalistan. It has also published a news sheet *Khalistan News* and has joined other organisations in demonstrations against 'police killings' of Sikh youth in the Punjab. Every January, it holds a demonstration against Indian High Commission. The Council has also published several pamphlets and reprinted reports of human rights agencies from Punjab and Delhi. Dr. Chohan has often written an open letter to Sikh leaders in the Punjab and advised them on the future course of action. During the recent elections in Punjab held in February 1992 he cautioned Sikhs against democracy in the Punjab. He argued it would be a step back from an independent Khalistan. The strength of Khalistan Council has now dwindled to a small number of Dr. Chohan's admirers. This has not stopped his campaign in *gurdwaras* where people listen to him eagerly. Every year, Khalistan Council holds an annual conference.

The second most important organisation to emerge in the wake of June events is the International Sikh Youth Federation (ISYF). When Bhai Jasbir Singh - a nephew of Sant Bhindranwale came to Britain, he helped to form it. On 23 September 1984 at Almvale Comprehensive School, Walsall, in the presence of 4,000 Sikh youths, the new constitution of International Sikh Youth Federation was approved and a 51 member panel was announced. ISYF units went up to twenty-one in different cities. Hundreds of youths joined Birmingham and Southall branches. ISYF leader Jasbir Singh was detained at Heathrow in December, and the Indian High Commission persuaded the authorities to expel him[10].

Conflict and struggle for power between the Federation and the local *gurdwara* management committees was inevitable. As the Federation was able to mobilise more successfully, it undermined the old leadership, sometimes leading to litigation and to court cases. In this battle, the Federation was successful in winning elections and imposing controls over the *gurdwaras* in Derby[11], Leicester Nottingham Southall, Smethwick, Luton, Huddersfield and Coventry.

The Federation has established its own Panjabi weekly paper, *Awaz-e-Quam* (The Voice of Nation) from Southall in 1986, and then from Smethwick. The Federation has also published several pamphlets including the Delhi riots report 'Oppression in Punjab'[12]. It has set up a Sikh Human Rights Group with the cooperation of some Sikh barristers in London. However, the Federation has also suffered some set-backs. Authorities have arrested some activists on various charges in the past five years as a spate of violent events have occurred within the Sikh community. The Federation president, Dr Pargat Singh escaped a violent attack on 7th November 1985, while the house of his successor was attacked by some unknown gang. The Federation has also split into separate factions. A section of its leadership parted company in late 1985 setting a rival organisation under the banner of Damdami Taksal[13] legitimising their status by their leaders in India. Many Sikh organisations, including IWAs have used this method of establishing their own credentials while upsetting the rivals' claims.

Babbar Khalsa well-known for its members' strict adherence to the Khalsa traditions, was set up in 1978. Prior to 1984, members of Babbar Khalsa were content with weekly recitations of Sikh scriptures and night-long hymn singing sessions. In the post 1984 period, they have been among the most radical advocates of Khalistan[14]. They have won high praise from Sikhs for their stubborn resistance and valour against the Indian army during the Golden Temple fighting. Their leader was on the Khalistan Council but now maintains a separate establishment in Birmingham.

The Pattern of Mobilisation

Most post-1984 British Sikh organisations would like to see the formation of Khalistan. However Sikhs do not support these organisations evenly. Caste and occupation differences within Sikh community influence the support for Khalistan. While Jat Sikhs are in the forefront of separatist movement, the Ramgarhias and Namdharis have shown little interest; indeed some of them are opposed to the movement[15] although they condemn the invasion of the Golden Temple. The Bhattra Sikhs, on the other hand, have shown enthusiasm for the separatist cause. They have held conferences in their *gurdwaras*. Of all the Sikh groups, the lower caste Ravidasi Sikhs have been unambiguous in opposing the Khalistan movement.

Gurdwaras have paid a central part in political mobilisation among the Sikhs and this explains the importance of religion in Sikh politics. A *gurdwara* is not just a place of worship but a community centre for religious, political and cultural concerns, where even family disputes are resolved. Births, marriages and death ceremonies are invariably concluded in the *gurdwara*. *Gurdwara* may be now more important for British Sikhs than ever before as it is the main focus of social and political activities. Along with other bodies, *gurdwaras* have reacted to news from Punjab either by placing advertisements in Panjabi weeklies or by calling meetings. When the Punjab Accord was signed by Indian Prime Minister, Rajiv Gandhi and Akali leader, Sant Longowal in September 1985, a majority of Akali leaders, the Khalistan Council, the ISYF and management committees of over seventy *gurdwaras* rejected it.

Internal differences, factions and conflict mark Khalistani organisations, undermining their unity and effectiveness. The earlier sense of unity between different organisations like the Akali Dal, IWAs, Communist Party and the Congress Party based as it was on the notion of common Indian nationality seems to have declined. It has presented difficult dilemmas to those who are torn between their Indian patriotic feelings and their desire to preserve an autonomous nation for the Sikhs as they see their homeland endangered.

Supporters of Khalistan have also had to confront those opposed to the movement. When the Indian Overseas Congress wanted to celebrate the Indian Independence Day in Derby on 14 August 1984, angry Sikh youth halted these celebrations and subjected the leaders to angry criticism and expelled them from the *gurdwara* committees. In 1985 when Swaran Singh, who had been a cabinet minister in Indian government, inaugurated Punjab Unity Forum, its first conference discussed the twin aims of keeping Britain's Sikh community loyal to India and to sustain unity among Indians abroad. The events to follow led to shooting of Sohan Singh Lidder, the president of Indian Overseas Congress. An International Sikh Youth Federation activist, Sulakhan Singh Rai was charged with murdering Tarsem Singh Toor, general secretary of Southall branch of Congress who had been shot dead. Mr. Rai was given a life sentence at the Old Bailey.

A Panjabi weekly newspaper *Sandesh International* had also sustained a campaign emphasising the unity of India and was the only Panjabi paper to support the Indian government in the aftermath of 1984. It described as traitors those Sikhs who had burned the Indian flag[16]. Supported by Sandesh International, a new organisation calling itself Sachkhand Nanak Dham (SND) which argued for the unity of all Indians and mankind entered into a violent confrontation with the Sikh Youth.   Some Sikh youths tried to set fire to the headquarters of SND in Birmingham. Sachkhand Nanak Dham launched an appeal to support its mission to install a gold-bound copy of Guru Granth Sahib in the Golden Temple. It asked the management committee of Southall *Gurdwara* to take this copy to India with proper ceremonies. However, Southall Sikh leaders were alerted to the 'propaganda value SND was trying to generate' and declined the offer. The continuing confrontation between SND and Sikh youth came to a boil when their leader, Darshan Das was murdered by two Sikh youths[17].

As a secular organisation, the IWA opposed the separatist tendencies among the Sikhs. Some of the communist leaders were well-known and well-regarded among the Panjabis. However, their inability to cope with the Punjab crisis brought their decline as they were rapidly removed from the position of power and authority in Sikh *gurdwara* committees[18].   In the aftermath of June 1984, IWAs issued statements denouncing the demand for an independent Sikh state. The statement reproduced Punjab Communist Party stand on the 'Punjab problem'. Some Sikh youths in Derby and Leicester resigned in September 1984 at a public meeting. When some of IWA workers tried to distribute a pamphlet condemning both Indian government and the Sikh leaders for the tragedy in Amritsar in front of Smethwick *Gurdwara*, angry Sikh youths gave them a severe beating. This was the first of a series of fights between Indian Workers Association and Sikh youths which took place at several places in the subsequent period. While IWA [GB] through stresses the unity of India, Sikh communists allied to the Naxalite movement are more critical of the Indian Government's handling of the Punjab situation. They propose a communist revolution to remedy all the ills of the existing order[18]. The Southall IWA took a different route to oppose the Sikh separatist ideas. Vishnu Datt Sharma and his associates appealed for the boycott of *Des Pardes* and *Punjab Times*, the two Panjabi weeklies, whom they branded as Khalistani papers[19]. The circulation of these two papers in fact went up due to the heightening of interest among Sikh readers. In another move, Sharma also launched a monthly *Charcha* aiming to woo 'the patriotic section of the Punjabi population' and to sway them away from the separatist ideas. His stand, however, was not shared by other Punjabi communists[20].

India and the British Sikhs

On 10th July, the government of India issued a White Paper on the army action in the Golden Temple. The Indian High Commission sent it to prominent *gurdwaras*. There was also a video of the Golden Temple showing Jathedar Kirpal Singh of Akal Takhat, declaring (under duress from the army authorities as transpired later) that the Golden Temple was unharmed. A glossy booklet titled 'Sikhs in their Homeland-India' was sent to a number of *gurdwaras*[21]. It showed several Sikh personalities, photos of some *gurdwaras* and concluded with the message of Giani Zail Singh, the President of India defending the army action as necessary to save the 'sanctity of the Golden Temple'. The Government of India also announced visa requirements for all visitors to India supposedly to curb Sikh extremism abroad. Many organisations including the IWAs called for the lifting of this requirement, but without any success[22].

The White Paper cites Jagjit Singh Chohan's connection with overseas Sikh leaders. Observers of the means employed by Indian Government in combating Sikh separatism abroad have commented upon such measures as inappropriate[23]. The alleged reliance on pseudo-religious movements such as Sachkhand Nanak Dham to undermine the Sikh revolt from within are too transparent to be effective. Similarly the tactics of 'divide and rule' policy applied to groups within Sikh community have also been counterproductive. The strict regulations, ill-treatment of Sikhs at Delhi airports for alleged connection with separatist leaders has fostered negative attitude among some Sikhs towards India. The list of Sikhs under surveillance in Britain, according to Kuldip Nayar was very long and he took some credit in scrapping some part of it[24]. The pressure on Punjabi media in Britain can also be cited as also another example of how Indian authorities have shown high-handedness abroad.

India has also been pressing upon governments of United States, Canada and Britain to deal severely with the 'Sikh extremism and separatism'. The charge that Sikh extremists were operating in Britain was reported to be the main agenda of the Rajiv-Thatcher talks. Four Federation Sikhs were arrested in Leicester on charges of conspiracy to murder the visiting Indian prime minister and Harwindar Singh Gill and Jarnail Singh were jailed for 16 and 14 years respectively on the charges brought against them. Bilateral trade and the arms deal with India possibly influenced the British policy[25]. The Indian government has also insisted on concluding a bilateral treaty of extradition in order to curb the activities of Sikh 'extremists'[26]. Thus both Labour and Conservative parties have taken a stand on the 'Punjab question'. In the case of Tory party, matters have been rather more urgent. The Anglo-Asian Conservative Association had to be dissolved by the Central Conservative Office due to what was alleged to be 'Sikh domination' of it[27]. Moreover some local members of Parliament have been involved in the lobbying of particular cases of Sikhs held in India[28]. Thus Sikhs are likely to remain an important issue in Anglo-British relations in the foreseeable future. The Labour party has also issued statements from time-to-time, concerning the human rights issue but shelving the question of independence. The Green Party's stand comes very close to endorsing Sikhs' right of self-determination[29].

Although some commentators may regard Sikhs as 'romantics and fools',[30] intervention by them into the political life of Punjab has a long tradition[31]. The Ghadr movement in the Pacific States of America and Subhash Chandra Bose leading the Indian National Army with many Punjabi soldiers in the Far East are examples how diaspora Punjabis have affected the political events at home[32]. Both Khalistan and the Ghadr movements suggest some striking parallels, in deployment of tactics and pattern of mobilisation. The Khalistan movement is now based on the religious symbolism and institutions confined to Sikhs only whereas the Ghadr rising was more secular in principle and concerned with freedom of India though most of its personnel came from Sikhs of peasant background who traced their origins to central Punjab.   These differences between two movements in separate historical contexts show that Sikh political consciousness has changed over a period of this century in response to variation in political changes.

Conclusion

Outlining the distinction between Sikh political organisation before and after the invasion of the Golden temple in 1984, this chapter has explained the complex rise of new Sikh organisations in response to this event and the consequent transformation of Sikh political self-consciousness. The champion of Khalistan, Dr Chohan, provides a good illustration of this process. He had hardly any support for his Sikh homeland ideas in Britain before 1984. But he was able to mobilise a great deal of political support for Khalistan after 1984. The Indian authorities and their insensitivity in dealing with the demand for Sikh autonomy has played no small a part in undermining the feeling of patriotism amongst British Sikhs. Dismissal of the Akali Dal ministry, direct central rule and human rights violation by paramilitary forces in Punjab have contributed to ill-feeling.   The Sikhs were already aware of unwillingness of the Indian authorities to give them proper recognition in public affairs before 1984.

The Indian army invasion of the golden temple and the consequent destruction of the Akal Takhat has been the most crucial factor in transforming the Sikh political organisations in Britain towards a demand for an independent Sikh homeland. A secure and independent Punjab may have been the 'imagined homeland' of a few overseas Sikhs prior to 1984. In the post-1984 period, this has turned into a serious and attractive scenario for many. A distinct minority within Sikhs is now committed to the achievement of an independent country. Whether the silent majority of ordinary Sikhs would be persuaded by their arguments depends upon two factors, namely, the sense of security they feel in Britain and the future events in Punjab itself. That both of these factors are outside the parameters of a migrant community points to the dilemma of its members. The Sikh reaction and the pattern of mobilisation in Britain to 1984 events in the Punjab reminds us how a secure ethnic minority could suddenly become conscious of a 'threatened' homeland'. Harry Goulbourne has argued that the Sikh sense of alienation stems from insecurity they experience in foreign lands and the unabated violence in the state they come from[33]. Sikhs have never felt homeless, though the history of the community shows how precarious its survival has been. Events since 1984, may have turned this confident ethnic community into a psychological state of 'homelessness' and the idea of a sovereign Khalistan has, perhaps for that reason, found a distinct chord of endorsement from a section of the community.

Footnotes

1   I am thankful to Rohit Barot, Harry Goulbourne and Gurharpal Singh for their comments on this material. I am also grateful to Sujinder Singh Sangha and the editors of Panjabi newspapers. I am grateful to Dr. J. S. Chohan, Dr. Pargat Singh, Dr. J. S. Rai, Balwinder Singh Dhillon, Bhai Gurmel Singh, Gurmej Singh Gill, Gurdeep Singh, Balbir Singh and Sewa Singh Lalli for their views on the Khalistan movement. None of them is responsible for my interpretation of their arguments.
     Khalsa or Panth refers to collective body of Sikh community, occasionally both are used together, Khalsa Panth. Shiromani Akali Dal is the main Sikh party in the Punjab, Akali/s refers to its member/s.
2   The call for IWA support was given by Narinder Dosanjh at a meeting in Beacon Cinema, Smethwick. Jaswant Singh Kanwal, prominent Panjabi writer visiting Britain chaired this meeting. See DeWitt, John for an account of Indian Workers' Associations.
3   Beetham (1970) who explored the 'turban issue' in 1960s did not explore the organisational structure of Sikh leadership.
4   This meeting took place in the presence of 300 Sikhs on June 1972 at Ealing Hall. See reports in *Des Pardes*, 3.2.1972.

5   See *Des Pardes*, 14.1.1983.
6   A spate of books on the Punjab Problem have appeared in the wake of 1984. Among these Kuldip Nayar and Khushwant Singh, *Tragedy of Punjab: Operation Bluestar and After* (1984), New Delhi, Vision Books; Amrik Singh (ed) *Punjab in Indian Politics* (1985), Delhi, Ajanta Publications; M. Tully and S. Jacob *Amritsar: Indira Gandhi's last Battle* (1985); Iqbal Singh, *Punjab under siege: a critical analysis* (1986), New York, Allen McMillan and Enderson; R Kapur, *Sikh Separatism: the politics of the faith* (1986), London, Allen & Unwin, are noteworthy.   None of these deal with overseas Sikh reaction in detail, though a number of them cite Dr. Chohan's activities.
7   For a study of reaction among Sikhs in Bristol, see Barot (1991).
8   Thus when Basant Kaur Khalsa, wife of Beant Singh arrived at Heathrow, in April 1991 she was warmly welcomed. She and her father were given 'siropas' (a characteristic Sikh from of honour) and substantial cash.
9   See Pettigrew 1991/92.
10   *The Guardian*, 7.1.85 reported the haste with which Jasbir Singh was deported from Britain. He was arrested at the Manila airport and taken to India.
11   This demonstration took place on 18th October 1985. See details in *Des Pardes* and *Punjab Times*.
12   This report was originally published by a Delhi based Human Rights organisation documenting violence against Delhi Sikhs after the assassination of Indian Prime Minster on 31 October 1984. See ISYF, Annual Report, Walsall, September 1986.
13   Sant Bhindranwale belonged to the Damdami Taksal which traces its lineage to a close follower of Guru Gobind Singh.   The Damdami Taksal gained prominence in the post 1984 period.
14   Babbar Khalsa came into prominence when 13 Sikhs belonging to Akhand Kirtani Jatha were gunned down in Amritsar in April 1978 during a clash with members of a dissenting sect called Nirankaris. Balbir Singh is the new chief of Babbar Khalsa in Britain replacing Gurmej Singh according to a recent announcement of the Babbar Khalsa from Punjab.
15   From 1983 the visiting Congress Party ministers were not welcome at major *gurdwaras*.   Some used the Ramgarhia *gurdwaras* to address the Sikh congregations. For more details of differentiation within the Sikhs, see Ballard (1989).
16   This Panjabi paper launched a vigorous campaign against Sikh separatists. However, its proprietor was sent to jail on charges of heroin smuggling and the paper was closed amidst controversy that the Indian High Commission partly financed it.
17   Sant Darshan Das was shot dead by two Sikhs in a Southall school when he was leading a prayer meeting on 11th November 1987. Two Sikhs Rajinder Singh Batth and Manjit Singh Sandher are serving life sentences for the murder.
18   At a meeting held at Summerfield school by IWA CPI(ML) Sikh youths came to disturb the meeting and as a result several people were hurt. Smethwick was the scene of another fight in July 1987.
19   *Lalkar* is the occasional publication through which such revolutionary solutions are offered.   For a general overview of Panjabi press, see Tatla and Singh 1989.
20   A Punjabi Marxist leader (Bains 1986) settled in Canada outlines his position on Sikh separatism.
21   *Sikhs in their Homeland*, India: Government of India, New Delhi, 1984
22   Strict visa regulations between Britain and India were relaxed with the arrival of the Janata Government headed by V. P. Singh.   The new Indian Ambassador, Mr. Kuldip Nayar took the credit for this relaxation. As a result,

the Indian ambassador was received by one or two *gurdwaras*, the first time an Indian diplomat was allowed inside a *gurdwara* since 1984.
23 A concerned scholar of Sikh diaspora had this advice to the Indian government: India . . . should develop policies that work on the psychological and cultural framework of the overseas community rather than resorting only to subversive activity and legal action.   Such policies could be developed with the cooperation of individuals who understand the thinking patterns and group processes of the overseas Sikh community. (Helweg, 1989).
24 See Nayar (1991).
25 A large Indian contract order with British Aerospace was reported to be cancelled due to Britain's soft policy towards the Sikh extremists.
26 The latest visits by British Home secretary to Delhi in February 1992, followed by his deputy was reported to be around this proposal. A treaty was signed in September 1992.
27 *The Guardian*, 20.8.86
28 Kuldip Kaur, wife of Mr. H. S. Bedi, one-time President of Anglo-Asian Conservative Association was arrested when she visited the Punjab and was released only after a personal petition from an M.P. and her case was raised in British Parliament.
29 See the Green Party statement issued in 1987.
30 See Jeffrey (1986) pp. 142-44, Chopra (1985), Nayar (1986) and Kshitish (1984).
31 See Barrier (1989) for an outline of relationship between Punjab and overseas Sikhs especially those in North America in the early part of this century.
32 For an account of the role of Indian revolutionaries abroad during the British rule of India, see Bose (1971). Juergensmeyer provides a cogent thesis of a tradition of 'revenge in order to restore honour' among the Sikhs and calls its overseas variant as 'the Ghadr syndrome'.
33 See Goulbourne (1991) who has argued forcefully for this framework.

References

Bains, H. (1987) *Call to the Martyrs*, London: Socialist Workers Party.
Ballard, R.   (1989) 'Differentiation and disjunction amongst Sikhs in Britain' in Barrier N G and Dusenbury, Verne, A (eds) *The Sikh Diaspora: migration and the experience beyond Punjab*, Delhi: Chanakya Publications.
Barot, R. (1991) 'The Punjab crisis and Bristol Sikhs' a paper presented to the British Association for South Asian Studies, Annual Meeting in Birmingham, 10-12 April.
Barrier, N. G. and Dusenbury, V. A. (1989) *The Sikh Diaspora: migration and the experience beyond Punjab*, Delhi: Chanakya Publications.
Beetham, D.(1970) *Transport and Turbans: a comparative study in local politics*, Oxford: University Press for the Institute of Race Relations.
Bose, A. C. (1971) *Indian Revolutionaries Abroad*, Patna.
Chopra, P. (1985) 'A turning point for Sikhs' in Amrik Singh (ed) *Punjab in Indian Politics*, Delhi: Ajanta Publications.
Dewitt, J. (1967) *Indian Workers Associations in Britain*, Oxford: Oxford University Press, for the Institute of Race Relations.
Dusenbury, V. A. (1989), 'On the moral sensitivities of Sikhs in North America' in Lynch, Owen M. and Kolenda, P. (eds) *Divine Passions: the social construction of emotion in India*, Los Angeles and Berkeley: University of California Press.
Goulbourne, H. (1991) *Ethnicity and Nationalism in Post-imperial Britain*, Cambridge University Press

Helweg, A. W. (1989) 'Sikh politics in India: the emigrant factor', in Barrier, N. G. and Dusenbury, V. A. (eds) *The Sikh Diaspora: Migration and Sikh Experience Beyond Punjab*, Delhi: Chanakya Publications, pp.305-336.
Jeffrey, R. (1986) *What's happening to India: Punjab Ethnic Conflict, Mrs Gandhi's death and test for federalism*, London: Macmillan.
Juergensmeyer, M. (1969) 'The Ghadr syndrome: immigrant Sikhs and nationalist pride', in Juergensmeyer, M. and Barrier, N. G. (eds) *Sikh Studies*, Berkeley, Graduate Theological Union, University of California Press, pp.173-190
Kshitish (1984) *Storm in Punjab*, Delhi: The Word Publications.
Nayar, K. (1985) 'After the accord' in Amrik Singh (ed) *Punjab Indian Politics*, Delhi: Ajanta Publications.
Nayar, K. (1991) *India House*, New Delhi: Penguin.
Pettigrew, J. (1991/1992) 'Songs of the Sikh resistance movement' *Asian Music*, Fall/Winter, pp.85-118.
Sheffer, Gabriel (ed.) (1986) *Modern diaspora in International Politics*. London: Croom Helm.
Singh, A. (ed.) (1985) *Punjab in Indian politics: issues and trends*, Delhi: Ajanta Publications.
Singh, G. (1987) Understanding the Punjab problem, *Asian Survey*, 27(12), December, pp.1268-77
Singh, K. and Singh, S. (1966) *Ghadr 1915: India's First Armed Revolution*, New Delhi.
Singh, U. (1987) *The waxing and waning of the Khalistan movement abroad* (Panjabi and English), Birmingham and Toronto: published by the author.
Tatla, D. S. and Singh, G. (1989) 'The Punjabi Press', *New Community*, 15(2), pp.171-184.

Panjabi Newspapers and Journals

Des Pardes (1965-) Panjabi Weekly from Southall.
Punjab Times (1965-) Panjabi Weekly from Southall
Awaz-e-Quam (1986-) Panjabi Weekly from Birmingham.
Sikh Pariwar (1987-) Panjabi Monthly, Birmingham.
The Unity: Journal of the Punjab Unity Forum (1985-) (Quarterly English from London).

9

Upanayana Ritual and Hindu Identity in Essex

Helen A. Kanitkar

The purpose of the *upanayana* ritual in Hinduism is to mark the transition from one mode of life to another, from childhood to student, as well as to prepare a child for the responsibilities of adulthood. Formerly both boys and girls went through the ceremony, but during the Brahminical period it gradually became confined to boys, and remained so until very recently, when a small minority of girls questioned this and some have undergone a version of this rite de passage.

Although a number of Hindu rituals feature thread-tying, symbolising the union of two people, prevention of a loss of spiritual worthiness or protection from attack by evil powers, only the *upanayana* has been so prominent as to have been translated into English as 'the thread ceremony. This translation does not relate to its literal meaning of a student being brought before his guru for *dharmic* instruction and religious training, but it does reflect the changing emphasis of the ritual, especially in recent years, from a request for the privilege of education to a purely bodily *samskara* in which the performance of ritual is sufficient for a boy to move to a new status. The sacred thread with which he is invested is a visible symbol of his new status, but it is, in fact, a substitute for the *brahmacharin*'s clothing formerly given to the student by his guru to replace his usual daily wear. The donning of the thread is not even mentioned in the oldest manual for the *upanayana*, the *Grhyasutras*, yet it is now regarded as the pivot of and reason for the ceremony.

The *upanayana* has always been most important for Brahmins, but it was never confined to this varna. It was performed for the three twice-born varna; twice-born because they were ceremonially born into a second stage of life through this ritual. Kshatriya and Vaishya castes shared in it, though the ages at which education was supposed to begin did vary. It was preferable for Brahmins to receive the thread, made of cotton, at the age of eight, though this could be delayed until they were sixteen; Kshatriyas went to their guru at eleven, or, at the latest, twenty-two; Vaishyas at twelve preferably, though up to twenty-four was possible. Changes in the rules affecting performance of *upanayana* illustrate the tolerance and flexibility that Hinduism is capable of; in the seventeenth century, for example, the scholar Mitramishra allowed Brahmins to undergo the thread ceremony as late as twenty-four, Kshatriyas up to thirty-three and Vaishyas up to thirty-six. For Hindus under

Muslim rule the period was one of *apad-dharma*, a time of distress and upheaval, during which some laxity in *dharmic* duty could be allowed. A time of migration and resettlement, with the challenges and demands of a new environment and social conditions may also be considered a period of *apad-dharma*, and the much later age of *upanayana* performance in UK would seem no less tolerable than it was in seventeenth century India.

Kshatriya threads were of wool, Vaishya of linen, but all now tend to be cotton, the traditional Brahmin material, perhaps an indicator that the ritual is now mainly performed in Brahmin households. It is among Brahmins, too, that the father of the initiate is qualified to act as guru to his son. The ceremony which is described in this chapter focuses on the important ritual rule of a Brahmin father in England. Such a Brahmin may equally qualify to perform the same ritual for individuals who come from one of the non-Brahmin varna.

The Traditional Ritual

A resumé of the orthodox *upanayana* may be useful at this point. The complete ceremony consisted of 15 stages: the initiate's father brought his son to the guru, asking him to accept the boy as his student. He would commend his son to the teacher's care, and he was also commended to the deities Savitri, Pushan, the Ashvins, Soma, Agni, and Prajapati. The guru took details of the boy, then touched his student's thumb, hand, breast, and shoulder to signify acceptance. He gave the boy upper and lower garments, the former of which used to be of deerskin, though now cotton is used, a mere fragment of hide (antelope for a Brahmin, spotted deer for a Kshatriya, goatskin for a Vaishya) acting as a symbol of the original practice. A three-stranded girdle (*mekhala*) was tied round the initiate's waist, and a staff (*danda*) was presented by the guru, symbolising life's long journey to spiritual perfection. Water poured into the guru's cupped hands was allowed to flow into his student's, a symbol of the passing of knowledge from one to the other, then the guru, intoning prayers, touched the boy's chest above his heart, indicating his position of authority over his student. The young man would then step on a firm stone while being urged to be steadfast and steady in his resolves; then he was given curds to eat, symbolically clearing his mind for the acquisition of new knowledge. He would be shown the sun, as a symbol of inspiration in seeking the light of knowledge. An important part of the *upanayana* was the repetition of the *Gayatri-mantra*[1] by the student after his guru; only after this was successfully repeated was he regarded as having joined the ranks of the twice-born.   The initiate demonstrated his newly-acquired ritual status and responsibilities by placing sacrificial wood on the sacred fire and asking blessings of Agni, thus symbolising his new right to tend the fire.   Traditionally he was supposed to gather the wood for this purpose, but nowadays it is provided for him. He would worship the sacred fire by circumambulating it, before beginning his *brahmacharin* stage of life by begging alms from those attending the *upanayana* ceremony. Traditionally 8-12 years of residence with and instruction by the guru now followed before the student would request his teacher for leave to return home, don his usual clothes again, marry and become a householder and family man, through the *samavartana* ceremony. This ceremony has now become an appendage to the *upanayana* in most cases, certainly when the initiate is already adult, as in the recently-performed ritual in Essex described below. The description is based on personal ethnographic observations made by the author during the entire ceremonial and close contact with various participants involved in this life cycle ritual.

An Essex Upanayana

The Maharashtrian community in Britain provided the *upanayana* examples in this paper. This group is small but well-established, and there are several families which have been permanently settled since before World War II. They are an elite group whose members are mainly professionals and business people. Nearly twenty years ago B. A. Chansarkar, himself of Maharashtrian origin, noted this in a short research paper. He claimed that

> The value-system and the relative cohesiveness of the community prevents its members from accepting or being known to accept jobs which are looked down on by other members of the community . . . This necessitates accepting white-collar jobs . . . (1973: 303).

In 1992 there is a settled 2-3 generation deep Maharashtrian community widely scattered throughout Britain, but maintaining a social network of lively and frequent contact. The career values of the parental/grandparental generations outlined by Chansarkar have been passed on to younger members, so that most of them have now an upper middle class lifestyle appropriate to their professional occupations. They are owner-occupiers of houses/flats[2] and have at least one car per household; they have been canny in choosing their places of residence, so that there are good schools nearby for their children (thus helping to secure their future) and other amenities in the form of libraries, sports clubs, open spaces, clubs to foster cultural interests, etc. Inter-generational ties are still strong, and parental interest in young people's career progress and marriage prospects, even if not always welcomed, cannot be ignored, even by young professionals living independently. As children they would be taken by their parents informally each weekend to spend days in the company of other Maharashtrian families, or to meetings of the Maharashtra Mandal (London), founded in 1932 and still a focus of Maharashtrian social/cultural activity in Britain. While parents gossiped about India and other Maharashtrians in UK, the children played together and formed lasting friendships, many of which have survived into adulthood and, in some cases, resulted in marriage.

This informal intra-group socialization has resulted in the survival of aspects of a traditional value-system deemed supportive when facing the challenges of a new socio-cultural environment. As a socio-cultural group the Maharashtrians have not pursued economic/political aims from an ethnic basis, but this does not mean that ethnic consciousness is not a lively force within the community vis á vis not only white society but also British Asians originating from other areas of the Indian sub-continent; for example, the *upanayana* ceremony described below conforms to a Western Indian pattern; the few guests who were invited were from the same area and the same socio-religious tradition.

The initiate at the ceremony, performed in June 1991, was Shyam, a young professional man, 27 years old, soon to be married to a Hindu girl of about the same age, who, like her fiancé, was Brahmin, professional, and born in UK of parents originating from Maharashtra, India. The young man's parents arranged the *upanayana* at his request; to him, it had become an obligatory rite to be completed before his religious wedding could take place. This had been impressed on him by relatives of his own generation during a holiday in India in 1990. His parents were not accompanying him at that time, so the ceremony could not be performed in Maharashtra; on Shyam's return his parents began to look for a suitable priest to officiate within their friendship circle in UK. Initially this proved difficult; the family wanted a Brahmin known to them, but outside India few have traditional family priests available to act on such occasions. The criteria voiced by Shyam's family for selection of a priest reflected closely those put forward by the sage Aunaka: 'A Brahmin who is well-read, of good family, of good character, purified by penance, should initiate a child', or, as is quoted in *Viramitrodaya-Samskara-Prakasha*, Vol.1: the initiator should be one 'who is of a good family . . . learned and . . . self-controlled' (Pandey, 1969: 125).

A family friend, a Brahmin and Sanskrit scholar, was finally requested to perform the *upanayana*; although it was not in his tradition to act as priest, he agreed. An auspicious day shortly before the marriage was chosen, and it was arranged that the ceremony would take place privately at the boy's home before a few relatives and close friends, all Brahmins. Although this ritual is traditionally home-based in Brahmin households, in Britain this need not be the case; some families, especially when more than one son is to receive the sacred thread at the same time, may hire a hall, perhaps attached to a temple or social centre, where a canopy can be erected over the shrine, and numerous guests invited for a feast of celebration. The ritual thus performed gives occasion for conspicuous consumption of family resources; for the turning of financial capital into social capital, thus increasing the family's prestige where it matters, i.e. the setting for its social, economic and professional activities, which is now Britain. The ceremony, too, is an announcement of potential marriageability of the initiates, if such arrangements have not already been made, while indicating, too, the socio-economic and religious attributes likely to be expected of a future bride and her family.

The home-based *upanayana* described here took place in the living-room of the initiate's home, one end of which was cleared for the purpose. All participants took purificatory showers before the rites began, and the shrine was prepared by Shyam's parents and other relatives. Large reed table-mats placed on the carpet served as seats for the major participants before the altar (a converted white plastic step-stool) and the sacred fire (placed in a barbecue tray for safety). For the ceremony the father's younger brother and his wife, as well as the mother's cousin (she has no brother) and his wife came from India, bringing a ready-prepared pack of necessaries for the performance of the *upanayana*. It is usual for the closest relatives, especially those with particular roles to play in the ritual, to come from India for an *upanayana*; by tradition it is one of the longest-surviving family rituals of the *Grhyasutras*, particularly among Brahmin families. Family members remaining in India may afterwards share in the ceremony by means of video recordings.

The ceremony began by propitiating the deity Ganesha and the family deity, the former being placed on the altar in the form of a *soupari* nut, accompanied by a picture of the goddess who has this family under her protection. A red swastika was drawn in the centre of the altar, and on each side of this a coconut rested in a bed of rice grains. Nine *soupari* nuts representing the nine planets[3] were arranged in a plate of rice grains, and a vessel of water placed before the altar, with a water-filled copper *kalash* (pot) holding a coconut resting on mango leaves, an offering to the goddess of the family. The propitiation began with offerings of water to the deities by Shyam and his father; the latter continued by adding drops of water to each *soupari* on the rice plate, while Shyam's mother followed by anointing them and the coconuts with *kum-kum*, the red vermillion powder, flowers and incense from a prepared *puja* (worship) tray. Finally a *dipam* (clay lamp) was lit before the altar. The *kalash* with its coconut, water and mango leaves was offered to the family deity; Shyam made his personal offering by placing coins given to him by his paternal uncle in the water. He then touched the coconut with his forehead, symbolically receiving back blessings of insight and inspiration from the deity. The priest announced in Sanskrit the day, time and place of the ceremony, and prayed that these would prove auspicious.

The propitiation being complete, the main *upanayana* began, starting with the eating together of mother and son for the last time, symbolising the cessation of his childhood status, when he would have spent much of his time with the women of the household, and the assumption of the ritual duties and responsibilities of manhood, which would take him more and more into the company of the men of the family. In strictly orthodox Brahmin families some fathers would not eat with their sons until their *upanayana* had been performed. On this occasion, Shyam's mother fed him with rice and *lahdoo* sweets with her own hands while music was played; this can be a very emotional rite, but on this occasion the atmosphere was cheerful, perhaps because of the age of the initiate. Seeing a fully-grown man fed in this childish way proved amusing.

Shyam's mother now moved away from the site of the ceremony; her part was over. The initiate and his father remained seated before the altar. Shyam's father then announced that he was performing his son's *upanayana*, and repeated the *Gayatri-mantra* ten times to confirm his eligibility to do so. A coin was dipped in water and offered to the deities by Shyam as a penance for unperformed childhood sacraments. A white scarf, brought from India with the *puja* equipment, was tied round Shyam's right shoulder, while a thread on which was tied a small piece of deerskin was placed round his neck. A three-stranded cord of white cotton was wound around Shyam's waist. The sacred thread was prepared by the priest, then placed round Shyam's neck by his father, over the left shoulder and under the right arm in the traditional way. Meanwhile the set *mantras* were intoned by the priest.

The sacred fire (*agni*) was now lit, using wood brought from India. Shyam's father offered nine oblations of clarified butter, *ghee* to Agni to remove the taint of omission of nine childhood sacraments; a further three oblations were offered to Agni and one to Prajapati. Throughout the ceremony his father wore a ring made of sacred *darbha* grass on his ring finger.

Shyam's father poured water into his son's cupped hands; the priest afterwards poured more water into the father's cupped hands; this was allowed to flow down into Shyam's. Father and son clasped hands and further water was offered before Savitri, the Sun God, was asked to protect the new student. His father touched Shyam's chest, just above his heart, indicating that it was he who now had authority over and direct charge of his son. Shyam proceeded to sprinkle water clockwise and anti-clockwise round agni, after which he offered two pieces of wood sent from India to the fire to keep it burning well. Shyam held his right hand to the flames and passed it over his face to receive spiritual grace. He prayed for health, intellect and children. Ash in a long spoon was touched to the initiate's forehead, throat, navel, both shoulders and the crown of his head to avoid untimely death.

Next came one of the most crucial points of the *upanayana* ceremony, symbolising the original purpose of this important rite de passage, the beginning of a young man's period of religious instruction at the house of his *acharya* (instructing priest). At this time the initiate is taught to repeat the *Gayatri* hymn, a plea to the Sun for enlightenment. Shyam first massaged his father's right leg, thus performing for his teacher a small service; as they sat facing each other their heads were covered with a white cloth, so that knowledge of the *mantra* could be passed on, as well as the initiate's secret spiritual name, to be used henceforward in prayer. Afterwards a *munja* grass cord was wound three times round Shyam's waist and he was also given a *palasha* staff, a wood which, in *ayurvedic* belief, stimulates the intellect. The staff is thus intended to strengthen and guide him in his spiritual pilgrimage.

His father reminded him of his duty to be diligent in his studies, to refrain from eating or drinking harmful things, and to lead a disciplined life. The father offered three oblations of *ghee* and rice to *Agni*, to the Sun, and to the sages of old. A shawl, held by the paternal and maternal uncles, was placed like a curtain between Shyam and his father while the priest chanted verses of blessing in Sanskrit. During this chanting the coconut and mango leaves offering to *devi*, the family deity, still in its *kalash*, was held behind Shyam by his sister, alongside a lighted lamp held by the daughter of his mother's cousin. When the curtain had been removed and the prayers were over, his sister dipped her fingers into the water in the *kalash* and anointed Shyam's eyes with it, thus transferring to him insight and understanding from the deity for his religious education. His cousin's daughter moved the lamp before him in a clockwise vertical circle to bring blessings, and protection from misfortune. Shyam then offered worship to the *palasha* staff to obtain sufficient enlightenment to learn the Vedas. Afterwards he listened to the priest chanting prayers to the Gods to endow the initiate with intellect.

The young man then prepared to depart on pilgrimage to Banaras or Kashi: he took up his staff, and begged from his mother and relatives present fruit and nuts for his journey, which were tied in a bundle and carried over his shoulder. As always, he responded to pleas, and gave up his pilgrimage, perhaps an indication that his life's journey will, in time, be that of a *grihastha*, or householder and family man, not renouncer. The priest gave his blessings for long life and prosperity. The completion of *upanayana* ritual was then followed by a further step which would mark a further transition in Shyam's life.

The Samavartana

Shyam, still wearing the visible emblems of his student status, sipped water three times while the priest uttered the 24 names of Vishnu, the beginning of every Vaishnavite ritual. The priest invoked various deities and stated the date, time and place of the ritual.   Shyam declared his intention to perform *samavartana*, to change his *ashrama* status from student to householder by spooning water into his right hand and allowing it to trickle into a copper tray. He offered *puja* to Ganesha to remove obstacles from the ritual. Fire was prepared; oblations of *ghee* were offered to Agni and Prajapati, Lord of All Creatures. Ten oblations of sacred wood were offered to Vishvedeva, the Gods of the Universe. Shyam then removed the deerskin, cotton girdle and grass cord, and laid them near the *palasha* staff before Agni. He took a symbolic bath (*snana*) by sprinkling holy water over his head from a flower, while the priest intoned the *Gayatri mantra* ten times. Shyam again donned his usual clothes, made *namaskar* (respectful greetings) before the family deity, his parents, older relatives and the priest, who gave his blessings for a long life. According to tradition, Shyam offered *dakshina*, or payment, to his guru in return for his care and teaching.

The ceremonies ended with a pre-marriage *puja*, since on this occasion the initiate's wedding was imminent. Ganesha, traditionally remover of obstacles, as well as the family deity and the holy rivers, were asked to make the way ahead smooth and free of insurmountable difficulties.   On the altar were *soupari* to represent Ganesha; the picture of the family deity; betel nut and more *soupari*; and the two coconuts on rice beds, anointed with vermillion, *kum-kum* and turmeric. Before the altar were the tray of rice grains set with nine *soupari* and the *kalash* with coconut, mango leaves and water, as before. A *puja* tray holding betel nut, ghee, *kum-kum* and *agarbhatti* (incense) was prepared, and while this was offered before the deities, the priest prayed Sanskrit *mantras* for the success of the wedding and a smooth passage through married life for Shyam and his future bride.

Appropriately, neither she nor her family members were present at the *upanayana* and *samavartana*, though, the day being an auspicious one, she and her relatives were simultaneously offering *puja* to her family deities.

The Upanayana as a Focus of Ethnicity

For this paper, ethnicity is viewed as a 'consciousness of kind' serving as both a socially positive, cohesive force within a group by promoting common identity, solidarity and mutual assistance when needed; and as a negative, divisive indicator of socio-cultural difference which can limit or prevent communication, exploitation of opportunity, and inter-group dialogue and understanding[4]. The focus of such ethnicity may be a regional-linguistic unit; a religious faith-group; or, in the South Asian context, a caste. Not all these collectivities may be readily or acceptably defined as 'ethnic groups', a term which has become increasingly confined to minorities who share normative behaviour patterns and common value-systems within a national framework that is both more powerful and challenging, with which they must interact and communicate. Such a conception of ethnicity implies competitiveness and eventual confrontation; but I would argue that this need not necessarily be so, though the potential is always there. Cohen (1974: xiv) has pointed out that there are degrees of ethnicity; he offers the example of Roman Catholics in Northern Ireland, who often demonstrate their ethnic adherence through 'violence and bloodshed'. We may compare the ethnicity of the London Welsh, who have sublimated hostility to the rugby field, and who express their cultural achievements in music and literary composition through acceptably institutionalised performances. An appreciation of difference in degree of ethnic manifestation, and of the varied ways of expressing it, is the starting point for understanding what is going on within the Maharashtrian community through the performance of the ceremony which is the subject of this chapter.

Cultural values, and the norms of socially responsible behaviour patterns, can equally well be demonstrated and passed on to younger generations by the institutionalised performance of religious ritual, and herein, I would suggest, lies the significance of the revival of the *upanayana* ceremony among Hindus of certain groups resident in Britain, and the willingness to participate in it and to understand its implications shown by young men and, sometimes, young women. Though mainly British-born, educated in Britain, and fulfilling a socio-economic role common to others of their age, class, and profession in UK, they can add to this cultural inheritance a real, active, operationally effective socio-religious tradition which, as they approach the responsibilities of adulthood, lays claim to them. The ritual acceptance of a new status, with new rights and duties, is a clear statement of an ethnic commitment which can be activated if, or whenever, group needs become evident. That both Brahmins and Vaishyas in Britain have used this ritual means of ethnic assertion is unsurprising, since these are also the sections of the Hindu community in India which most frequently still find the rite is a valid marker of progression to adult status. A parallel use of ritual performance to emphasize ethnic distinctiveness and maintenance of cultural values is described by Shlomo Deshen when writing of the revival of the *hillulot* (memorial ceremonies) among Tunisian Jews in Israel. He claims that there can be '. . . ethnic manifestations that are primarily cultural, and perhaps not relevant at all to problems of conflict and competition. Such manifestations might better be interpreted primarily in terms of strategies to solve problems of identity, belief, and culture . . .' (1974: 282). That this may be the case with the young Asian professionals of whom we have been speaking, surrounded as they are during work and in much of their leisure time by the customs and normative values of white British society, is undeniable. Rituals such as the *upanayana* serve as reminders of moral values sacred in Hindu society, at a time, just before marriage, when young adults may be expected to be especially aware of new responsibilities, to each other, to the newly-related family, and to any future children. Parental values and authority are reinforced, as well as the traditional hierarchy of the family based on age and gender, and the apparently self-sufficient younger generation is reminded of the duties owed by each member of a Hindu family to the others. Ritual pointers to these values recur as the *upanayana* progresses stage by stage. Individuals who participated and witnesses this occasion were aware of the expression of following values:

(a) The interest and support of the wider family group, some of whom will have travelled from India to take part in and observe the ceremony, and to report back to relatives still in India, showing photographs or videos of the event. Gifts will be brought for the initiate, for which he, when his chance comes, will be expected to make return, thus establishing the reciprocal principles which keep family ties alive, operative and international.

(b) The duties of the initiate to the family deity, who, it is believed, has the whole family under her/his protection, are made clear. Future worship will benefit both him and the larger family unit, and his responsibilities in this regard are made clear.

(c) The mother's role in the Hindu family is enacted during the ceremony, firstly by sharing with the boy's father in the propitiation of the family deities, then by feeding her son by hand for the last time. The feeding, care and welfare of children as the primary duties of a wife, as well as her unity with her husband before the deity, are the values being passed on. A woman's role in ritual appears to parallel her role as a housewife, and the young man about to be married is here shown what to expect of his wife in her turn[5].

(d) After the feeding of her son the mother moves away from the ritual area, leaving the male members to continue the rite, indicating the permanency of males as family members, and the responsibilities towards it that arise from this.

(e) This permanency, and the desired unity of male members of the family is stressed by the clasping of hands by father and son, which also symbolises the inter-generational tie that maintains the family and its interests.

(f) Throughout the ceremony a father's authority as guide, instructor and moral mentor is reiterated through offerings of water passing from the father's hands to those of his son, and by the father's touching the boy's chest. Respect and service is due from a young man to his elders, as is shown from the massage of the father's feet, and the way the initiate touches the feet of older family members present after the ceremony is over.

(g) A son's responsibility towards the female members of the family is symbolised by the blessing given to him by his sister, which will earn reciprocation in future years as he looks after her interests in her matrimonial home, and which will be renewed annually at *raksha-bandana*.

(h) By honouring and offering payment to his guru the initiate takes on the responsibilities he will have in future towards his community, and especially to those who perform services for him.

The satisfaction and appreciation of seeing a young man take his place ritually in his family and community was summed up by a friend at the end of the ceremony in the words: 'He's one of us now!'

But there is yet another factor to be taken into account, one pinpointed by Michael Banton when discussing the sanctions that can be employed by an older generation against the younger members of a minority who threaten to abandon sacrosanct tradition in the face of majority challenges (Banton, 1979: 327). He suggests that those who conform win support and reward from the older generation; those who do not are left to their own devices. In this time of unemployment and recession, when jobs have to be struggled for and firmly held on to, the participation of young British Hindus in ceremonies such as the *upanayana* is confirmation to their parents and the community generally that they still hold to proved values and are deserving of help should this be needed. The challenges posed by majority group competition drive young adults to re-affirm by ritual participation their membership of the minority community within which, if they make overt acceptance of its expectations, their security ultimately lies.

There appears to be a growing interest among young Hindus as well as their parents in the performance of the *upanayana* ceremony in UK, as a necessary precursor of the pre-marriage, or *samavartana*, rite, which marks the return of the *brahmacharin* from his guru to home life, his acknowledgement of his debt to his teacher, and his forthcoming social rôle as *grihastha*, or householder. Logically, until a young man has been 'brought to' his guru through the *upanayana*, he cannot 'return' through the *samavartana*; in India, as in Britain, the two ceremonies are increasingly being performed in close sequence, the *upanayana* absorbing the *samavartana*, rather than with an interval of approximately twelve years for the process of religious education. The significance of the *upanayana* is thus changing from a protective, instructive ritual marking the liminal period of change from childhood to adolescence, to an acknowledgement of maturity and imminent assumption of marital responsibilities. Though voicing his deep regrets, Pandey (1969: 116; 152) acknowledges this change of emphasis and perceived purpose in both ceremonies, calling the *upanayana* today 'a ceremonial farce which is performed sometimes before the marriage of a twice-born', and the *samavartana* 'an absurd simplicity . . . performed either with the *upanayana* or the *vivaha* in (a) hurry'. That this can be the case in India today is corroborated by Tom Selwyn (1979: 689), who finds that in Madhya Pradesh, as in other areas of India, the *brataband*, or *upanayana*, is often 'merged into' the cycle of marriage rites.

Among Hindus in Britain during the 1960s and 1970s *upanayana* and *samavartana* ceremonies were rarely performed, and given scant attention, except among some devout families. Even in the case of such families, children would often return to India to their father's relations for the *upanayana*, and, as brides were usually sought in India and weddings performed there, the *samavartana* could conveniently accompany the *vivaha* rites. As more Hindu children were born and educated in UK, childhood *samskaras*, particularly the naming ritual or *namakarana*, began to be performed, though on a less lavish scale than in India, because the full circle of relatives was not present to fulfil the traditional rôles, and learned priests and other ritual specialists were not plentiful. In many cases the rituals of childhood were ignored completely. At five years old young Hindus began their schooling along with all other children, and formal Hindu religious education was rare in the early years of migration, neither was it felt necessary to mark the commencement of school attendance, with its strongly secular emphasis, by any religious ceremony. As a result, no urgency was felt regarding the performance of the *upanayana*. Now, however, young Hindus born in Britain are of marriageable age, and are likely to seek partners from among other British-born Hindus; many of them have a lively curiosity, if little experience and knowledge, about their family faith and its practice. As marriage approaches, relatives and friends in India bring up the question of the traditional ceremonies of *upanayana* and *samavartana*, so that a growing awareness of and need for these ceremonies is noticeable. Their significance is still not fully understood in many cases: the query 'Why are you having this ceremony?' is generally met by a blank expression and the response: 'I thought it had to be done before we got married', or 'My friends in India teased me because I hadn't had it; they said I couldn't marry without it'. There is no doubt that young people appreciate a full explanation of the ceremony, and a translation of the Sanskrit *mantras*; they are dissatisfied and impatient with being steered through a ritual performance in a language they do not understand. What is sought is what would have been supplied during *brahmacharin* years, not simply the text and bodily enactment of the *samskara*, but an understanding of its significance, its intention. Traditionally this would have followed the ceremony; now it is presented within the pressure of unfamiliar ritual performance, or, as Pandey would say, in a hurry.

The home-based *samskaras* of the Grhyasutras are, by definition, usually performed at, or near, the homes of the participants. Home, for the young British Hindus, is the UK, so it is in the UK that they have come to expect the relevant rites de passage to be performed. Interchange of visits between India and Britain is now speedy, so the arrival and assistance of relatives from the sub-continent is to be expected. This is, perhaps, a factor in the maintenance of tradition found in the material substances used in the ceremony; clearly some of these are available in Britain, but as they are supplied in the *upanayana* pack brought from India, they are kept specially for the ceremony. Household items of Western origin can be converted to ritual use when necessary, nevertheless; in the *upanayana* described above, for example, the step-stool as altar, the barbecue tray to hold agni.

Indications are that there will be a growing need for pandits with a knowledge of ritual procedures and the ability to perform them; linguistic skills in Sanskrit and English, and a facility of communication to explain the *samskaras* to young British Hindus who are anxious to maintain and express their Hindu religio-cultural identity. The continued performance of these *samskaras* can only contribute to a positive self-image, self-worth and personal dignity for young Hindus in Britain, as well as a reinforcing of community bonding and identity, and a preservation of the unique richness of a great tradition expanding amoeba-like to absorb and incorporate the adaptations and changes that present themselves while retaining the substance of an innate meaning.

Footnotes

1. The *Gayatri-mantra* is one of Hinduism's oldest daily prayers, said, in Sanskrit, every morning. It is a prayer to Savitri, the Sun God, written in the Gayatri metre, hence its name: 'We concentrate our minds on the most radiant light of the Sun God, Who sustains the Earth, the Interspace and the Heavens. May the Sun God activate our thoughts'. Trans.: V. P. (Hemant) Kanitkar, (1989: 23).
2. The trend towards private ownership of housing was noted by Chansarkar in *New Community* as early as 1973.
3. The nine planets referred to are: Sun, Moon, Mars, Mercury, Venus, Jupiter, Saturn, Rahu and Ketu.
4. This theme is developed further by H. A. Kanitkar, 1972a and 1972b.
5. For a detailed examination of women's rôles in Hindu religious ritual see F. M. Smith (1991).

References

Banton, M. P. (1979) 'Gender Roles and Ethnic Relations', *New Community*, 7: 323-332.

Chansarkar, B. A. (1973) 'A Note on the Maratha Community in Britain', *New Community*, 2: 302-305.

Cohen, A. (1974) 'Introduction', in Cohen, A. (Ed), *Urban Ethnicity*, London: Tavistock Pubs.: ix-xxiv.

Deshen, S. (1974) 'Political Ethnicity and Cultural Ethnicity in Israel during the 1960s', in Cohen, A. (Ed), *Urban Ethnicity*, London: Tavistock Pubs.: 281-309.

Kanitkar, H. A. (1972a) *The Social Organisation of Indian Students in the London Area*, Ph.D. Thesis, London: University of London.

Kanitkar, H. A. (1972b) 'An Indian Elite in Britain', *New Community*, 1: 378-382.

Kanitkar, V. P. (Hemant) (1989) *Hinduism*, Cheltenham: Stanley Thornes & Hulton.

Pandey, R. B. (1969) *Hindu Samskaras*, Delhi: Motilal Banarsidass.

Selwyn, T. (1979) 'Images of Reproduction: An Analysis of a Hindu Marriage Ceremony', *Man*, 14: 684-698.

Smith, F. M. (1991) 'Indra's Curse, Varuna's Noose, and the Suppression of the Woman in the Vedic Srauta Ritual', in Leslie, J. (Ed), *Roles and Rituals for Hindu Women* London: Pinter Publishers: 17-45.

10

A Place for our Gods:
Tradition and Change among
Hindus in Edinburgh

Malory Nye

This chapter attempts to explain the development of Hindu religious traditions within a 'Hindu community' in Scotland. This expression of culture is usually labelled 'ethnicity' - which tends to mean very different things to different writers. It usually refers to the sense of identity which belongs to a social-cultural group existing in a poly-ethnic situation. It can often be used, however, to describe reactive developments to situations of culture-conflict. Many writers nowadays follow Barth's (1969) interpretation of ethnicity - that it is not the culture itself that one should look at, but rather the boundaries that exist between different cultures. Thus ethnicity is the result of interaction across cultural boundaries.

Such a view tends to exclude an important part of the equation, however. Cultures are, of course, dynamic products of complex social situations. But too often the stress is put upon looking for cultural change in terms of reaction to external influences, rather than looking at the internal dynamics within cultures that lead to change. This is especially true of the study of religions among minority ethnic groups, where complex traditions are reduced to being mere expressions of a vague sense of ethnic or cultural identity.

When Hindus in Scotland conduct some religious worship, they are not attempting to express some vague notion of their cultural identity - rather they are living out aspects of their cultures. That is, religious expression is automatically a cultural expression, the two are indivisible, one is not merely an attempt to recreate the other. And although religious behaviour is often directed towards the expression of some notion of identity, it is not always so - people are religious for a multiplicity of reasons.

In this chapter, I shall be highlighting a few alternative reasons for the maintenance of religious practices among Hindus in an ethnic minority situation. Religious activity among ethnic minority groups is not solely the product of reaction to external influences - it is a complex amalgam of many different forces.

Hindus in Edinburgh

There is a population of approximately 1,000 Hindus living in Edinburgh[1], which is internally divided into several different groups.   Despite this division into factions, there is a general consensus that the various groups constitute a 'Hindu community'.   The two main factions within this community are Panjabis (from north-west India), and Gujaratis (from the west coast, north of Bombay).   About forty percent of the total Hindu population of Edinburgh are Panjabi, and another forty percent are Gujarati.   The remainder are from other areas of India (such as Bengal, Bihar, Tamilnad, Kerala, and so on).   The two main groups - the Panjabis and Gujaratis - tend to dominate the community.

Most Hindus in Edinburgh are professional and middle-class doctors, teachers, accountants, architects, etc.   There are some who are engaged in profitable businesses.   In terms of residence, they are spread throughout the city, usually living in the desirable middle-class suburbs.   Their socio-economic position thus makes them rather different from many other South Asian groups in Britain who are in a much less favourable situation.[2]

The Hindu community is small, and it is quite new.   Indians began to settle in Edinburgh during the 1960s and 70s.   Communal institutions for Hindus did not emerge until the mid-70s, and are still in the process of being developed.   The fact that there is such a thing as a 'Hindu community' is worth considering - Hindus in Edinburgh live in a number of different social groups and communities, some of which are based on notions of ethnicity, whilst others are focused on the workplace, or a residential area, or on a special interest.

Alongside the Hindu temple community, there is also an Indian institution in Edinburgh, called the Edinburgh Indian Association (EIA).   This Association has roughly the same membership as the temple, and there is some overlap in leadership, and yet the two groups remain distinct.   The EIA is a based on a quasi-nationalist principle of allegiance - its aims are secular and so-called 'cultural', so that non-Hindus may participate in its functions.   In practice, however, it tends to be predominantly Hindu in membership and so it overlaps to a considerable extent with the Hindu temple.   As my interest here is in the religious behaviour of Hindus in Edinburgh, I will be focusing primarily on the Hindu community and the temple.

The heterogeneity of the Hindu community provides an important dynamic to its activities.   Panjabis and Gujaratis have distinct cultural traditions - their languages, food, styles of dress, and religious outlooks are all different - and in Edinburgh their social origins and backgrounds are also different.

The majority of Panjabis migrated directly from India to Britain, settling in Edinburgh after having first lived in some other town in Britain.   Edinburgh Gujaratis are quite different: a large proportion of them are 'twice migrants' (c.f. Bhachu, 1985); they lived in East Africa before coming to Britain.   Their reasons for migration were quite different - they were forced to leave East Africa at the time of decolonialisation.   Their migration stemmed much more from political changes in

East and Central Africa. It was these changes rather than economic necessity which stimulated their migration to Britain. Unlike the Panjabis, many of the Gujaratis have never been to India - for them being 'Indian' has a very different meaning.

The Hindu temple

The temple project is the result of a pooling of resources by the various sections of the community - Panjabi, Gujarati, and others. Although the temple institution was founded in 1981, it is still in the process of being constructed - both physically and perceptually.

Among other British Hindu communities, such as in London, Leicester, and the West Midlands, different regional groups - particularly Panjabis and Gujaratis - have formed separate temples (e.g. Bowen, 1981; Jackson, 1981; Michaelson, 1987; Teifion, 1984; Vertovec, 1992). In towns where the Hindu population is relatively small, joint temples (such as the Edinburgh one) have been founded - for example, in Leeds (Knott, 1986; 1987), and Bristol (Barot, 1991).

The Edinburgh temple is by no means the only place in which Hindus maintain and express their distinctive cultures[3]. Neither does it have any privileged position as the main ethnic/cultural arena. It is worth bearing in mind Michaelson's point that Hindu temples are very different from Christian churches, and that it can be a matter of western bias to look at temples as the centres of religious communities (1987: 33, 48). Her point is rather overstated, however, especially when describing British Hindu temples, since many of these do have important communal roles to play - as this chapter attempts to show.

I have used the temple as the centre of my study of Edinburgh Hindus mainly because of its accessibility, but also because it is an arena in which several potentially conflicting strands of Hindus are coming together to create a pan-Hindu institution. Even though temples are not usually communal organisations in India, many are adopting such a role in Britain. In all cases this newly formed temple tradition is being fed by, and also feeding into, other aspects of life among the community. The most important relationship is between religion at the temple, and religion in the domestic sphere - both of which strongly influence each other.

It must be stressed that there is not one single religious tradition among Edinburgh Hindus. On the contrary, there are a number of traditions - regional, local, sectarian, and caste based - which co-exist alongside each other within the temple arena. There is a general agreement that all these traditions are subsumed within a greater tradition - that is 'Hinduism' - and it is this which unites them all as a 'community'. What this Hindu tradition actually consists of is very hard to determine; its most salient feature appears to be its inclusiveness. The creation of a 'Hindu' temple, however, appears to be an attempt to construct a new Hindu tradition for all Edinburgh Hindus, which has a definite form.

The temple is establishing itself as a 'community centre' - its leaders are attempting to put it at the centre of the Hindu community. Such a role for a Hindu temple is quite new. In India, *mandirs* have very different roles, which are focused much more on the worship of particular gods, rather than on serving communities (see Fuller, 1988; Basham, 1971).

By making the Edinburgh temple a community centre the temple leaders are also helping to construct the notion of the 'Hindu community'. If there was no communal religious institution, then there would be no real motive for defining a social group in terms of their religious affiliation. There are many other ways in which they could define themselves. They could be defined in terms of their cultural/national origins (i.e. as Indian), or into a larger group as South Asians, or into smaller groups according to the diverse regions from which they originated (Panjab, Gujarat etc.). Religious affiliation as Hindus is only one factor out of many possibilities.

It is possible to argue that the choice of religion as a defining criterion is a reaction to majority-western cultural influences upon members of the Hindu community in Edinburgh. In Britain, there is a common notion that religious organisations should be community centres. Thus Hindus see that Christians have communal social organisations (churches), and that other groups organise themselves similarly (such as Muslims in mosques), and so they should also create temples that fulfil the same role. In fact this argument was suggested to me by the son of the founder of the temple, when he told me that:

> The Muslims build their Mosques everywhere they go, and the Christians have their churches . . . So we need a place where our gods can live and be cared for everyday, otherwise how can we expect the gods to come to us?

But although this man gave a 'reactive' argument for temple building, he also combined it with a 'traditional' Hindu notion that temples are not only about congregations, they are also about gods. Thus, Hindus are constructing temples in Edinburgh only partly to serve a community - they are also doing it for other reasons, which come from within the traditions that they (or their parents/grandparents) brought from India. Thus, the temple is very much within the traditions of sub-continental Hinduism. At the same time, however, it is also the product of an ethnic minority group's attempt to establish themselves as a 'community', bound together by a 'common' religion.

The temple leaders are attempting to use the temple as the main arena where the community comes together. Of course, they are doing this for more than simply disinterested devotional reasons. If the temple is at the centre of a large community, then the leaders of the temple will have authority over a lot of people. Thus the temple is not only catering for their cultural and religious needs, it is also providing them with a power base. There are many good reasons for them to encourage its growth as a congregational institution.

Satsangs

Since its foundation in 1981, Hindus have been meeting together as a temple regularly every month. These monthly meetings, called *satsangs*, were held in people's homes, and then later in a community centre. It was not until 1989 that a temple building was actually opened; this building - an old church - has not been formerly dedicated, and a substantial amount of work still needs to be done before it will be complete. However, since its opening the monthly *satsangs* have been held regularly in the new building. Portable images of various Hindu gods have been set up for worship, and a large space has been cleared where worshippers can sit.

The transferral of the *satsang* to the temple building did not affect the structure of the meeting at all, it simply meant that it could be held in a more permanent situation. There is as yet no pandit (priest) for the temple - and so worship and temple business is attended to by members of a committee. The presence of a pandit is not essential to lead *satsangs*, his role (when he is appointed) will be to conduct other rituals and to maintain the temple building.

Other writers on Hinduism in Britain have observed that new temples have to establish a form of worship which satisfies the main groups contributing to the temple (Knott, 1986, 1987; Vertovec, 1992). If the temple is mainly to serve a particular regional or sectarian group - for example a section of Gujaratis, Swaminarayans, or Arya Samajis - then the choice of worship is fairly straightforward. In other instances, however, the choice is more difficult - particularly when there are several distinct groups cooperating in the temple project.

Thus the Hindu temple in Leeds, which is a joint Panjabi-Gujarati project, has had to find a focus of worship that appeals to both of these groups (Knott, 1987). Their solution is to have two major forms of worship regularly performed in the temple - one is a Vedic fire sacrifice called *Hawan*, and the other a less complicated lamp waving ritual called *arti*. *Hawan*, which is associated with Arya Samaj, mainly appeals to Panjabis in Leeds. *Arti*, however, is more popular amongst Gujaratis. The regular weekly temple meeting in Leeds consists of both *hawan* and *arti*, which enables each regional group to attend the form of worship that most appeals to them.

Some form of compromise has also been necessary at the Edinburgh temple. There is a similar mixture of Panjabis and Gujaratis, and a similar desire to find a 'lowest common denominator' form of worship which will appeal to all potential worshippers. The result in Edinburgh has been quite different to that in Leeds, however. Instead of conducting two different forms of ritual which appeal to separate groups, there is one main religious form, which both Panjabis and Gujaratis join in together. This is the monthly *satsang*.

The *satsang* is a gathering at which religious songs (*bhajans*) are sung, and the lamp-waving ritual of *arti* is performed. Members from many different regional traditions take part in this form of worship - there are no trends in which Panjabis or Gujaratis favour one or other part of the *satsang*. In fact, the *satsang* has developed into an integrated whole whereby the performance of *arti* concludes the singing of *bhajans*; it is not perceived as being distinct from what precedes it[4].

In this sense, therefore, members of the various regional traditions at the temple have agreed upon a common form of temple worship which is acceptable to most members of the community.   In fact, the dominance of two north Indian groups (Panjabis and Gujaratis) within the temple has created a temple which is predominantly north Indian in style and character.   Indians from southern districts (Tamils, Keralans, etc.), and also those from the east of India (such as Bengalis and Biharis), do not always find the temple to their taste.

There is a general agreement amongst the dominant groups that the chosen form of temple worship is acceptable, appealing, and appropriate.   The present form of the *satsang* appears to have remained unchanged for the past ten years - despite changes that have occurred within the temple itself (changes of personnel, organisation, and the actual place of worship).

Arti and *bhajan* singing are thus traditional 'Hindu' forms of worship.   Both of them are found within religious traditions of Panjab and Gujarat.   Although Panjabis and Gujaratis have different traditions of *bhajan* singing (e.g. both the words and music of most songs in these regions are different), the actual use of *bhajans* is common to members of both regional groups.   *Arti* is also found throughout much of north India (and in different forms in south India also), although again there are regional variations.

But these types of worship are not only perceived as being common traditions which are shared by the various groups in the temple.   The performance of them can - potentially - encourage communality, the development of a shared or communal religious tradition.[5]

Bhajans are usually performed in groups, with one or more persons leading the singing, and others participating in any way they like.   Anyone can sing, or provide percussion, or simply listen to the words and music as a means of devotion.   The songs are not restricted to any particular language - songs may be sung in Hindi, Panjabi, Gujarati, Sanskrit, Tamil, or whatever.   Hindi is the most popular language for *bhajans* at the Edinburgh temple - there are a large number of Hindi *bhajans* (many based on film songs) which are known to most of the regular worshippers, regardless of their regional origins.

Arti can also be performed as a form of group-based worship - the waving of the lamp is open for all worshippers.[6]   The song that accompanies *arti* is also in Hindi (*Om Jai Jagdish Hare* . . .), so that most people can sing it, and photocopied (Roman) transcripts of the song have been produced for those who do not know the words.

This does not happen in all contexts: in India and in other British Hindu temples, both *arti* and *bhajan* singing can be exclusive and non-communal activities.   *Arti* is usually performed by family groups, who visit temples in the evening, perform *arti* and then leave, without meeting any of the other worshippers present - who are doing exactly the same.   *Bhajans* may be sung exclusively in one language, or in a dialect, and when this happens it encourages sectarianism, rather than communalism.

But in Edinburgh there appears to be a deliberate attempt to overcome sectarian and regional differences, and to develop a form of worship which can unite the various groups. Thus the leaders chose a style of worship common to both Panjabis and Gujaratis, and which could be performed as a group, or congregation. By doing so, they were recognising that worshippers should be using the temple as a congregation - and that the temple should take on a role as the centre of the Hindu community.

By combining two influences - tradition with communalism - the temple leaders have created a reinvention of the religious tradition in the context of the Edinburgh temple (c.f. Hobsbawm, 1983). Communal and inclusive *bhajan* singing has now developed into a 'traditional' form of worship. The concept of tradition is changing in new circumstances - new styles or arrangements of worship are being presented as 'traditional'.

The association of *bhajan* singing with mainstream temple worship is at the heart of this reinterpretation. There are traditions of *bhajan* singing among many different Hindu groups, in India and abroad[7]. Although *bhajans* are sometimes sung in temples, they are more usually sung at religious meetings conducted in homes, or in public halls. What appears to be happening in Britain[8] is that *bhajan* singing is becoming the main form of temple worship, that a new temple tradition has developed out of a collection of other traditions.

There are a number of reasons why this is occurring, and so it is simplistic to explain the development merely in terms of 'reactive ethnicity'. The change of temple tradition is not a major change - *bhajan* singing is sometimes associated with temple worship in parts of India. The reinvention of tradition has come from within the ethnic group, whilst the formation of the group itself (i.e. as a 'Hindu community') is part of this change although it is possible to argue that some external influences do have some bearing on this development.

Temple Festivals

Besides *satsang* and *bhajan* singing, there are a number of different festivals Hindus celebrate at their temple. But the great cultural diversity within India means that groups from different parts of India celebrate different festivals - even though they all claim to belong to the same religion of Hinduism. Even when different groups celebrate the same festival, they may be worshipping different gods, or worshipping in very different ways.

This can be a problem among a community of Hindus in Edinburgh. The assumption that there is a common religious tradition for all members of the community does not easily encompass the desires of different regional groups to conduct festivities and worship in their own particular and distinctive styles. This problem has been overcome to a certain degree in the monthly *satsang*. But festivals are different from this - they are 'one-off' occasions, and for many individuals these may be the only times in the year when they actually attend the temple.

The main conflict in this respect is between Panjabis and Gujaratis. As it is they who dominate the temple, these two groups can set the terms for other members. But finding a suitable compromise is not always easy.

There are three main festivals which are celebrated at the Edinburgh *Mandir* on a regular basis - a fourth was added in 1991, but as yet it has not become very popular. The three festivals are *Krishna Janamasthami* (usually in August)[9], *Nawratri* (in September), and *Diwali* (in October). *Janamasthami* and *Diwali* are festivals which both Panjabis and Gujaratis celebrate, *Nawratri* is one which is particular to Gujaratis. The fourth festival is *Ram Nawmi* - which is more popular among Panjabis. This most recent addition seems to be an attempt on the part of the Panjabi faction of the community to add one of their own festivals to the temple calendar, to redress the balance. Whether or not this will become permanent is hard to judge at this stage.

Janamasthami and *Diwali* are shared festivals, and it is perhaps for this reason that compromises have been made about the form of worship at these festivals. The format of *bhajan* singing and *arti* have been transferred to both festivals, although other elements are added to highlight the special occasions.

Janamasthami is an evening festival, directed to the god Krishna, as it is the celebration of his birth. *Bhajans* are sung for several hours, and then a small cradle is worshipped at the stroke of midnight. This is followed by *arti*. There is little differentiation between the worship of Panjabis and Gujaratis at this festival - it is a 'communal' affair.

Diwali is considered the main festival of the year. It is seen by most members of the community as the beginning of the Hindu New Year. The Diwali celebration - usually held at the weekend after the festival day itself - is very well attended. Worship involves the singing of *bhajans* and the performance of *arti*. Other activities are based around this worship - there is a meal, and music, and dancing, which all help to make up a 'proper programme'. But there is little elaboration of worship beyond the model used for regular temple meetings.

Nawratri

Nawratri is a festival which extends over nine different nights, followed by a tenth night of festivity. It is dedicated to Ambaji or Mataji - the 'goddess' - in her various forms. Ideally it is expected that there should be some form of worship on each of the nine nights, as well as on the tenth night. Before the opening of the temple building in Edinburgh, it was not usually possible to find a room that could be booked for so long. Many people were also sceptical that worshippers would take the trouble to attend for the whole festival.

Thus in past years it was usual for only two *Nawratri* nights to be celebrated in Edinburgh - on consecutive Sundays in a local community centre (the place where the regular *satsangs* were held). Once they had use of the new temple building, however, a few members of the community decided that there should be some celebration on every night of *Nawratri* - and this is what occurred in 1990. Attendance during the weekday meetings was quite sparse, but most people were pleased by the mere fact that something was happening, that the festival was being celebrated properly.

The association of *Nawratri* with Gujaratis appears to have encouraged a different approach to organising the worship for this festival. Many Panjabis attend *Nawratri* celebrations, but few of them consider it to be an important festival, and thus do not rank it as highly as *Janamasthami* or *Diwali*. Gujaratis, on the other hand, place a great emphasis on it - it is they who ensure that the festival is celebrated at all, and it was Gujaratis who provided the incentive for holding nightly meetings in 1990.

This autumn festival is also important to Bengalis and Biharis - who call it *Durga Puja*[10]. Their style of worship is very different from that of Gujaratis, and interestingly they have not attempted to create a compromise form of worship for the festival. Edinburgh Bengalis who wish to worship at *Durga Puja* (and there are a reasonable number of them) drive fifty miles to Glasgow - where a 'Durga Puja committee' (run by the Bengali Association of Scotland) organise celebrations for the event in a proper (i.e. eastern Indian) style. Their lack of co-operation in the Edinburgh temple is perhaps because they are outnumbered by Gujaratis - thus there is no chance that events for this festival will be organised to their liking in Edinburgh.

Because much of the impetus for celebrating *Nawratri* comes from Gujaratis, the festival in the Edinburgh temple has a distinctively Gujarati form - there is far less emphasis upon the common forms used at other times. The main form of worship is dancing rather than singing (although songs are incorporated into the dancing), and these dances are exclusively Gujarati. The dances - particularly *garba* and *dandya* - are performed in a large circle around a small shrine, on which have been arranged pictures of Ambaji, along with other items of worship. The dancing is accompanied by music - a drum to mark time, maybe some other percussion and some recorded music, and also one or two people singing *bhajans*. Unlike in *satsangs*, however, most worshippers dance rather than sing - this is the focus of the worship[11]. At the end of the meeting, after the dancing is completed, *arti* is performed in the usual fashion - although the *arti* is dedicated to *Ma Jagdambe*, a female form of the usual *arti* god Jagdish (the 'Supreme Lord'; c.f. Knott, 1986: 121; Jackson, 1981: 84).

Panjabis at the temple appear to have allowed a concession to the Gujaratis over this festival - there is little conflict about the fact that the worship is predominantly Gujarati in style, and is in marked contrast to the usual compromise forms of worship. A number of Panjabis make the effort to attend *Nawratri* meetings, and some even join in the dancing (although the majority of them choose to sit and watch Gujaratis dance).

It is worth considering the reasons why dancing has been chosen as the main form of worship for *Nawratri*, when it is not performed at other times of the year. Most Gujaratis stress the fact that the way that they organise *Nawratri* in Edinburgh is traditional, that they are doing it the way that it should be done. Most of them refer to East Africa to justify this - rather than to India - describing *Nawratri* festivities that they experienced in their youth in Kenya and Uganda. There is often a complaint expressed about the fact that although they are recreating the tradition, somehow it is nowhere near as well done as it could be - that in East Africa the dancing went on all night, that there was more competition between the dancers, and that the men and women should really be dancing separately.

In fact, there appears to be a recognition that although the festival is being performed in a 'traditional' way, it is also having to be modified to take account of the new circumstances. The modifications appear to be small in this respect, but there is a general feeling that some changes are necessary for the Edinburgh situation.

It is also possible to argue that the use of dancing at *Nawratri* is an expression of cultural/ethnic identity by Gujaratis. By performing 'their' dances they are helping to maintain and demonstrate the continuance of a sense of their distinct ethnicity. Other elements are involved with this - women wear new clothes on each night of the festival, often spectacular saris which they would rarely wear at other times. Thus by participating in the festival they are marking out their cultural distinctiveness vis-a-vis the other cultures that they live alongside[12].

But this is not only an expression of 'Indian/Hindu' identity, the ethnicity is not only a reaction to white-Asian cultural contact. At *Nawratri* there is an emphasis on Gujaratiness, as opposed to other regional forms of 'Hinduism' - they are expressing their identities as Gujaratis in relation to non-Gujarati Indians (particularly Panjabis). This is tacitly accepted by most Panjabis, who are happy to be at the celebrations, but do not attach much significance to the whole affair.

If *garba* and *dandya* are performed at other festivals - particularly at Diwali, where it often forms part of the 'programme' - then this has to be balanced by some Panjabi-style dancing, called *bhangra*. This *bhangra* is quite different from *garba* - although it was originally a Panjabi 'folk dance', it has developed new forms in Britain, where it has become discoised and associated with night clubs. It is this modern *bhangra* which is performed in the temple at Diwali, not the 'original' folk dance, and is thus very different from the Gujarati dances, which are devotional in orientation. The emphasis appears to be upon balancing a Gujarati dance against a Panjabi dance, rather than matching like for like.

It is important to stress the devotional element of *garba* and *dandya*. The word *khelnaa* in Gujarati and Hindi meaning 'playing' expresses this. There are words in Gujarati and Hindi which can be directly translated as 'dance' (*ras* in Gujarati, *naacnaa* in Hindi), and these are used in other contexts[13]. But *garba*, *dandya*, and other Gujarati religious dances are always forms of *khelnaa* or playing. It is this concept that is most stressed by worshippers at the Edinburgh temple when they would insist that I should participate in this playing. This notion of *khelnaa* has many complex associations. It defines dancing as a form of devotion - somewhat like *bhajan* singing, but obviously distinct from it. There are links with other devotional ideas, such as the dance of Krishna (also called 'play' or 'sport', although this is *lila*, not *khelnaa*). *Khelnna* is at the heart of the festival - *Nawratri* would not be the same without the dancing/playing. It is the most appropriate way of worshipping the goddess as well as an enjoyable form of entertainment. The festival is both a social gathering and a time of worship - the one feeds the other.

There are three main types of dancing associated with *Nawratri*, although there are variations on these types. The most common dance is what is generally referred to as *garba* - it is performed in a large circle, ideally with men and women dancing in separate circles. Different forms of *garba* have different rhythms and tempos, and also different footsteps. The second type of dance is *dandya*, which is usually translated as the 'stick dance'. This dance is very well known, and the sight of two women knocking sticks together is often used to symbolise Gujarati culture in tourist brochures. These first two types of dance are used most often at the Edinburgh temple - they are both quite easy to learn, and both men and women can participate easily.

The third type of dance includes several distinct styles, which are all linked by the fact that they are almost exclusively performed by women. One of these is a fast and rather dangerous dance, in which two women face each other grasping hands and spin around deftly on their feet. This is usually performed on very hard surfaces - particularly in India, where I have seen dancers spin extremely quickly over hard concrete floors. The other women's dance that I have seen performed at the temple is quite different from any of the other dances - again it involves two women facing each other, but they hop in crouching positions in rhythm with the drum, clapping with their hands very close to the floor.

This latter dance is not performed very often in the Edinburgh temple, and when it is done I have found that most men are quite baffled by it. It is something that is quite out of their usual experience. This type of dance is more usually performed in all-female groups of worship, such as the large scale *Nawratri* gatherings that used to occur in Nairobi, or in specially sponsored festivals held in worshippers' homes. These women's dances are obviously distinct from the *dandya* and the *garba*, and it appears to be a recent development for them to be performed in the temple in mixed company. Both of these dances are associated with worship of Mataji, and so they are particularly appropriate for *Nawratri*. Notwithstanding variation in dance forms at the temple, the participants I spoke to were keen to emphasise that all the dances expressed the adoration of the goddess and, to both men and women, they symbolised the essence of devotional worship they had known as a part of their living religious tradition.

Religion, Culture, and Community

Ideas of cultural boundary maintenance can be useful for understanding this account of temple behaviour.   Worship (of any type) at the temple in Hindu styles is obviously different from the behaviour of other religious or cultural groups in Edinburgh (particularly white Christian groups), and so participation in such worship helps to reinforce a sense of difference.   At the same time, the worshippers construct an 'ethnic' community which is based on the notion of a shared religion. I do not think that this is specifically a reaction to external influences, however, instead it is the result of a sense of a shared religious tradition across regional and other cultural boundaries.   The construction of the Hindu community is also a development which is being encouraged by its political leaders.

Nawratri celebration suggests that the processes of ethnicity are quite complicated.   At this festival there is a clear regional bias, the worship is distinctly Gujarati.   Many Panjabis do attend the temple for this festival, and a significant number of these participate in the dancing.   But this does not alter the fact that the worship is derived almost solely from Gujarati traditions.   This cannot be reduced to a simple case of reactive ethnicity - indeed it is not clear who Gujaratis are reacting to in this instance.

By organising *Nawratri* in this way the Panjabi faction in the temple are conceding much to the Gujaratis, whilst the Gujaratis themselves are working against the ideals of compromise and Hindu communality which usually prevail. There is no simple explanation for this, and certainly none which relies on notions of ethnicity and boundary maintenance.   It appears that in the case of *Nawratri* the need to maintain regional traditions is greater than the need to construct a 'Hindu' community.   Perhaps the Panjabis allow this to happen because it gives their faction the opportunity to force concessions in other areas of temple organisation.

But the way in which *Nawratri* is organised is not exclusively a matter of Panjabi-Gujarati relations.   Worshippers at the festival - particularly those from Gujarati backgrounds - dance 'for the gods', not to express their sense of regional ethnicity.   Devotion is an important element of religious behaviour which cannot be ignored.   Perhaps related to this is the notion of having fun - dancing and singing are very enjoyable, and added to this is the food that is often provided at festivals. Worshippers often go to the temple simply to enjoy themselves and to please the gods.   Others may cynically comment on this, and complain that people 'only come to dance and to eat', but such motives are important.

Religious change among a minority group in Britain is fuelled by internal developments, it is not only a reaction to external influences.   Thus it is not only boundaries that are important - the intra-cultural context must also be recognised as an important element in the development and reinvention of traditions.

If we reconsider the three notions with which this paper began - religion, ethnicity, and community - it is worth considering how we can relate these to each other.   In Edinburgh it is possible to argue that the religion and community are both partial constructions, whilst there are several related but distinct cultures within the groups which are each helping to feed into both the 'common' religion and the 'community'. So what is creating the community? Is it a reaction to religious values in Britain? Christians have church communities, and so Hindu religious communities may be a reactive development arising out of the multicultural experience. But the idea of Hindu (i.e. religion based) communalism is very strong in India at present, so it must also be part of some Hindu/Indian tradition.

The development of a temple based Hindu community may, however, simply be the result of people wishing to preserve a religious/cultural tradition, and in so doing they are creating a community out of the process of preservation. But does a common religion necessarily create a common community? And is there not also a creation of religion occurring at the same time? At the Edinburgh temple Hindus are coming together as Hindus - which is itself a notion with very ambiguous meanings. The only explanation appears to be that the process is circular, and that the notions of religion, ethnicity, and community all help to construct the other.

Footnotes

1   The fieldwork for this chapter was collected between May 1989 and November 1990. The research was funded by a University of Edinburgh Postgraduate Studentship.
2   Recent research into population statistics has shown that most British Indians do in fact belong to this middle-class/professional economic niche (Robinson 1990).
3   The Edinburgh Indian Association is a rival 'cultural' organisation, while many other cultural activities occur within the homes of community members.
4   It should be noted that there are other elements of the *satsang* which are not being detailed in this account. In particular there is the individual *puja* and *darsan*, which each worshipper performs on entering the temple, and the later *puja* and distribution of *prasad*, which follow *arti*. For more details about each of these see Knott, 1986: 108-110, 119-123). These elements, however, are also integrated into the process of worship, and are performed equally by the various regional groups.
5   I am using the terms communal and communalism to refer to the creation of a sense of common identity. In India the term communalism is often used to mean something different - there it refers to differences and factionalism between social groups, and is often a euphemism for Hindu-Muslim tensions.
6   It is more usual for *arti* in temples to be performed by a pandit, but as the Edinburgh temple has no pandit, this ritual has to be performed by worshippers.
7   There are numerous accounts of *bhajan* singing in India, perhaps the most famous of these is Singer (1972), who wrote about 'bhajana' groups in Madras. For *bhajan* singing in East Africa, see Bharati (1972). For use of this form of worship by Hindu groups in various parts of Britain, see Knott (op cit.), Bowen (1981), Jackson (1981), O'Keefe (1980), Teifion (1984).
8   In Edinburgh, in particular, but this is found in other British temples.
9   Hindu festivals are dated according to a lunar calendar, and so they occur at different times in the western calendar each year. *Janamasthami* fell on 24th

August in 1989, 14th August in 1990, and 2nd September in 1991. For more detail about the exact timing of Hindu festivals, see Knott, 1986: 271-294; Freed & Freed, 1964; and Sinclair-Stevenson, 1920: 263-342.

10   Durga is another form of the goddess.

11   The singing of *bhajans* as a prelude to dancing is also common during *Nawratri*. But this singing is usually quickly superseded when the dancing begins. Most - if not all - *bhajans* sung are directed towards Mataji (in one of her many forms).

12   This argument of ethnicity is supported by the fact that many Gujaratis were pleased when I (as a non-Indian outsider) made the effort to learn the dances. This was taken as a compliment - that I was learning and performing 'our dances'. But they were taking the compliment not only as Indians, but as Gujaratis in particular.

13   Nobody was able to tell me why they did not use these other words. To complicate the situation further, however, this type of dancing is also called 'ras' (i.e. dance) although the act of performing it is always referred to as 'khel' (playing).

References

Barot, R. (1991) 'The Bristol Indian Association'. Paper presented to the fifth annual conference of the British Association for South Asian Studies, March 1991, SOAS, London.

Barth, F. (1969) 'Introduction'. In *Ethnic Groups and Boundaries: The social organisation of cultural difference*, London: Allen and Unwin, pp.1-57.

Basham, A. L. (1971 [1954]). *The Wonder That Was India* London: Sidgwick and Jackson.

Bhachu, P. (1985) *Twice Migrants: East African Sikh Settlers in Britain*, London: Tavistock.

Bharati, A. (1972) *The Asians in East Africa: Jayhind and Uhuru*, Chicago: Nelson Hall.

Bowen, D. (1981) 'The Hindu Community in Bradford'. In Bowen, D. G. (ed.) *Hinduism in England*, Bradford: Bradford College.

Freed, R. S. & Freed, S. A. (1964) 'Calendars, Ceremonies and Festivals in a North Indian Village: The necessary calendric information for fieldwork', *Southwestern Journal of Anthropology*, 20: pp. 67-90.

Fuller, C. J. (1980) 'The Hindu temple and Indian society' in M. V. Fox (ed.) *In Temple in Society*, Winona Lake: Eisenbrauns.

Hobsbawm, E. (1983) 'Introduction: Inventing Traditions'. Hobsbawm, E. and Ranger, T. (eds.) *In The Invention of Tradition*, Cambridge: Cambridge University Press.

Jackson, R. (1981) 'The Shree Krishna Temple and the Gujarati Hindu community in Coventry', in Bowen, D. G. (ed.) In *Hinduism in England*, Bradford: Bradford College.

Knott, K. (1986) *Hinduism in Leeds: A study of religious practices in the Indian Hindu community and in Hindu related groups*, Leeds: Department of Theology and Religious Studies, University of Leeds.

Knott, K. (1987) 'Hindu Temple Rituals in Britain: the reinterpretation of tradition' in Burghart, R. (ed.) *Hinduism in Great Britain: The perpetuation of religion in an alien cultural milieu*, London: Tavistock.

Michaelson, M. (1987). 'Domestic Hinduism in a Gujarati trading caste' in Burghart, R. (ed.) *Hinduism in Great Britain: The perpetuation of religion in an alien cultural milieu*, London: Tavistock.

O'Keefe, B. (1980) *Hindu Family Life in East London*,   London: University of London (London School of Economics and Political Science Ph.D. thesis).
Robinson, V. (1990) 'Boom and Gloom: the success and failure of Britain's South Asians' in Clarke, C., Peach, C. and Vertovec, S.   *South Asians Overseas: Migration and Ethnicity*, Cambridge: Cambridge University Press.
Sinclair-Stevenson, M. (1920) *The Rites of the Twice Born*.   London: Oxford University Press.
Singer, M. (ed) (1972) *When a Great Tradition Modernizes: an anthropological approach to Indian civilization*, New York: Praeger.
Teifion, M. B. (1982) *A Way to God: Hindu beliefs in Leicester and Leicestershire*, Leicester: University of Leicester, M.Phil. dissertation.
Vertovec, S. (1992). 'Community and Congregation in London Hindu Temples: divergent trends', *New Community*, 8(2), pp.251-264.

11

Surinam Hinduism in the Netherlands and Social Change

Corstiaan J.G. van der Burg

In an article on religious change Mark Holmstrøm states that existing Hindu societies and Hindu history can only be understood by paying attention to the interplay of two radically different kinds of religion, associated with two kinds of morality and of social relations (Holmstrøm, 1971: 28). On the one hand he discerns a religion which consecrates the existing social order, values of submission and hierarchy, and a relativist morality of closed groups. On the other hand, he meets with a devotional religion with values of choice and equality, and a tendency towards a universalist 'open' morality. In his opinion these two types of religion exist in unstable combination in every Hindu community, traditional as well as modern. They correspond to values of heteronomy and autonomy, which coexist in every social morality. He argues, then, that innovation in the field of morality, influenced, but not directly determined by (changing) circumstances, upsets the equilibrium between the two types of religion, which in turn involves a change in the nature of the social relations.

In broad terms Holmstrøm refers to the views of Louis Dumont, who in a famous article on world renunciation in Indian religions (Dumont, 1960) distinguishes two types of religion: 'group religion' and 'religion of choice'. The latter is, according to Dumont, associated with - and on the whole even derived from - the thinking of the *sannyasin*, the renouncer who has broken bonds with society in an attempt to reach *moksha* or liberation from rebirth. Thus Dumont sees in Hinduism the polarity of 'social religion' and 'religion of choice' as an elaboration of the polarity in the ideas of the heteronomous 'man-in-the-world' over against the autonomous renouncer.

Both Dumont and Holmstrøm see devotional religion as a very specific combination of elements from these structurally opposed forms of religion. Dumont calls this combination an 'invention of the renouncer', for it is a way of applying the renouncer's views to life in the social world (Dumont, 1960: 57). It is the coexistence of the idea of *moksha* - or, alternatively, of the idea of continual communion with a personal God - with a stay in a society which is shaped according to the values of the caste ideology. Thus, such a devotional religion contains a set of heterogeneous religious values which exist in this unstable combination.

Dumont's approach to religious change is problematic. He states, as we saw, that innovation comes from the renouncer, who is seen as the 'agent of change' and as the 'creator of values' (Dumont, 46). In his view, innovations would be absorbed in the group religion. The result would then be an ideology which renews and adjusts itself again and again. According to Dumont, however, when innovation is attended with change, it is an autonomous process. In his analysis, he seems to exclude the possibility that other factors - socio-economic or political ones - could influence this change.

Holmstrøm, however, regards, as we saw, other factors not so much as direct causes, but as reasons for change, which should be taken into account. He does not rule out the possibility of an inherent pattern in the process of religious and ethical change, although he considers this process as the result of a dialogue of ideas and of action which expresses ideas (Holmstrøm, 1971: 30). Besides, he notes that analysis in terms of social structure and function, of class relations or psychology, should not be a reduction, but a further commentary, deepening our understanding of what is going on.

Apart from Holmstrøm, others, like Richard Burghart (1987) and Timothy Fitzgerald (1990) also elaborated and improved Dumont's typology. The gist of the distinction they make is between (type I) the ever present moral order of the universe, a *dharma* to which all beings are subject, a religious outlook, stressing ritual order and hierarchy and (type II) a soteriological religion, a path of salvation. Type I stands for the traditional 'mainstream' Hinduism, which is 'group-tied', simply meaning: embedded in the social relations of a group or a set of groups. Its ideology is that of 'hierarchy or ritual order that embraces the whole mythical cosmos, but which is manifested to the observer most evidently in 'caste' (Fitzgerald, 1990: 112ff), based on the principle of purity. *Dharma*, as the fundamental unifying principle of traditional Hinduism, defines the status and obligations of all beings in the cosmos, from the gods to inanimate matter. It can also be called 'karmatic' Hinduism, because 'the importance of correct ritual action *karma* in the fulfilment and maintenance of cosmic order is paramount'. It is not a 'World Religion' and not for export; it is neither a soteriology nor is it a system of meaning available for non-Hindus. Analytically speaking, it is the 'centre of gravity, the context within which the other phenomena, the sectarian soteriologies, the potential 'religions' for export, are rooted'.

The other kind of Hinduism, type II, comprises the ideologies which are generally centred around a personal soteriology. It is sectarian rather than caste-based, it inclines towards free choice of personal devotion instead of ascribed status and duties; it is 'other-worldly' rather than 'this-worldly', and it tends towards egalitarianism and individualism, rather than hierarchy (Fitzgerald: 113). Authority lies not with the Brahmin, the traditional religious specialist, but with the ascetic who has achieved some personal realisation of transcendent deity.

Historically, these two ideal types have been interwoven and dynamically related. Since empirical Hindu reality is a mixture of these types, then the latter type, comprising doctrines and practices explicitly focused on devotion and salvation can never be presented as 'Hinduism' *tout court*, 'as if [these doctrines] existed in abstraction from the wider ritual context in which they are anchored' (Fitzgerald: 114). The influence emanating from this type II Hinduism can hardly be underrated. This more or less 'abstract', extra-cultural form of Hinduism seems to correspond most to the Western and Christian conceptions of religion, and is therefore appealing to non-Hindu Westerners as an equivalent alternative. This may not so much appear from the great numbers of disciples from non-Hindu origin it attracts, yet there seems to be a constant interest in, and a growing acquaintance with whatever this form of 'universal' Hinduism has to offer. As a consequence, this kind of Hinduism has gradually become the measuring rod with which type I Hinduism is being judged, not only by non-Hindus but also by educated Hindus themselves. For example, the difficulties Surinam Hinduism - which might, for reasons we will discuss later, just as well still be labelled a type I Hinduism - experiences in the Netherlands can be partly attributed to this circumstance (Burg, 1989).

An analytical differentiation between type I and II Hinduism may help to provide a framework within which the relation between Hindu traditions and social change could be explored and problems of continuity and discontinuity, in particular between Hinduism in India and *diaspora* Hinduism could be assessed (cf. King, 1989: 90ff.; Fitzgerald, 1990: 115). In other words, it may help in analysing not only how social change could influence religious change, but it could in particular be useful for examining the viability of the distinct Hindu traditions in a new social and cultural environment.

In this respect, the recent history of Hinduism in Surinam and the Netherlands offers ample opportunity to test the serviceability of our typology. Since it will make no sense in this context to study a religion abstracted from its specific sociological setting (cf. Fitzgerald, 1990: 115), the history of the community of Surinam Hindustanis will be of central concern in this article. It reveals a succession of changes in the social and cultural situation which also the Hindus amongst them had to deal with. We found that these changes created a series of varying adaptive strategies, with their concomitant ideologies and identifications, in particular with regard to religion. We could distinguish several phases in this process of change.

First phase: Ethnic Identity in Surinam

The fact that a considerable part (37 per cent) of Surinam's population is of South Asian origin has its cause in its colonial history. Ten years after the abolition of slavery in Surinam in 1863, the Dutch Government could get so-called 'indentured labourers' from the Central Eastern part of British India who were shipped from Calcutta to Surinam. On June 5th 1873 the first transport vessel 'Lalla Rookh' (the 'Rosy Cheeked') disembarked in Paramaribo. By 1916 about

33,000 men, women and children from all strata and occupations of the Indian population came to Surinam. The major part of them did not return after their five-years' contract period. It was they who constituted the basis of the Hindustani community.

In the process of reconstruction of Hindustani identity after the severe shock it experienced from the migration, Hinduism gradually lost one of its most distinctive features, namely the caste system which had up to then controlled all social relations and styles of living of these British Indians.

While traditional ('South Asian') Hinduism - as we saw - has a dual structure of meaning and organisation, that is Brahmanism and sectarianism (similar to our Hinduism type I and II), each with its own relationship to the caste system, Surinam Hinduism lost this duality as well as its close relationship to the caste system, which could not be maintained after the migration to Surinam. There, a new kind of Hinduism developed which contained elements derived from both forms of the religion.

The gradual disappearance of social distinctions between castes in the Surinam plantation economy was one of the reasons for the integration of the Hindu community. Already during the passage to Surinam the caste rules for commensality were almost literally muddled up. In the plantation period, the caste distinctions, concerning profession and marriage, could not be maintained either. Even the Brahmans - about five per cent of the workers - could no more abide by their strict rules. Moreover, this integration put an end to the religious differentiation which was attended with the social differentiation in traditional Hinduism. In India the higher castes adhere to a Brahmanic form of Hinduism while folk religion is the variant for the low-caste majority of the population. Although the Brahmans had equally been incorporated in the plantation economy like all other indentured labourers, they managed to retain their distinct position after the plantation period. Mostly simple *karam kandis* (officiants) by origin, they were able to monopolise not only the ritual expertise, but also the sacred knowledge which, in their homeland was the domain of the *gurus* and their ascetic communities. These *gurus* were completely absent in Surinam, so that the Brahman priests, the so-called *pandits*, the religious specialists, became the only exponents of Hindu religion and sacred lore from the community's formative period onward.

Thus, it was not the folk religion which survived in Surinam, although the majority of the former indentured labourers were not from high caste origin (17.75 per cent) but belonged to the middle castes (33.25 per cent), the lower castes (nine per cent) and to the casteless (22 per cent) (De Klerk, 1953: 103-108). In fact a process of Brahmanisation took place, by which all Hindus were integrated under the banner of Brahmanic Hinduism. After the period of indentured labour the Brahmans not only resumed their position as ritual specialists, but they were even able to extend their authority to areas hitherto closed to them, such as healing practices and exorcism, - areas which had been the prerogative of non-Brahmanic Hinduism (cf. Van der Veer, 1987).

This rise of a Brahmanic priestly hegemony in Surinam Hinduism seems to be closely connected with a conspicuous absence of sectarianism, that is, ascetic monastic orders. These monastic communities, as exponents of a philosophical attitude of world-renunciation (our type II Hinduism), counterbalance the wordly attachment of 'social Hinduism' (our type I Hinduism) which is based on the caste system. The fact is that in Hinduism these ascetics are the ones who guard the purity of the doctrine and who provide it with a theological basis. The absence of such ascetics in Surinam and later on in the Netherlands, unlike for example some major Indian communities in the U.K. like the Gujaratis (Pocock, 1976; Burghart, 1987), deprived Hinduism of its most important religious authorities and spokesmen. As a consequence, not only has Surinam Hinduism enjoyed for more than a century a great doctrinal liberty which was hardly limited by the rather arbitrary standards applied by the individually acting and self-employed Brahman priests, (the only extant religious authorities), but also it has suffered right from the beginning from the absence of a distinct religious institution which was in charge of the perpetuation of religion.

What made the Brahmans' social position even stronger was the fact that their religious expertise went together with a central position in an informally structured network of hereditary patron-client relationships mainly concerning officiating in rituals. Even in the Surinam situation this network is still called the *jajmani* system but it differs from what is known in India by that name, because Surinam lacks a caste-structured economy. In the Indian caste society the dominant castes operate as *jajmans* ('patrons of the sacrifice'), for the specialist castes of the Brahmans in exchange for ritual services on their behalf. According to Brahmanical tradition most of these services were family bound house rituals, like e.g. the *samskars* (rites de passage), *jags* (offerings) and *kathas* (recitations). Surinam Hinduism is in essence a family centred religion, which explains why congregational temple cults were until recently of secondary importance. In Surinam, the building of congregational temples started only after the religion was given a formal organisational structure. Even today, in the Netherlands, we can hardly see the beginning of the fully-fledged temple religion some Hindu spokesmen so eagerly want us to believe there should be. We will revert to this matter later.

The *jajmani* system is the best known Indian example of mutual dependence through service-rendering. Another related one is the traditional Indian royal patronage of court priests or of ascetic communities. Formerly, the king representing worldly power had a close relationship with the 'clergy' representing the spiritual authority. Both were mutually dependent in the execution of their office. Perhaps it was the Dutch authorities' religious subsidy arrangement of the 1970s, discussed later, which reminded the Surinam Hindus of this way of supporting religion. Anyway, in turn-of-the-century Surinam, the *jajmani* system made the priests the central figures in the only form of organisation religion knew at that time. So, vested with authority as religious experts, their social status was equally unassailable.

In short, we can say that in the first place the levelling of the caste boundaries effected the social and religious integration of the Hindus - up to a certain level - under the canopy of Brahmanical religion, while it also enabled the Brahmans themselves to rise to a central position in the religious and social organisation of the community.

Second phase: Religious Ethnic Identity in Surinam

Although the foundations for a Surinam Hindu identity had been laid by then, this situation was not going to last long. The arrival of the missionary fundamentalist reform movement Arya Samaj (the 'Society of Nobles'), initiated in India in 1875 by Svami Dayanand Sarasvati, put the newborn unity among the Hindus in jeopardy. In its call for a return to the Vedas (the oldest class of authoritative religious scriptures in Hinduism), its condemnation of the caste system and in particular its anti-Brahmanical stance, the Arya Samaj had a significant success among the British Indian communities in the Caribbean. In Surinam, the movement obtained in a short time a following of sixteen percent. A majority of its supporters came from the lower classes (Dew, 1978: 10), because these people could connect the Aryan ideology of emancipation from the Brahmans' dominance to their own aspirations to upward mobility. This meant a serious threat to the power position of the traditional Brahmans. These hereditary Brahmans on their part closed ranks and received the support from certain reactionary Brahman circles in India, in particular those of the conservative freedom fighter Malaviya (Klimkeit, 1981: 160). In order to hold their ground against the massive propaganda of the Arya Samaj, the Brahmans founded in 1929 a formal association of followers of mainstream Hinduism under the name of Sanatan Dharm, the 'Eternal Religion'. A few months later the Arya Samaj officially founded its Surinam branch, naming it the Arya Dewaker, the 'Aryan Sun' (De Klerk, 1953: 193-196).

This formalisation of Surinam Hinduism and the split into two contesting factions gave rise for the first time to a growth of a consciousness of religious identity with the Hindustani laity, an awareness which had hardly existed until then. Before that time only secular interest organisations could rally the Hindustanis against the vicissitudes of post-indenture life in Surinam. These first welfare organisations of Surinam Hindustanis were differentiated merely on the basis of conservative and progressive criteria (De Klerk, 1953: 192). Besides, by this formalisation the laity got some say in religious matters, its organisation and its activities. This made these religious organisations more rooted in society and therefore more equipped to play a part in later political developments.

After the formative years, a new period set in by the end of World War II, a period which was characterised by hopes and fears for an impending autonomous status of Surinam, as had rather prematurely been promised by Wilhelmina, Queen of the Netherlands, in December 1942 (Dew, 1978: 53). This induced an unprecedented political activity in which all ethnic communities were involved.

Between the two World Wars, most Hindustanis had become peasants, staying behind in the rural areas. Their counterparts, the Creole former slaves had previously left the plantations for Paramaribo, Surinam's political and cultural centre. Ethnic competition, so crucial in the period to come, hardly played a role in this situation yet. The Hindustanis contented themselves with agricultural labour in the rural areas, while the Creoles found jobs in the administrative and educational sector. So far, isolation as the consequence of geographical and occupational separation promoted the undisturbed and rapid development of the Hindustani community.

From World War I onward, the Hindustanis managed to make up social and economic arrears. In less than fifty years the former British Indian 'coolies' were emancipated into a community with vested interests in agriculture, trade and transport. This emancipatorial development was attended with increasing westernisation and secularisation, in particular in the field of education and food habits.

Internally, inside the Hindustani community, the divergent religious identifications with the Sanatan Dharm and the Arya Samaj, supported by their respective formal religious organisations, fostered a fully-fledged communalism. Still the priests remained the grass-root leaders of both religious communities. They kept religious factionalism alive so that a pronounced religious partiality structured the Hindustani community.

Thus, it is not surprising that when, after World War II the Hindustanis entered the political arena it was the religious organisations which supplied the basis for the formation of the political parties. When the development of the Hindustani community led to increasing confrontations and antagonism with the Creole community in every field of public life, one came to realise that ethnic unity was more important than religious discord. So, when in 1949 the 'Verenigde Hindostaanse Partij' (United Hindustani Party) was formed, it had for its basis a Hindustani ethnic identity (Dew, 1978: 75). Because religious factionalism continued to exist internally, the Brahman leaders were no longer acceptable to represent the Hindu community as a whole to the outside world. Religious authority had to make way for non-Brahmanic secular professionalism in that, for instance, a non-clerical professional politician became the most important political leader: the low-caste 'praktizijn' (advocate) J. H. Lachmon.

So far we have noticed that the process of religious formalisation had been started off by a heterogeneous factor, the Arya Samaj. The formal religious organisations set the stage for the entrance of an all-Hindustani political party inside which they themselves remained central. We have also seen that along with the emancipatorial growth of the Hindustani community, ethnic identification became increasingly important in Surinam society.

Third phase: Ethnic Identity in the Netherlands

In the seventies a third of the Surinam population emigrated to the Netherlands. The exodus reached its maximum in the years preceding Surinam's independence, in 1975. Although this massive emigration cannot be interpreted in terms of labour migration comparable to the West Indian migration to Britain (cf. Peach, 1968; Bovenkerk, 1983) or to the migration of Mediterranean workers to North Western Europe, there is no doubt that it was the economic security and political stability of Dutch society at that time which encouraged both Hindustanis and Creoles to migrate. For the Hindustanis an added consideration was the threat of Creole oppression after independence, such as in British Guyana. To them this migration undoubtedly had ethnic aspects, in spite of the fact that the Creole migrants actually outnumbered the Hindustanis.

It was Hindustanis from all economic and social sectors of society, Brahman pandits included, who migrated to the Netherlands. To prevent the new immigrants from all settling in the big cities - which is what generally happened with the Mediterranean workers - the Government pursued a policy of deconcentration. The Hindustanis had to undertake the arduous task of rebuilding their community, socially as well as religiously. In this respect their situation was not unlike the state of affairs in colonial Surinam in the last decades of the previous century.

Since, amongst other considerations, survival inside their own community had been the *rationale* for the Hindustanis' migration, ethnicity seemed to be the most natural principle for the construction of organisational instruments aimed at their integration into the plural Dutch society. The Government, however, appeared to have a different opinion on ethnic identity. It sought to implement its policy by addressing the only existing Surinam welfare organisation. This agency, although it was officially based on an all-ethnic principle, was in fact controlled by the Creoles. Initially, the Government clearly neglected the ethnic differences among the Surinam immigrants, showing its almost total ignorance of ethnic sensibilities. Therefore, the Hindustanis decided to set up their own welfare organisation on a pure ethnic basis and named it Lalla Rookh, after the first transport ship which brought them to Surinam. The organisation was born from sheer necessity, as the outcome of a particular political development, which, as we saw, was characterised in its Surinam beginnings by enduring ethnic antagonism and rivalry and now, in its Dutch continuation, by a too pragmatic policy on the part of the authorities.

Thus we can distinguish yet another phase in the process of identity formation - this time on Dutch soil - marked by an ethnic identification along with its appropriate ethnic organisational set-up. Initially, this ethnic stance of the

Hindustanis proved to be successful, for a variety of external and internal reasons, some of which we will now mention.

First, the Government at that time had an interest in maintaining calm on the minority front and avoided - practically at any cost - unrest amongst the Surinam immigrants after a period of difficulties around Surinam's independence.

Secondly, since a purely secular ethnic identity was a popular theme in the Socialist-controlled Government's policy of the period, the prevailing political climate was favourable to the Hindustanis' ethnic stance. This would not have been the case had the Hindustanis stressed more strongly the religious aspect of their identity. For, when they came to the Netherlands in the seventies they entered a 'pillarised' society in which religious identity had been for a number of decades a dominant principle of articulation in the formation of interest groups. Thus, both major Christian denominations - Protestant and Roman Catholic - had not only fostered their own political parties, but had also developed comprehensive systems of denominational organisations, covering almost the entire field of social and occupational activities including state aided welfare organisations, supported by the parties' MP's. In the sixties, however, though religious affiliation was an important factor, in the welfare associations secular professional expertise came to be more valued than religious ardour. In spite of the ongoing 'de-pillarisation' and professionalisation of the Dutch welfare sector, the Hindustanis as well as other minority groups continued to claim their own welfare organisations on a purely ethnic basis, so far without the obligation of keeping up a professional appearance. As a social determinant, religion had indeed become suspect; this was not the case, however, with the new phenomenon of ethnicity. Dutch society in the seventies had grown accustomed to the idea that foreigners should organise themselves ethnically, to make a better stand for themselves, as foreign communities, against social and economic exploitation and discrimination.

Thirdly, since the Government was only too anxious to mobilise a kind of leadership inside the migrant communities in order to implement its policies, it could not neglect Lalla Rookh, as an ethnic organisation. As an agency representing all Hindustanis, Lalla Rookh united Hindus as well as Muslims. The parallel with the 'Verenigde Hindostaanse Partij' (United Hindustani Party) in Surinam is obvious. By now it was able to play the same role, that is, as an intermediary between the Government and the Hindustani community. Here we see an interesting transformation in that a political party in the Surinam context came to function as a welfare agency in the Netherlands.

Inside the community the religious organisational structure had for the greater part collapsed. Although the doctrinal distinction between the Sanatan Dharm and the Arya Samaj continued in the Dutch situation, the formal organisational set-up of religion largely dissolved, due to the Government's policy of deconcentration. The only kind of religious organisation which more or less continued to exist was the pandit-centred informal network of personal *jajmani* relationships. But, compared to the Surinam situation, the laity had little involvement with the priests, much less a certain degree of social control over them. This process of virtual deformalisation of the religious organisation gave the priests a free hand in their entrepreneurial activities on a religious market of supply and demand. The gradual loss of control by the laity over the priests (and *vice versa*) proved to be detrimental to the religious life of the Hindustani community. Attempts to change this undesirable situation ended in failure for a variety of reasons. Initiatives to organise the priests got stranded in talking shops lacking the authority to control their members. It was these very members who refused to give up their unchallenged position as free entrepreneurs in religious services. This also applied to the formal religious organisations Sanatan Dharm and Arya Samaj. They lacked strong leadership and realistic goals, although in general the Arya Samajis were more able to organise themselves.

The Foundations

The Dutch Government too had a hand in this general organisational disorder. The lack of co-operation and reluctance to organise on the part of the Hindustanis can also be seen as the side-effect of the Government's failing welfare policy, which gave rise to a new phenomenon: the religio-cultural foundations. Since Lalla Rookh and other foundations came to be more firmly established as ethnic welfare agencies, the Government had begun involving them in its policies, in particular as distributors of funds for cultural purposes. The end of the 1970s saw a proliferation of cultural foundations, which could profit by this funding policy. This phenomenon is to be partly accounted for by the fact that through the intermediary of the ethnic welfare agencies and their local counterparts, the authorities granted funds to any foundation which produced a plan to spend money for cultural purposes in a very general sense. A patronage like relationship between the granter, the intermediary and the spenders seemed unavoidable. This entrepreneurial flowering, even in the field of culture and religion, can be explained by the same commercial spirit in the Hindustanis which also led to remarkable successes in ethnic enterprise (Boissevain and Grotenbreg, 1986). It cannot be denied that the opportunity to acquire money so easily and with little control over its spending, combined with a spirit of enterprise and independence - most of the foundations are family-based businesses - created an atmosphere of competition and mutual distrust in circles of the cultural and religious foundations. The almost uncontrollable mechanism of distributing these funds led in the long run to such odd situations (cf. Latham, 1982; 1983; Boedhoe, 1980: 3-6) that 'cultural activities' came generally to be looked upon with increasing scepticism by the Dutch welfare authorities.

The general discomfort with the way in which the funds were shared out called for more unity and joint action on the side of the Hindustanis. It was obvious that the urge for unity could no longer be based only upon the usual 'ethnic identity' employed so far, that means, in the form it had taken in Surinam. Such an ethnic stance, inspired by Hindustani-Creole antagonism in Surinam, made less sense in the Netherlands since the two communities became part of contemporary pluralistic Dutch society. It had become ineffective in the new situation because it was no longer a clear and honourable enough principle of distinction, to be used for the promotion of Hindustani ethnic interests.

A new substance for 'ethnic identity' was looked for and found: religion. A religious stance appeared to be preferable for a variety of reasons. As a social determinant, religion had recently begun to enjoy a new popularity in the Netherlands. Although the Christian religious institutions had for the most part lost their social relevance, religion remained an important source of power in national politics in the 1980s. Moreover, due to the immigration of large numbers of Mediterranean Muslims, Islam had become the widest spread non-Christian religion in the Netherlands. This enhanced the general interest in their religion and equally in the religions of other minorities.

In spite of its formal secular stance of 'no preference and no interference' the then Government, controlled by the Christian Democrats, continued to maintain a certain relationship with the established religious institutions, and with religion in general. In an attempt to reconsider its position towards the minorities' religions, the Government published in 1983 and in 1988 two reports concerning the continuation of subsidising the 'Religious Provisions for Ethnic Minorities in the Netherlands' (Werkgroep, 1983) and about the relation between Government and religious denominations (Commissie, 1988). This shows that religion was still regarded by the Government as a matter of concern in minority politics.

It is therefore not surprising that, by then, it was religion which was starting to provide a focal point for a common Hindustani ethnic ideology. This is one of the reasons why we will distinguish a final phase as yet in the ongoing process, in which the secular, welfare-inspired ethnic ideology had been replaced by a religious, that is a Hindu, ethnic ideology. What was new about this was that the religious aspect of this ideology was no longer stressed in the antagonism between the distinctive religious denominations inside the Hindustani community. Rather, this time religion played a part in the confrontation of the entire community with the surrounding society.

Fourth phase: Religious Ethnic Identity in the Netherlands

Lalla Rookh responded well to this new political interest in minority religions. The agency started to present itself as 'the' advocate of religion. The fact that up to then there were no religious provisions whatsoever for Surinam Hindus and Muslims (whereas Mediterranean Muslims could indeed benefit from these opportunities) increased the motivation of the agency in pursuing its religious claims. The recent building of a mosque in Amsterdam by Mediterranean and Surinam Muslims, which had been made possible through municipal aid and that of other organisations, gave the agency all the more reason to teach the authorities their duty in religious affairs. The municipal Spring elections of 1986 were an additional opportunity to make a political issue of religion. Some members of the agency's board offered themselves as candidates for the Christian Democratic Party. We would say that the agency had special reasons to come to the fore itself as the advocate of religion.

The official religious organisations should have been the first to undertake this task. But as we have seen already, in the Netherlands they were not yet sufficiently developed to represent the Hindus in this matter. (The same holds - though to a lesser degree - for both Muslim denominations, the Orthodox and the Ahmadiya.) Mutual rivalry obstructed joint action. In this sense the Hindus are more badly organised in the Netherlands than in Surinam. Earlier we noted that in fact a process of religious deformalisation had started with the massive influx of Hindustanis into the Netherlands.

As a second alternative, the traditional religious leaders, the *pandits*, could have been qualified representatives. We have established, however, that they do not constitute a firm enough group. They tend to act too much as independent entrepreneurs. Even their councils are not weighty enough to hold a firm grip on them. Besides, the *pandits* would not benefit from a religion gradually developing a church-like structure, which they fear to be the case with a Government-aided Hinduism. For them this would be fundamentally alien to Hinduism (Girjasing, 1984: 12-15; Lalla Rookh, 1985). An even more important reason is the fact that, generally speaking, the person of the priest and his role in religious matters are increasingly being criticised by the laity. In this respect priests are no longer acceptable to the more progressive and educated members of the community, in particular to the younger generations. Their willingness to use religion for enterpreneurship and to increase commercialisation of the priestly service as a result of the unsteady *jajmani* relationships (cf. Van der Veer, 1985: 319) in the Dutch context are particularly open to serious objections. Moreover, the priests' lack of religious training and their unfamiliarity with what is going on in the lives of their following often result in communication breakdown (Ramsoekh and Baldewsingh, 1985). Besides, the *pandits* use a language which does not appeal to the younger generations. Their religious parlance makes it difficult for the latter to familiarise themselves with the traditional religious culture of their community (cf. Pocock, 1976: 347ff.). Since the younger generations have to keep their foothold in Western society, also in respect of their religion, the *pandits* need to be sufficiently skilled to keep them involved in matters religion.

In short, we cannot help but conclude that those institutions in Surinam Hinduism which should have been the first to stand up for the religious rights of the Hindus in the Netherlands, appear to be unfit for a variety of reasons.

So, it had to be Lalla Rookh - the only institution inside the Hindustani community which was more or less qualified - to undertake this task. Having started as a categorial welfare agency in 1975 it gradually developed into an 'identity organisation'. As a public relations agency, pleading the Hindustanis' cause with government and municipal authorities, it came to be an influential party in minority affairs. At the end of 1984 it arranged a meeting with all (i.e. about 100) representatives of the cultural and social organisations with which it is associated. The most important outcome of this meeting was that Lalla Rookh's proposal to form a 'Committee of Hindu and Muslim Congregations' was given unanimous approval. This committee should act in the interests of both Hindus and Muslims as an adviser to the Government in religious matters.

A good case to test the strength of the Hindustani religious unity under the leadership of Lalla Rookh presented itself in the form of the issue on Government-aided religious provisions. Lalla Rookh made this political question into a religious one with ideological overtones. The major argument for subsidising mosques and temples was that Islam and Hinduism, unlike Christianity, were 'ways of life', in which no clear distinction could be made between the religious and the secular, between a congregation and the pagan world at large (Lalla Rookh, 1985; 1986). This is the reason why Surinam Hinduism never had an organisational structure which should enable it to administer funds for the maintenance of temples or the appointment of priests (Girjasing, 1984: 15). Following this line of argument, these religions should get government aid. With good reason, Peter Van der Veer has expressed his doubts on the supposed unity of culture and religion among the Hindustanis (Van der Veer, 1984: 10). Surinam did, contrary perhaps to India, show indeed the beginnings of a split into a religious and a profane culture inside the Hindustani community. This is likely to be also the case in the Netherlands, as may be gathered from our notes above.

The second argument was that temples were a great necessity for Surinam Hinduism in the Netherlands, because 'religion forms an integral part of the cultural identity of the ethnic minorities' (Werkgroep, 1983: 75). Apart from the fact that we would welcome the building of temples, because we consider them as indispensable points of convergence of Hindu identity in the Dutch context, we view this argument as striking in its negation of the historical reality as we observe it. In fact, this Surinam/Dutch form of Hinduism is still a house-and-family religion. Therefore, it needs sacral provisions for religious occasions in the first place, like the two Government Commissions suggested, who in their reports appeared not insensitive to the religious claims of the Surinam Muslims and Hindus. The Hirsch Ballin report received an elaborate and positive response on the part of the Hindustanis (Lalla Rookh, 1988). So far, this is what this kind of Hinduism seems to afford itself because of its informal organisational structure. In Surinam, congregational temples were built only as soon as Hinduism started to organise itself formally, that is, after World War II. Unless such a formalisation will start in the Netherlands, we may not expect the number of temples to increase very much in the near future.

In a word, then, we could say that the changes in the external circumstances we described in our review of the Surinam Hindus' recent history account to a great extent for the changes in identification we noticed.   Not completely, however, because there appears to be also a relationship between the option of a certain kind of identification and the varying power relations within the community itself.   In particular, the eventual use of religion as the symbol of ethnicity in a surprisingly late stage in the identity formation process, can be regarded as the outcome of an internal struggle for power, i.e. between the Brahman elite and the welfare elite, an outcome which was favoured indeed by external circumstances, not in the last place by the religious policy pursued by the Dutch authorities.

Conclusion

In our account of the history of Surinam Hinduism we highlighted the impact of migration and socio-economic change on processes of identity formation and transformation of religion.   Focussing on the latter process, we hope the relevance of our analytical distinction between 'group religion' and 'religion of choice' to our approach to Hinduism in the Netherlands has become clear.   The distinction is artificial and made for research purposes, and is therefore non-existent in the faith of the Hindus themselves.

The typology has enabled us to locate at least three important changes Hinduism underwent right from the beginning in the *diaspora* situation in Surinam.   By far the most obvious effects of the migration were the gradual breakdown of the caste system and the change of Hinduism into an ethnic religion. Not so conspicuous but no less fundamental was the disappearance of the ideological side of the religion, the 'sectarian', other-worldly aspect of Hinduism. The result has been, as we saw, that, on the one hand, the 'type I' part of Hinduism was no longer 'anchored in society' in the traditional way, while, on the other, it came to be deprived of its sectarian, 'type II' part, its major source of inspiration.   As was noticed earlier, we regard Hinduism I and II as ideal types, which are complementary to one another, dynamically related and interwoven in one empirical Hindu reality.

Concentrating first on the 'group religion' aspect of Hinduism, we found in the first place that, in spite of the disappearance of the caste-system, the power and authority of the Brahman priesthood largely compensated for this loss.

Next, we found that the official Hindu spokesmen, laity as well as clergy, gave hardly any evidence, as far as their attitude and public statements were concerned, of viewing their own religion as an ethnic religion amongst others in a plural society, and of coming to terms with the fact that they do not live any more in a religious culture embedded in society, which was the case in India and might, to some extent, have been so in Surinam for some time after the period of indentured labour.

This attitude appears to be in striking contrast to what a spokesman of Hinduism in the United Kingdom has advocated to his fellow believers for years.

In an article on the religious life of Hindu immigrants in England, Pocock tells us how the *Pramukh Swami*, spiritual head of a certain Gujarati *sanstha* (religious society), advised the devotees resident in the United Kingdom to 'emulate the Jews' in making their adjustment to British society (Pocock, 1976), by developing a distinctive religious culture capable of co-existing with a secular one. Curiously enough, it is precisely such a distinction between religion and society (or culture), between the sacred and the secular, which is contrary to the reports of what 'eternal Hinduism' has always advocated to the faithful. This leader of a British minority religion apparently saw the separation of religion and society (or culture) as the only possibility for his religion to survive.

This opinion seems absent in the minds of the spokesmen of the Surinam Hindus in the Netherlands. These authorities do their utmost - as we saw - to maintain that such a separation of 'Church' and 'State' or between 'religion' and 'culture' is thoroughly inappropriate in Hinduism's case. Netherlands Hindus are quite far from 'emulating the Jews' as yet, and far from adapting, let alone examining, what is essential to their religious identity. In the case of Lalla Rookh the notion of the inseparability of 'religion' and 'culture' seems to fit well in its ideological perspective, as its official terms of reference are limited to religious policy making, that is: providing for the prior conditions for the preservation of the religion as an organisation, without interfering in matters with respect to religious content. The other religious spokesmen, like the priests and the boards of the religious organisations, seem - as we saw - to benefit more from a Hinduism as it once has been and as it still should be in their eyes, as an ideal type that is, than from a Hinduism as a religion which can be 'lived by' by its believers in an alien setting.

Turning now to the 'religion of choice' aspect of Surinam Hinduism, we have seen that there are virtually no official authorities concerned with the substantial aspects of changing religious beliefs and practices in terms of redefinition and re-interpretation (King, 1989: 90). Such a structural absence of religious experts who guard the doctrine and guarantee its transmission, could be seen as 'detrimental', especially in the new environment. Once more, 'sectarian', that is 'religion of choice' Hinduism of our type II, this time in the form of new religious movements, like e.g. Transcendental Meditation, ISKCON, and Sathya Sai Baba seems to become increasingly attractive to a great number of Surinam Hindus in a situation of growing cultural insecurity, to which their own religious tradition does not always have a ready answer, mainly for reasons we elaborated upon earlier.

Now that this traditional religion has been designated the most important resource in the community's identity formation, one would expect indeed, that these developments would induce the Hindu authorities to react appropriately. However, nothing of the kind is happening yet. This could be explained by the fact that they obviously do not view these movements as a real danger to the continuance of their religion. The reason for this lenient attitude is that the

Surinam Hindu spokesmen, as descendants of British Indians, see themselves as natural and rightful heirs to the 'timeless culture' of Indian civilisation (cf. Burghart, 1987: 248ff.). This includes all neo-Hindu accretions in the form of soteriologies preaching a universalised Hindu spirituality, which claims to transcend social and cultural boundaries (cf. Fitzgerald, 1990: 115).

However, if we look these days behind the façade of formal Hindustani representation and religious authority, we can perceive indeed new developments inside the community, both in the organisational set-up as well as in terms of ideological substance, which could lead to more radical changes in conceptualizing an interpretation than so far.   In spite of the stagnancy in the process of organisational *aggiornamento*, new initiatives are coming up in areas such as formal education which as yet have been looked down upon by the official welfare authorities as inaccessible, undesirable or of minor importance.   The recent founding of Hindu primary schools by a group who did acknowledge the separation of 'Church' and 'State', requires a timetabled formal instruction in Hinduism.   Next, one of the own Hindu foundations, with the longest record of opposition to Lalla Rookh's policy, officially declared itself a 'religious denomination on Vedantic principles' in order to disseminate Vedantic spirituality among Hindus as well as non-Hindus in the Netherlands (Ganesh, 1989: 8).

Such new developments inside the community, together with the growing popularity of non-traditional forms of Hinduism (Burghart, 1987: 225), will unavoidably play a part in the future of the religion in terms of perception and self-description (King, 1989: 91).   The question of how they will play this part cannot be answered, because of the multiplicity of the factors involved.   One of the problems will be how the two types of 'Hinduism relate to each other, and in what way both of them are linked to the dominant religion in the Netherlands? Will both continue to exist next to each other in unstable combination?   Or will it be necessary to mould the divergent ritual and spiritual traditions into one viable religion, which should be appealing enough to Hindus from all sorts of religious background so as to ensure its continuance in the new environment?

Whatever the direction, scope and content of these religious transformations will be in the end, from our findings and those of Burghart, King and Fitzgerald, we may conclude that, next to the role of the spiritual authority, the traditional autonomous renouncer, the part of the individual layman will be crucial in the process of change.   Whether this transformation will be accompanied by a conscious high-level debate, or by an endless, uncontrolled and almost subconscious process of redefining the own tradition - or of adjusting it to the other tradition - religion will increasingly become a matter of personal choice of the Hindu laity.   In that sense, a new 'autonomous man', this time 'of-the-world' is likely to be more and more the creator of his own values.

154   Corstiaan J.G. van der Burg

References

Boedhoe, N. (1980) 'Graven in de macht van Surinaamse organisaties', *Aisa Samachar* 6(7): pp.3-6.
Boissevain, Jeremy en Hanneke Grotenbreg (1986) 'Culture, structure and ethnic enterprise: the Surinamese of Amsterdam', *Ethnic and Racial Studies* 9 (1): pp.1-23.
Bovenkerk, F. (1983) 'De Vlucht, Migratie in de jaren Zeventig', in Glenn Willemsen (ed.), *Suriname, de schele onafhankelijkheid*, Amsterdam: Arbeiderspers, pp.152-181.
Burg, Corstiaan J.G. v.d. (1989) ' Religion in an Alien Context: the Approach to Hinduism in a Western Society' in Jerald Gort etc. (eds) *Dialogue and Syncretism: an Interdisciplinary Approach.* Grand Rapids/Amsterdam: Wm.B.Eerdmans/Rodopi.
Burghart, R. (ed) (1987) *Hinduism in Great Britain: the Perpetuation of Religion in an Alien Cultural Milieu*, London/New York: Tavistock Publications.
Commissie (1988) *Overheid, godsdienst en levensovertuiging. Eindrapport van de Commissie van advies inzake de criteria voor steunverlening aan kerkgenootschappen en andere genootschappen op geestelijke grondslag*, 's-Gravenhage: Ministerie van Binnenlandse Zaken.
Dew, E. (1978) *The Difficult Flowering of Surinam*, Den Haag: Martinus Nijhoff.
Dumont, L. (1960) 'World Renunciation in Indian Religions', *Contributions to Indian Sociology* 4: pp.33-62.
Fitzgerald, T. (1990) 'Hinduism and the "world religion" fallacy', *Religion*, 20: pp.101-118.
Ganesh (1989) 'Stichting Ganesh treedt op als Kerkgenootschap van de Vedanta', *Ganesh informatie-bulletin*, 4(12): pp.4-12.
Girjasing, Soeshil K. (1984) 'Behoort de Hindoegemeenschap in het bestaan van de pandit te voorzien'? *Aisa Samachar*, 10(8): pp.12-15.
Holmstrøm, M. N. (1971) 'Religious Change in an Industrial City of South India, *Journal of the Royal Asiatic Society* , (1): pp.28-40.
King, U. (1989) 'Some reflections on Sociological Approaches to the Study of Modern Hinduism', *Numen*, 36(1) pp.72-97.
Klerk, C. J. M. de (1953) *De immigratie der hindostanen in Suriname*, Amsterdam: Urbi et Orbi.
Klimkeit, H.-J. (1981) *Der politische Hinduismus: indische Denker zwischen religiöser Reform und politischem Erwache*, Wiesbaden: Harrassowitz.
Lalla Rookh. (1985) 'Kongreseditie Kultuur/Religie', *Lalla Rookh* 10(2/3).
Lalla Rookh. (1986) 'Surinaams Inspraakorgaan bracht advies uit inzake verhouding kerk - staat m.b.t. hindoes en moslims', *Lalla Rookh* 11(5): pp.23-28.
Lalla Rookh. (1988) 'Commissie pleit voor formatieplaatsen t.b.v hindoes en moslims; Lalla Rookh doet voorstel', *Lalla Rookh* 13(2): pp.7-11.
Latham, E. A. (1982) *Verslag van het onderzoek ten behoeve van het ontwikkelen van de toekomstige structuur van het welzijnswerk in Breda e.o.*, Breda.
Latham, E.A. (1983) *Verslag van het onderzoek ten behoeve van het ontwikkelen van de toekomstige structuur voor het welzijnswerk voor Surinamers te Tilburg*, Tilburg.
Peach, C. (1968) *West Indian Migration to Britain, a Social Geography*, Oxford: Oxford University Press.
Pocock, D.F. (1976) 'Preservation of the Religious Life: Hindu Immigrants in England. A Swami Narayan Sect in London', *Contributions to Indian Sociology*, (NS) 10(2): pp.341-365.
Ramsoekh, Wiresh en Rabin Baldewsingh. (1985) 'Over Hindoegeloof, *pandits* en jongeren', *Aisa Samachar*, 11(3): pp.6-7.

Veer, Peter van der (1984) 'Hoe bestendig is "de eeuwige religie"?.   Enkele vragen rond de organisatie van het Surinaams Hindoeïsme', in P. van Gelder e.a. (red.), *Bonoeman, rasta's en andere Surinamers*. Amsterdam: Werkgroep AWIC, pp.111-124.

Veer, Peter van der (1985) 'Brahmans: their Purity and their Poverty. On the Changing Values of Brahman priests in Ayodhya', *Contributions to Indian Sociology (NS)* 19(2): pp.303-321.

Veer, Peter van der (1987) *'Religious therapies and their valuation among Surinamese Hindustani in the Netherlands'*, Paper for the 'Conference on South Asian Communities Overseas', Oxford: Mansfield College.

Werkgroep (1983) *Religieuze voorzieningen voor ethnische minderheden in Nederland*, Rapport, tevens beleidsadvies van de niet-ambtelijke werkgroep *ad hoc.*, Rijswijk: Ministerie van Welzijn, Volksgezondheid en Cultuur.

The Transmission of Christian Tradition in an Ethnically Diverse Society

Eleanor Nesbitt

This chapter is based on ethnographic fieldwork conducted in Coventry between November 1990 and July 1991 as part of the Religious Education and Community Project[1]. The purpose of the research was to document the religious nurture, both formal and informal, of children associated with churches of twelve Christian denominations[2]. Care was taken to include a range of ethnicity of Christians in the city, drawing upon material on four ethnic groups. While detailed research will be reported elsewhere[3] this chapter focuses upon denominational allegiance and ethnicity in religious nurture. It takes up issues such as mother tongue and liturgical language, music and iconography, the calendar and significant days, lifecycle rites, the role of the country of origin in children's religious heritage and the values and assumptions they encounter. The examination draws attention to the differing relationship of home, school and church to the cultural identity of Christian children from different ethnic groups. I hope that the complex nature of Christian nurture in a multicultural society will be apparent.

For some, a Christian is a person whose life reflects the principles of behaviour apparent in the life of Jesus as recorded in the four canonical gospels. For others it refers to those born to Christian parents and/or baptised into the church. Some believe people are not Christian unless they have personally committed their lives to Jesus Christ. Thus by this definition Christians are people who have 'asked Jesus into their life' or 'accepted Christ as their Lord and Saviour'. In this study, Christian children are children who receive instruction and/or take part in congregational worship in a church. I have excluded those churches such as Spiritualist, Mormon, Jehovah's Witness and Christian Scientist, which are generally regarded as heterodox by the churches that constitute the Council of Churches for Britain and Ireland.

After preliminary participant observation in sixteen churches from twelve denominations I conducted structured interviews with fifty children. These took place in each child's day school, eighteen in all. Questions were open, allowing children to range over many aspects of religious belief and practice[4]. The study also included children of indigenous families from major Christian denominations (Church of England, Baptist, Methodist, etc.) as well as children of Irish, South Asian, Jamaican, Ukrainian and Greek Cypriot origin[5]. Others described themselves as being Jewish because their mothers were Jewish (2), Spanish (1), Greek (1), having a Chinese mother from Singapore (1) and half Croatian (1). Adults with special responsibility for religious teaching were interviewed in each denomination.

An earlier research on the religious nurture of Punjabi and Gujarati Hindu children[6] provided helpful points of comparison with the processes of religious transmission observable in ethnic minority Christian families. Among the Hindus, the home, family and community values were not compatible with values of school and wider society and they largely depended on the home, temple and the community rather than on school. In contrast, the school does provide a basis for religious activity to Christian children from ethnic minorities. In their case both the school and the church confirm values and practices, such as Christmas activities, which are associated with the traditions of their ancestral homeland.

By looking, albeit cursorily, at the experience of children from four communities, namely the Roman Catholics of Irish descent, the Greek Orthodox of Greek-Cypriot background, the Ukrainian Catholic (Uniate) community and Christians (including members of a Church of England congregation) of Indian Punjabi descent, I hope to illustrate the ethnically specific patterning of religious nurture in each community and highlight some of the differences which appear to be significant for particular groups, especially the Punjabi Christians. Their affiliation to Christianity has to be understood in the context of cultural differences on the one hand and their visibility distinguished by the majority with a focus on the colour of their skin. However, for most minorities, the school reinforces home tradition less than in the case of the ethnically English Christian children.

Homogeneous Religious Nurture: The Irish Catholics

The Irish constitute the largest ethnic minority in Coventry[7]. Irish settlement in the city has a history of over 150 years. By 1881 there were already 2,500 Catholics living in Coventry, most of whom must have been of Irish descent[8]. West Midlands is one of the six major conurbations which together account for over half of the Irish-born population in Britain (Gay, 1971: 92). There are now sixteen Roman Catholic churches in Coventry, nineteen Roman Catholic primary schools and three Roman Catholic comprehensives[9]. As a result Irish Catholics experience the greatest consistency in the religious teaching and cultural practice which are passed on by their home, church and school in contrast to children who come from Hindu or Sikh backgrounds. Children attend the Roman Catholic parish church where the priest and the congregation are of Irish Catholic descent. Home, church and school share a common language, the same assumptions and religious calendar.

To take a small example, St Patrick's day, commemorating the life of Ireland's patron saint, is celebrated in school.

Greek Cypriot Orthodox

The transmission of culture and religion is less homogeneous for new ethnic minorities. Home, church and school are not so mutually reinforcing. Many Christian children from ethnic minorities are growing up in more than one religious system, or more than one sub-system of Christianity. They are receiving information (verbal and behavioural) from different sub-systems[10].

There are no precise figures for the Greek Cypriot population in Coventry. The local Greek Orthodox church lists one hundred and twenty households as members. Most of them are of Cypriot origin, the rest being Greek or 'British'. Families live in Coventry as well as in Kenilworth, Leamington, Rugby, Nuneaton, Stratford-Upon-Avon and neighbouring villages[11]. Most of the early settlers (i.e. from 1955 onwards) were men who took jobs in restaurants and factories of various industries eventually followed by their wives. Most local Cypriot families now consist of three generations with some of the men running most of the city's fish and chip shops. Many young men and women are entering the professions such as law and accountancy.

A Greek-speaking Cypriot almost invariably belongs to the Greek Orthodox church. In Cyprus orthodoxy and Christianity were seen as identical. The priest knew everyone in the village. The Orthodox liturgy was celebrated amid a wealth of local tradition. Kotsoni describes the central role of the Orthodox church in the preservation of socio-cultural and ethnic identity (1990: 19).

At first Cypriots worshipped in the Anglican church of St. Anne in Acacia Avenue from 1963 to 1964 and then in St Alban's church at Barras Heath until funds enabled the purchase of a disused school building in Westwood Heath in 1974 (Hellenike Orthodoxe Koinoteta, Coventry, 1989: 27). The priest conducts the liturgy each Sunday and during the week on days of major significance e.g. daily in Holy week. Church services officially started on 7th March 1977 and the church was consecrated on 28th May 1978 as the Church of the Holy Transfiguration in the Archdiocese of Thyateira and Great Britain which belongs to the Ecumenical Patriarchate of Constantinople[12]. The church is one of the over fifty in Britain outside London.

While the Irish did not have to worry about the language problem, the Greek Cypriots did. Since 1965 the Greek school has run on Saturdays to instruct the children in the Greek language[13]. At present sixty-five children, aged five to fifteen, attend. They are divided into six classes, each with its own teacher. The school is one of the eighty-six in Britain which are under the jurisdiction of the Archdiocese (Kotsoni, 1990: 3, 23-24). Before lessons start on Saturday the priest, who is from mainland Greece, not from Cyprus, speaks to the children in Greek and starts the class with fifteen minutes of prayer in the church.[14] He also teaches one of the classes.

Children attend church on Sundays with their parents, although few go every Sunday. When about seven, boys are trained to serve the priest during the liturgy, initially by carrying the *lampada* (lantern). On Great (Holy) Friday girls scatter flowers and spray perfumed water on the *epitaphios*, a wooden replica of the sepulchre in which is laid an embroidered icon of Christ's body taken down from the cross. Boys read key parts of the service (e.g. Gospel) in English. Elders try hard to involve children in worship but some children feel bored by the long service. The liturgy is in old Greek, adding to the difficulties of children who do not all easily understand even contemporary Greek. The style of Byzantine singing continues unaltered except that in the Coventry church a group of women sing in response to the male cantor. Like the words the music is remote from the rest of children's experience.

The Greek Cypriot children in Coventry are growing up in a minority tradition. Their friends and teachers are often more aware of non-Christian ethnic minorities in the city than of the Greek Orthodox community. In school, the child hears of Christianity and of other faiths but nothing of traditional Greek Orthodox practice. The biblical knowledge passed on by the school supports that of the home and church. However children also become aware of significant differences. Those who attend private Catholic schools learn to cross themselves in the Roman Catholic way rather than in the Greek Orthodox way practised at home and in church[15]. Children also see differences associated with Holy Communion between Roman Catholic and Greek Orthodox traditions.

Ukrainian Catholics

The experience of children in Coventry's Ukrainian Catholic (Uniate) community is comparable with children from other groups[16]. Nevertheless significant differences in the community's history affect the transmission of religious belief and practice. Coventry has an estimated population of five hundred residents of Ukrainian origin[17]. Men arrived as refugees from Europe just after the Second World War. Most were from Western Ukraine, an area in which Ukrainian Catholics (Uniates) far outnumbered members of the Orthodox church (Diuk, 1985: 16).

Until the recent dissolution of the Soviet Union Ukrainians were more cut off than the Cypriots from their homeland[18]. Many Ukrainian men married non-Ukrainians as the Ukrainian men outnumbered the Ukrainian women who came as voluntary workers from Germany[19].

As Soviets had suppressed the Ukrainian language and culture, many Ukrainians wanted to preserve their culture. In 1947/1948 Coventry Ukrainians founded the Association of Ukrainians. In 1954 they purchased a building in Foleshill to serve as a community centre. In 1961 a wooden church hall in Broad

Street was purchased which was converted into the church of St Wolodymyr the Great and a community centre was set up nearer to the city centre in Leicester Causeway.

The Ukrainian children, aged three to fifteen, attend the Ukrainian Saturday School. Classes have been held since 1954. They are divided into five classes according to age and there are seven teachers. Children learn to read and write Ukrainian, a language written in Cyrillic script (Dmytriw and Wasyluk, 1982: 30-31). The community centre is about a mile from the church. The present priest does not participate in the children's classes. In a number of instances children have been prepared for their first communion by a priest in a nearby city. Currently most children attend church only on major festivals. Whereas Cypriot boys, like Irish Catholic boys, are trained from an early age to assist the priest in the liturgy, the present Ukrainian priest is generally served by elderly men. The present British-born generation in Coventry is not being enabled to play this role.

Through the community centre and the Ukrainian Youth Association (SUM), children are involved in religious aspects of their culture. They learn to paint *pysanky* (Easter eggs) and to recite poems on *Den' Materi* (Mothers' Day). They enthusiastically participate in the dramatic sketch, recitation of poems and distribution of presents on the day of Svyati Mykolaj (St. Nicholas' Day) which falls on December 19th December[20].

The church remains somewhat detached, although for those children who attend there is continuity of Ukrainian language and sense of community[21]. Like their Cypriot peers, children reported boredom related to difficulty in understanding the language of the service. Both the language and music are potentially remote as far as children are concerned.

Unlike the Greek Orthodox children, some Ukrainian children attend Roman Catholic aided schools. Here they have a similar feeling of separateness to their Greek Cypriot peers in private Catholic schools. This is because while owing allegiance to the Pope, the Ukrainian Catholic (Uniate) tradition maintains distinctively Orthodox practices. Also the liturgy is performed not in English but in Ukrainian. Although Ukrainian Catholics do not receive their first communion until about the age of seven (like their Roman Catholic peers), they receive confirmation at baptism (as do the Orthodox and as newborn Roman Catholic children do if their life is in danger). They too, like the Orthodox, receive the communion in both kinds (bread mixed in wine) from the Ukrainian Catholic priest but, as Catholics, they also receive the Communion wafer from the Roman Catholic priest. Like the Orthodox at school they have to unlearn their traditional way of crossing themselves.

Ukrainian Catholic calendar diverges further than the Greek Orthodox calendar from the Western (Gregorian) calendar. The Cypriots celebrate Christmas on December 25th like the majority of Christians in Britain[22]. They observe Easter and its related days, however, in accordance with the Julian calendar which predates the Gregorian calendar. The Ukrainian children not only celebrate Holy week,

Palm Sunday ('Willow' Sunday) and Easter on the Julian dates but also Christmas (on January 7th) and Jesus' Baptism (Jordan) on January 19th. This means that Christmas usually falls on a working day during the first week of the school term. This limits the celebration possible and increases a sense of belonging to a religious minority[23]. As a consequence the school does not, any more than British society at large, support the culturally or denominationally specific aspects of children's home and church life. Both Greek Cypriots and Ukrainians have to depend on home church and the community to sustain their tradition.

Fasting and Feasting

Both Ukrainian Catholic and Cypriot Orthodox children celebrate religious festivals in ways unknown to most of their peers. This too confirms a sense of separate identity. Both traditions combine regional custom, probably of pre-Christian origin, with their ancient liturgy.

For example certain foods come to symbolise for children here not only annual religious observance and family celebration but also a difference from their peers at school. Ukrainians look forward to the priest blessing their Easter baskets. These contain items such as a *pysanka* (uncooked, intricately coloured egg), Easter *paska* (a light-textured, rich bread containing egg yolk and saffron which is prepared specially for Easter), sausage, hard boiled eggs and cream cheese or butter studded with whole cloves in the shape of a cross[24]. On *Sviata Vechera* (Christmas Eve i.e. January 6th) twelve meatless dishes are eaten at a family meal rich in symbolism[25]. Cypriot Orthodox children look forward to bashing each other's hard-boiled, red-dyed eggs on Easter morning to see whose is hardest. In the church for St Basil's day slices of *vasilopita*, a cake with a coin hidden in it, are distributed. At certain times, in memory of the dead, *kolipha* a mixture of pomegranate, cracked wheat, sesame and aniseed, is distributed with blessed bread:

> People eat it and say 'God rest their souls'. It is a way of lightening their sins after death[26]. (Cypriot woman)

My Greek Orthodox interviewees also all mentioned a weekly and annual pattern of abstention from certain foods[27] and the way they train children to avoid them. The children made it clear that they knew about the requirement to fast but they did not observe the fasts as strictly as the most observant adults:

> We're not allowed meat on Wednesdays and Fridays because Christ died on a Friday[28]. When we fast forty days before Christmas and fifty days before Easter I don't actually go straight into the fasting.

Punjabi Christians

Punjabi Christians began to migrate from the Indian state of Punjab in the 1950s largely from Jalandhar like many Punjabi Hindus and Sikhs. The Punjabi Christian community differs both from the pattern of religious and cultural transmission in the three communities which have been examined so far and from the pattern evident in non-Christian communities[29].

In Coventry there are about sixty Punjabi Christian families[30]. Children use their mother-tongue, Punjabi, in the home to a greater extent than the groups discussed so far. Social and cultural differences mark them more clearly from the majority English community. However formal efforts to perpetuate a Punjabi or even South Asian form of worship are minimal. None of the Christian children growing up in Coventry is literate in Punjabi or in the related languages of Urdu or Hindi. The Punjabi Christians of Coventry do not have a separate place of worship[31]. They do not hold mother tongue classes for their children.

Most of these families attend the Anglican church and the Punjabi girls make up the church choir. In a nearby Roman Catholic church, one of the lay ministers of the Eucharist is a Punjabi woman while a Punjabi preacher holds weekly Sunday afternoon worship in Punjabi and Urdu in the Baptist church. In the Anglican church parts of the service, such as the sermon, are usually translated into Punjabi or Urdu for the benefit of older Punjabis. This is in contrast to the Greek Orthodox church in which boys read the gospel and creed in English while the language of the rest of the liturgy is unintelligible for most children.

As for schooling, almost all of those in the Anglican congregation go to a state primary school and subsequently to a voluntary aided Church of England comprehensive. In both cases church and church school have a mutually reinforcing ethos, with none of the minor disjunctions experienced by Ukrainian and Cypriot pupils. Supplementary religious teaching takes place in English with a non-Asian teacher in the Anglican Sunday school each Sunday afternoon. However, neither the Catholic school nor the Church of England school reinforces the Punjabi ethos of the home.

The Church of England Sunday school raises questions about the relationship of cultural values and norms to religious belief and practice. While the Sunday schools approve the knowledge of scriptures, it is a lively affair with an emphasis on Christianity as 'fun'. Children address the vicar and Sunday school teacher by their first names in a familiar, joking way - a manner which contradicts South Asian norms of respect for elders and teachers.

The weekly bible studies which occur in relatives' homes of a weekday evening provide another strand to the children's religious nurture. Here children of all ages are present, but quiet, and much of the singing, prayer and bible reading is in Punjabi and Urdu. The melodies and the *tabla* (drum) and harmonium accompaniment of the devotional songs are Indian. The children clearly prefer English words and western tunes. By contrast for members of their parents' generation in Britain at their age, the Indian hymns had provided a valued continuity with their earlier life.

The negative attitude to the formal perpetuation of 'mother tongue' stems from British missionary activity and the colonial history of India. By contrast with Goan and South Indian Christian traditions, few Punjabis were converted more than a century ago (Caleb, 1974: 11). Since the missionaries were British, their Punjabi converts learned a British style of Christianity and so Punjabis joined the congregations of British denominational churches on their settlement in Coventry from the 1950s onwards.

In contrast to the experience of Cypriots and Ukrainians with old Christian traditions, the Punjabis' first contact with Christianity was with British Protestant missionary activity[32].   This has profound implications for the perceived importance of the promotion of mother tongue. The fact that British missionaries brought Christianity to Punjab probably makes English appear a primary language for the scriptures. It appears that the script used for a community's religious texts, rather than its oral form, influences the desire for formal provision of 'mother tongue'. Thus, out of Coventry's Punjabi-speaking people, Sikhs run classes in Punjabi in Gurmukhi script and Hindus run classes in Hindi in Devanagari script. With Punjabi Christians there is no clear association between scriptures and script. Older Punjabi Christians have bibles in Urdu (Persian script) and Punjabi (Gurmukhi script) and hymns in Urdu (Roman script) and Punjabi (Devanagari script). There is no one written language or script strongly associated with their religious tradition.

Differences of skin colour and family custom combine to give Punjabi Christian children a greater sense of solidarity with fellow Punjabis than with Christians of other ethnic backgrounds. Racist attitudes, prevalent in many white congregations, will help sustain Asian Christians' sense of a distinct identity and the desire for the establishment of Indian language churches. Relatives in other cities tell of their involvement in Asian churches. The growth of an Asian Christian Fellowship with branches nationwide points to a growing sense of Asian Christian identity. Children will probably continue to prefer English songs but feel with other Christians of South Asian origin a strong bond of a shared ethnicity and ethos within the wider church. This ethos is evident not only in such matters as mother tongue, women's dress and diet but in religious practices which distinguish Punjabi Christians from fellow worshippers in their local denominational churches. I will take three - iconography, blessing the house and funerals.

Even when Punjabi Christian children attend Protestant churches, the walls of their living rooms are hung with colourful religious pictures of a type readily available from Catholic church shops. When they move, the Punjabi Christians ask the priest to bless the house. No other parishioners do so. When a member of the family dies, the uncovered coffin is kept in the house, amid wailing and praying. Before the funeral cortege sets out the vicar is expected to come to the house to lead prayers. Men and women sit separately in the church, men at the front, women, in white, at the back.

For the Punjabis neither church nor school in Coventry reinforce community preoccupations. For example, the arranging of marriages is alien to the practice and assumptions of teachers, church leaders and others in the congregation. Neither church nor church school have on their agenda answers to the questions raised for Punjabis by having social intercourse with non-Christian relatives. For example the question of how to respond to the distribution of *prashad* (food offered in front of the holy books) in the Valmiki temple attended by their cousins is a live one for Punjabi Christians but not for the churches or schools which they attend.

Pointers to the Future

A number of factors will influence the Christians of ethnic backgrounds. One is the extent to which young people marry within their ethnic community. The Punjabis expect their marriages to be arranged by their elders. In practice this means that a spouse will be a Punjabi of the same caste even if not of the same religion. Many spouses from India reinforce Punjabi cultural behaviour. Denominational difference is of minimal importance although for committed Christians a shared faith is seen as essential. Similarly Cypriots and Ukrainians expect to sustain endogamy based on the religious principle to sustain cultural identity[33]. Greek Cypriots plan to build a community centre by the church to ensure that their children marry within the community to preserving their traditions.

The extent of contact with the ancestral homeland will influence religious behaviour. Spouses from the homeland play an important part in this. Immigration controls make this a difficult option for Punjabi Christians. Many also feel it is preferable to choose a partner locally as both the spouses may have grown up in Britain. Several Cypriot and Irish interviewees reported yearly holidays in their home country. Now the Ukrainians will increase their visits home. It is likely that more people will leave Ukraine to marry and settle in Britain.

The investigation also showed that grandparents can play an important part in passing knowledge of religion, language and culture to the young ones, an issue which was confirmed by Cypriot and Ukrainian respondents. A Cypriot mother, talking about how the stories of saints are passed on, strongly emphasised the part grandparents were able to play in religious and customary socialisation of children.

Some respondents also referred to videos which depict religious themes. Cypriot families try to circulate videos of religious events and miracles that have taken place in Cyprus. For example a thirteen year old boy spoke enthusiastically of the video of the miracles associated with the martyrdom of Saint Theodora. A Ukrainian mother drew my attention to a video of supplies being sent for the relief of hardship in Ukraine.

From the evidence collected for this study, it is evident that Christians from minority ethnic backgrounds and their churches will survive in Britain. It is likely that most people will attend the main festivals and life cycle rites. However, only a few of them will understand the liturgical language where this is not English and some Roman Catholic and Protestant churches will become increasingly multi-racial. The ability of priests to respond to the need of ethnic minority church goers will determine continuity of congregations.

It is the denominational distinctiveness of Cypriot and Ukrainian Christianity that has encouraged the founding of separate churches. These churches continue as centres of cultural continuity, as reminders of children's separateness from mainstream British Christian traditions and as reminders of the linguistic gap between children and their older relatives. Here there are strong parallels with the Catholic churches in Britain which are ethnically at least eighty per cent Irish and where most priests, being Irish, strengthen the people's link with Ireland (Gay, 1971: 91).

If Punjabis establish separate churches the reasons are likely to be cultural rather than denominational. They will be responding to an institutional racism of the type which has precipitated so many Caribbean Christians into black led churches in Britain[34]. With pastors and leaders from Pakistan and India, or at least of South Asian origin, these churches will perpetuate ethnic norms and reinforce people's connections with their family's homeland.

As far as language is concerned, Punjabi children have greater access to bible and church worship than Greek or Ukrainian peers have to their own services. For Cypriot and Ukrainian children, their religious tradition is locked into a decreasingly familiar language. However, in schools and through the English media, they encounter more of their scriptures than most minority non-Christian children. They are distanced by language and their British upbringing less from the scriptures and ethical teaching than from the Greek Orthodox and Ukrainian Catholic expressions of the Christian tradition. In both cases, denominational distinctiveness and nostalgic maintenance of homeland culture are inseparably combined.

Footnotes

1   Robert Jackson has led this project at the University of Warwick since 1983. This study, 'Religious Education and Ethnography', has been funded by the Economic and Social Research Council (Project No.R00232489).

2   'Religious Nurture' refers to the process whereby children born into a particular faith community acquire its characteristic practices and beliefs or some adaptation of them (Hull, 1984). Formal nurture refers to classes run by religious bodies while informal nurture refers to less organised ways of learning religious behaviour.

3   See Nesbitt 1993a and 1993b, Nesbitt and Jackson, 1992 and forthcoming

4   The questions for this investigation benefited from similar work in Leeds by Kim Knott and Peter Woodward in Birmingham.

5   These groups came to Coventry in the 1950s and 1960s. Except for one child of Ukrainian descent, all children described themselves as British and English. The term South Asian applies to people from the Indian subcontinent.
6   For details of findings see Jackson and Nesbitt (1986), Jackson and Nesbitt (1993), Nesbitt (1991).
7   Gay (1971: 97) suggests that in 1961 Catholics (of whom most were Irish) formed 10% of the total population of Britain. Population figures are from Department of Economic Development and Planning (1989: 21).
8   This figure is cited by Simson (n.d.: 33) in a history which pays tribute to the life of Mother Margaret Hallahan, born 1803 'of good Irish parents' (p.25) and refers to the exodus of Catholics from Ireland in 1845 (p. 30). We know however, that by 1894, there were nearly 300,000 Irish born residents in England and Wales, because of the demand for cheap labour created by the Industrial Revolution (Gay, 1971: 89).
9   Figures for churches and schools are taken from Grady (1989).
10 Besides words, style, method, wisdom, insight, technique, behaviour, action, liturgy, silence, ritual, dance, decoration and so on are transmitted in a religious context (Bowker, 1987: 11).
11 Details supplied by the president of the church committee.
12 For details of Greek Orthodox Christianity in Britain see Constantinides (1977: 286-287). Up-to-date information is listed in Hemerologion 1990.
13 Constantinides (1977: 284-286) outlines the role of Greek classes in forming Cypriot children's identity.
14 Constantinides op.cit. mentions the fact that most clergy are from mainland Greece.
15 Elias (1984: 88-89) explains the symbolic meaning of each movement involved in making the sign of the cross.
16 The congregation of the church of St Wolodymyr the Great, Coventry refer to themselves as Ukrainian Catholic. They do not object to the term Uniate which means 'in union' (with Rome). In Ukraine they are called Greek Catholic. The churches in this Eastern rite tradition acknowledge the primacy of the Pope and are allowed to use Orthodox liturgy, to have married clergy etc.
17 Petro Diuk (Coventry Reminiscence Theatre, 1990: 7) Population statistics for people of Ukrainian origin in Britain are very hard to estimate as explained by Diuk (1985: 14).
18 Diuk and Karatnycky (1990: 72-104) describe Ukraine's changing circumstances.
19 Subsequently Ukrainian women from Poland and Yugoslavia married Ukrainians in Coventry. Some men married Italian women, believing they had more in common with them than with English women. I am grateful to Petro Diuk (spoken communication) for this information.
20 The 'j' in Mykolaj and in the Ukrainian word 'Jordan' below is pronounced like English 'y' in 'yes'.
21 In the 1980s Ukrainian replaced Old Slavonic in St Wolodymyr's church as the language of the liturgy.
22 Only the Russian and Serbian Orthodox and 'old calendar' Greek churches, which are not part of the Diocese of Thyateira and Great Britain, follow the Julian calendar for Christmas and the significant days associated with it. Orthodox in the Greek, Arab, Roumanian and Bulgarian churches all now follow the western (Gregorian) calendar at this time of year.
23 In the Westminster diocese of the USA a majority of Ukrainian Catholics decided to transfer to the Gregorian calendar for both Christmas and Easter.

Priests there are authorised to celebrate according to both calendars.   So far discussions in Britain have not resulted in such a change.

24   See Ukrainian Women's Association of Canada, Daughters of Ukraine Branch (1987: 24-44) for recipes and explanation of the symbolism of each item in the basket.

25   *Op.cit.*: 8-21.

26   In accounting for this practice, Woods (1991) suggests the continuity of pre Christian Greek tradition:

'At home before the funeral the women prepare kolipha, soul food. It's made of all the seeds, wheat, barley, nuts, raisins and the blood red seed of the pomegranate, the seed which Persphone ate, binding her to the world of the dead, when she could only return for part of the year, bringing Spring and new life back to the earth.'

Kotsoni, in contrast, writes:

'Wheat germs are traditionally thought to symbolise the resurrection of the souls' (a conception which is based on the *Holy Bible*, see John 12.24 or I Corinthians 15)' (1990:18).

27   The formerly comparable pattern of fasting no longer continues among the Ukrainian Catholics.   The second Vatican Council removed the earlier requirements.

28   The Wednesday fast commemorates the betrayal of Jesus on the Wednesday before the crucifixion.

29   For a study of religious nurture in Coventry's Punjabi Hindu families see Jackson and Nesbitt (1993).   For a detailed account of cultural transmission in the families of Coventry's Punjabi Christians' non-Christian relatives see Nesbitt (1991).

30   This figure was given by the Anglican parish priest, quoting a Punjabi Christian who has been actively involved in the church for over twenty years.   The priest, however, preferred to define Christians by reference to their involvement in church life.   All the 'families' are related to each other by blood and/or marriage.   These Punjabi Christians are not Punjabis who had been converted to Christianity in Britain (East, 1991).

31   Centre for Ethnic Studies in Education (n.d.) lists Indian language churches in Britain and includes two Punjabi churches in Bedford, one Punjabi church in Slough and three in Southwark (probably a misprint for Southall) and six or seven Hindi/Urdu language churches in London.   These figures were collected by Prabhu Guptara on the board of the Asian Christian Alliance.

32   For an account of Christian mission in Punjab see Jones (1976), Juergensmeyer (1982) and Caleb (1974).

33   See Josephides, 1988: 36-37 for an account of *proxenia*, 'a modified form of arranged marriage' and *op.cit.* p.35 for contemporary attitudes to this. Constantinides 1977: 277 reports, on the basis of research two decades ago 'Greek Cypriots tend largely to marry Greek Cypriots' and (*op.cit.* p.294) reports the views of marriageable second generation Cypriots.   My interviewees are third generation.   Kotsoni (1990: 21) reports that approximately 40% of Greek Cypriot marriages in Leeds are with outsiders although children of such marriages are baptised into the Orthodox church.

168   Eleanor Nesbitt

34 See for example Howard, 1987: 9-10, Hill, 1971 and Jackson, 1985. For a
    Gujarati Christian convert's criticism of the British church's denial of Asian
    Christians' culture see Patel, 1990.

References

Bowker, J. (1987) *Licensed Insanities*, London: Dalton, Longman and Todd.
Caleb, M. (1974) 'Christian Sunday Worship in a Punjabi Village' in Webster, J.
    C. B. (ed) *Popular Religion in the Punjab Today*, Batala: The Christian
    Institute of Sikh Studies, pp.119-126.
Centre for Ethnic Studies in Education (n.d.) *The Challenge and the Dream*,
    Manchester: University of Manchester.
Constantinides, P. (1977) The Greek Cypriots: Factors in Maintenance of Ethnic
    Identity' in Watson, J. L. (ed) *Between Two Cultures: Migrants and Minorities
    in Britain*, Oxford: Blackwell.
Coventry Reminiscence Theatre (1990) *We Came to Coventry: Memoirs of People
    from Many Lands who Made their Homes in Coventry*, Coventry: Coventry
    Reminiscence Theatre.
Department of Economic Development and Planning (1989) *Ethnic Minority
    Statistical Digest*, Coventry City Council.
Diuk, A. M. (1985) *Assimilation or Segregation? The Ukrainian Ethnic
    Community in Coventry*, unpublished dissertation, Oxford, St. Hugh's College.
Diuk, N and Karatnycky, A. (1990) *The Hidden Nations: The People Challenge the
    Soviet Union*, New York: William Morrow.
Dmytriw, I. and Wasyluk, J. (ed) (1982) *Ukraine and the Ukrainians: A Collection
    of Selected Articles*, London: The Association of Ukrainians in Great Britain.
Elias, Rev. Nicholas, M. (1984) 4th Ed. *The Divine Liturgy Explained*, Athens:
    Astir.
Gay, John, D. (1971) *The Geography of Religion in England*, London: Duckworth.
Grady, Rev. F. J. (1989) *Archdiocese of Birmingham Directory 1989*, Liverpool:
    Archdiocese of Birmingham.
Hellenike Orthodoxe Koinoteta Coventry (1989) *1964-1989 25 Eterida tes
    Hellenorthodoxes Koinotetas Coventry* (twenty-five years of the Greek
    Orthodox Community, Coventry).
Hemerologion: Hiera Archiepiskope Thyateiron kai Megates Bretanias, (Year-book
    of the Holy Archdiocese) (1990) London: Thyateira House.
Hill, C. (1971) 'Pentecostalist Growth Result of Racialism,' *Race Today*, 3(6):
    pp.187-190.
Howard, V. (1987) *A Report on Afro-Caribbean Christianity in Britain*, Research
    Paper (New Series) 4, University of Leeds, Community Religious Project.
Hull, J. M. (1984) *Studies in Religion and Education*, Lewes: Falmer Press.
Jackson, A. (1985) *Catching Both Sides of the Wind*, London: British Council of
    Churches.
Jackson, R. and Nesbitt, E. (1986) 'Sketches of Formal Hindu Nurture', *World
    Religions in Education, The Journal of the Shap Working Party*, pp. 25-29.
Jackson, R. and Nesbitt, E. (1993) *Hindu Children in Britain*, Stoke-on-Trent:
    Trentham Books.
Jones, K. W. (1976) *Arya Dharm: Hindu Consciousness in 19th Century Punjab*,
    Berkeley: University of California Press.

Josephides, S. (1988) 'Honour, Family and Work: Greek Cypriot Women Before and After Migration' in Westwood, S. and Bhachu, P. (eds) *Enterprising Women: Ethnicity, Economy and Gender Relations*, London: Routledge, pp. 34-57.

Juergensmeyer, M. (1982) *Religion as Social Vision (the Movement Against Untouchability in 20th Century Punjab)*, Berkeley: University of California Press, 181-192.

Kotsoni, K. (1990) *The Greek Orthodox Community in Leeds*, Research Papers (New Series), 6, Community Religious Project, University of Leeds.

Nesbitt, E. (1991) 'My Dad's Hindu, My Mum's Side are Sikhs' *Issues in Religious Identity. Arts, Culture and Education Research and Curriculum Paper*, Charlbury: National Foundation for Arts Education.

Nesbitt, E. (1993a) 'Photographing Worship: Issues Raised by Ethnographic Study of Children's Participation in Acts of Worship'. *Visual Anthropology*, 5(3): pp.285-306.

Nesbitt, E. (1993b) 'Drawing on the Ethnic Diversity of Christian Tradition in Britain', *Multicultural Teaching*, 11(2): pp.9-12.

Nesbitt, E. & Jackson, R. 'Christian and Hindu Children: Their Perceptions of Each Other's Religious Traditions', *Journal of Empirical Theology*, 5(2): pp.39-62.

Nesbitt, E. & Jackson, R. (forthcoming) *Christian Children in an Urban Setting*.

Patel, R. (1990) 'Why Do Christians Wear Ties?' in Grant, Paul and Patel, Raj (eds) *A Time to Speak: Perspectives on Black Christians in Britain*, Nottingham Racial Justice and Black Theology Working Group, pp. 87-93.

Simson, D. S. (n.d.) *A Centenary Memorial of St Osburg's Coventry 1845-1945*.

Ukrainian Women's Association of Canada, Daughters of Ukraine Branch (1987) *Ukrainian Daughters Cook Book*, Regina: Saskatchewan.

Television

(1991) *East*, BBC2; August 30th.

Woods, Michael (1991) *The Sacred Way*, Channel 4; August 5th.

13

Ideological Contradictions and Cultural Logic:
A Case Study

Marianne Freyne-Lindhagen

The pattern of migration which has become common to countries like Britain, France and Germany has now become increasingly familiar in Scandinavian countries. Now there are many groups of foreign origin who make up the total population in Sweden. Amongst people of European and non-European origin in these groups, there are the Suryoyos, a Christian Orthodox group. They are now established in Sweden for two decades. As an ancient ethnic minority spread out in several Middle Eastern countries, they have a complicated historical, political and religious background. As a minority in exile they are represented in many European countries as well as in the United States, Australia and Latin America.

The first Suryoyos came to Sweden in 1967 with the support of United Nations High Commissioner for Refugees. Although the Swedish authorities mistakenly labelled them 'Assyrians' in 1970s, throughout this paper I refer to them as Suryoyos which is their own self-designation. Suryoyo migration to Sweden increased in 70s as they were not allowed in West Germany after the introduction of more restrictive immigration policies there. The Suryoyo immigration to Sweden was a matter of great public discussion in 1976 and 1977 and resulted in a legal change that degraded the refugee status of the group - a point which is elaborated later in the paper. Today there are about 20,000 Suryoyos living in Sweden in 35 cities.

The Research Project

I have periodically carried out research among the Suryoyo group in Örebro from 1985 to 1989. I have been especially interested in the conditions women from this group encounter in Sweden with a focus on their socio-economic situation. To collect ethnographic information on this topic, I also followed the work of the Women's Committee in the Suryoyo Association for two years.

In order to get a more comprehensive picture, I lived in one of the suburban areas of Örebro for five months near 50 of the Suryoyo families. The case study presented in this paper describes how a seriously handicapped Suryoyo woman in her exile related to the specific culture of the Swedish social welfare system and to the authorities. The analysis of the encounter between this woman and Swedish society highlights the differences in cultural assumptions between two different ways of life. In this narrative, I attempt to show that the cultural situation of this Suryoyo woman is barely understood by those who are responsible for her welfare in Sweden. I also show what it is that is critical and necessary for the Suryoyo woman herself and the communication gap between her and the Swedish welfare system workers. The analysis explains the nature of power relations which makes it difficult if not impossible for the Suryoyo woman to fulfil *her* cultural expectations in a Swedish cultural milieu. It is this contradiction, difference and the inequality which very much lies at the heart of the structure that underpins the logic of cultural differences. Dialectical relations between the religion/culture component and the power/gender component influences migrants and their lives. As an individual, the Suryoyo woman in question is affected by these dialectical components both in her own society, as well as in the society of her reception in Western Europe. It is the relationship between a single migrant individual and her own experiences of the institutions vis-a-vis the immigration and welfare systems of the state that informs much of the methodology of this paper.

Immigration to Sweden

As in many European countries, the multicultural character of Sweden has its roots in the global political and social changes following the Second World War. Sweden received many refugees who were victims of the Second World War during 1940s. Sweden has also refused to accept some refugees, a fact that has been debated many times during the 70s and 80s. The question of how could Sweden maintain its own solidarity and at the same time extend generosity and support to outsiders has been raised as an issue from a historical point of view. Further, the question of Sweden as a generous welfare state and a refugee receiving country has surfaced in public debate in the late 80s when the government changed the immigration regulation in a more restrictive direction in December 1989.

The labour force recruitment in the 50s, 60s and 70s brought a large number of Europeans of different origins to Sweden - many of whom settled permanently in the country. From the beginning of the 70s the global political situation created an increasing number of refugees. Most of them came spontaneously from Latin America, Greece and Turkey. Sweden also started to receive annually about 1250 refugees who were sponsored by the United Nations High Commissioner for refugees.

During the 80s the refugee population has become radically more diverse in terms of its origin in many different countries. Today the multiethnic structure of Sweden is more heterogeneous with a very broad ethnic and language representation from Asia and Africa as well as Eastern and Western Europe.

The Swedish Immigration Policy After the Second War

1968 is an important year with regard to Swedish immigration policy and immigrant policy. This year the Swedish government for the first time in history formulated the guide-lines for *an integrated immigration and immigrant policy*. The introduction of *Immigration policy* was concerned with legislation that regulated the 'input' of migrants and *immigrant policy* was designed to concentrate on social conditions for the immigrants who were permitted to stay. As the formal document stated:

> *The immigration ought to be controlled in order to co-ordinate it with other resources and policies within the society*[1].

As in the case of other metropolitan societies like Britain which introduced immigration controls in 1960s, the Swedish immigration policy also changed from 'free' to 'regulated'. The quotation above also underlines a connection between the systems of *immigrant policy* and *social welfare policy*.

In 1968 the government also adopted the principle that immigrants should be entitled to the same standard of living as the native population. At first the Swedish Government had pursued an assimilationist policy towards outsiders. However, this changed as the authorities abandoned this integrative approach to a policy in favour of a more permissive attitude towards the cultural traditions and identity for the ethnic minorities. These changes were later, in 1975, confirmed in three goals setting out guide-lines for policy with regard to immigrants and ethnic minorities. The goals were adopted by all political parties in the government and were formulated in a slogan like manner as *Equality, Freedom of choice* and *Co-operation*[2].

In outlining this individual case study, I hope to point out the contradictions between praxis and adopted ideology and between *immigrant policy, immigration policy* and *social welfare policy*. This analysis shows the cultural logic behind an individual case and explains the suffering of a particular individual who finds herself between contrasting cultural realities. The narrative is also constructed to show that disparity and contradiction arise in the context of Swedish social institutional framework. The case helps us to grasp the situation for a specific ethnic minority as it comes to terms with its changing historical and political circumstances.

Inci: Suffering of a Suryoyo Woman

In 1979 Inci comes to Sweden accompanied by her uncle's family and the families of four neighbours from her village. She is 30 years old and seriously disabled by progressive muscle dystrophia. She is a Christian Suryoyo woman from the south east of Turkey, brought up in a small village in her uncle's family. Her mother became a widow when Inci was three years old and her older sister five. According to Suryoyo cultural norms, when a woman becomes a widow, her father's brother takes over the economic responsibility for the children and   their upbringing as Inci's uncle did.

In her new position as a widow, Inci's mother moves to her parents' home situated a few kilometres away in another small village. While growing up, the two girls keep up their contact with their mother - the villages stand close together in this part of Turkey. As soon as the Suryoyo rules allow, after the passage of few years, the mother remarries. In the new marriage she has three more children. In the new family, she lives to the full for her husband and their three children but still keeps up the contact with Inci and her sister. The two girls are by now old enough to belong to their stepfather's 'labour force' on his small farm.

Inci goes to school for a few years - a short and interrupted schooling, 'normal' for both Christian and Muslim girls in this feudal part of Turkey. She learns to read anyway and improves her reading when she stays in the Syrich-Orthodox nunnery situated in the neighbourhood because of her disease. Concerning the work on the uncle's farm Inci says:

> We worked very hard, men and women and children, like this (she illustrates this to me with a picture in a book). It was very hot in the fields. We were five girls from different farms. We were neighbours and we were asked to look after the farm animals. I watched my uncle's sheep, four or five of them. Sometimes they ran away and we could not find them. We went out very early in the morning and came back late in the evening. Sometimes conditions could be dangerous.

When Inci is 12 years old the symptoms of her disease begin to show. When she carries heavy burdens her legs are more shaky than before. Her uncle forces the girls to work hard without any regard for Inci's health. She gets more easily tired by physical work than before. However she still has the task to watch the sheep and take them to new pastures. She had always carried out this duty and carried it out joyfully. But now as her legs grow weaker, the duty is more and more burdensome.

As the years pass, some of her relations recognise the fact that Inci's physical condition is getting worse. A cousin takes the initiative to contact the Greek Orthodox hospital in Istanbul. At the age of 17 Inci is taken there for an examination. The diagnosis is progressive muscle dystrophia but the doctors have no treatment to offer. Inci goes back to the village and to the uncle's family to live a more and more immobile and painful life.

In the middle of the 70s the Suryoyos began to leave their homeland from the villages around the provincial capital Midyat. Inci's uncle and his family decide, together with some other families in the neighbourhood, to emigrate to West Germany as many Turks had done during the 60s and 70s. Inci, her uncle, her mother, and a sister who was already married, came to Germany in 1978. Inci is taken to a hospital in Hannover where she gets the same diagnosis as in Istanbul. She is offered some treatment - but the West German authorities did not allow the family to stay. According to restrictive West German immigration *gastarbeiter* policy, members of the family were not capable enough to become good workers. The hospital recommends Inci to seek asylum in Sweden and a doctor writes a certificate to the Swedish immigration authorities confirming the diagnosis and appeals to them to consider family's application for a long term stay in Sweden. As the Swedish authorities responded with some sympathy, Inci and her family as well as the families of four neighbours from the village were allowed to enter Sweden in 1979 for permanent settlement.

The Context of Migration

From a religious viewpoint, the Suryoyos are a Christian Orthodox group established in Sweden for more than two decades[3]. As an ancient minority spread out in several Middle Eastern countries (Turkey, Iraq, Syria, Lebanon, Iran) the group has a complicated historical, political and religious background. As a minority in exile they are represented in many European countries - besides Sweden and Germany, Netherlands, Switzerland, the U.K., Greece and Austria - as well as in North America, Australia, Latin America and India.

The Swedish exile story started in 1967 when the United Nations High Commissioner for Refugees supported the arrival of 200 Suryoyo refugees. Following this event, the number of Suryoyos coming to Sweden increased throughout mid 70s. There were two main causes for this development. First of all, restrictions which West German authorities imposed compelled Suryoyos to look elsewhere. They turned to Sweden as some members of their group had already settled there. Secondly, the presence of Suryoyos in Sweden created a pattern of chain migration. As a consequence, Suryoyos based in Sweden were able to sponsor their relatives and neighbours to come to Sweden.

The Suryoyo immigration to Sweden caused great discussions at the end of the 70s because of the spontaneous 'mass invasion' of Suryoyos in a short space of time and due to anxiety about rising levels of further immigration. At the end of 1977 the group included about 10,000 persons. The popular concern with their immigration was reflected in social and political discussions on the issue. There was sufficient public pressure to bring about legal changes necessary to ensure that further Suryoyo migration to Sweden was put to an end.

Today there are about 20,000 Suryoyos living in Sweden in about 35 cities. Most of them are still to be found in Södertälje, the episcopate centre for the Syrich Orthodox Church in Scandinavia, and in some of the suburban areas of Stockholm. About 2000 Suryoyos live in Örebro, a city of 120,000 inhabitants. The internal movement of Suryoyos from Södertälje to other parts of the country has its roots in the policy of the Swedish authorities to counteract residential concentration and 'ghettoization' tendencies. The increasing concentration of Suryoyos in Södertälje was looked upon negatively because of racial riots which occurred in 1977. 'Racism' and open ethnic conflicts were at that time almost an unknown phenomena in what was regarded as a culturally homogeneous Swedish society. Björklund

(1981) comments on the racial incidents in 1977 as 'a milestone' in the Swedish ethnic history. In many aspects the Suryoyos can be seen as a stigmatized minority in exile in Sweden, most of the time described as 'a problem' by the Swedish authorities.

The Wider Context of Cultural Encounter

The Suryoyos have in their exile rapidly moved to a modern industrial society characterised by a mixed economic structure - capitalistic economy of western type with planned economic sectors. The Turkish society that the Suryoyos have left behind them, i.e. the modern post-Ottoman Turkey, is mostly characterized by uneven development. The capitalistic model of production is superior and dominates the country as a whole. Those who hold power at the centre turn their face to Europe. At the same time, in the periphery, the pre-capitalist economy, and life style and culture associated with it, dominates the more distant southern and eastern areas. The Suryoyos in Sweden come from this less well-developed area. Their migration has occurred in a series of steps with a short or fairly long residence in Istanbul. Combination of 'push' and/or 'pull' factors have stimulated their migration further to countries in northern Europe. Some of them have also come directly from their village or the provincial city Midyat.

Over a period of time, especially during the period when Western European countries recruited a large number of migrant workers, we can clearly see certain changes in the distribution of Suryoyos. As the number of Suryoyos increase in Sweden during this period, there is a proportionate decline in their number in West Germany as the Germans restricted Suryoyos from long term residence. The Swedish policy towards migrants and refugees was still generous at the time and Suryoyos were able to benefit from this liberal policy.

Less developed parts of Turkey are characterized by slowly changing modes of production, lifestyles and structures of consciousness and ideas. Of course, this slow change is influenced by both national and international economic and political conditions. In the long run, the global change, as it filters through urban centres, also influences rural population, although the rural people are affected by the urban changes slowly and in different ways. Uneven technological development is, however, going on since the 60s in the south eastern Turkey from where various generations of Suryoyos descend. A most salient feature of the area is extremely high rates of unemployment, as well as the history of political antagonism between the local groups - Kurds against Christians and between the superior central power and the provincial power centres[4]. It is obvious that the Suryoyo encounter with a highly technological, modern and urbanized Swedish culture with its specific organization, bureaucracy and 'rationalism', is an encounter between men and women with very different day-to-day experiences and 'structures of consciousness'. This is also evident with regard to strategies to meet the challenges of life in exile as a whole, problems in the everyday situation, and life, looked upon from an existential perspective.

There is a specific phenomenon, that the exile *per se* makes this confrontation even more complex, sometimes even dramatic and traumatic. In many contexts the migration process and the exile existence at the individual level is described as a double-sided process implying a heavy burden on one hand and a positive challenge on the other. At the ethnic group level, in light of the cultural history and geographical origin, it is more problematic to look upon the exile *per se* as a positive phenomenon. The total exodus of Jews, Armenians and Gypsies, to use some familiar examples in Europe, are negative cases where forced exclusion dominates the reason for exile in the first place. The negative or positive result of the exile, in shorter or longer perspective, for the individual, the family or the ethnic group, is a question of many interrelated elements in the native country and in the receiving country. Although the case I present here concerns a single Suryoyo woman, the description and analysis show significant cultural and structural relations which influence the destiny of a single individual.

The Exile Career in Sweden

After she settled permanently in Sweden, Inci sees the possibility of leaving her uncle and his family. She had felt that she had been forced to join his family and had to abandon her own 'mother's family'. Inci subsequently decided to follow the four families of neighbours from Turkey. Initially all of them get jobs in Motala and later in Örebro. In Örebro Inci leads an independent but isolated life in a suburban area. The professional care system puts her in the "service-living" for disabled and elderly people. She gets her own flat, technical aid and a group of home help service personnel who assist her with her daily life. The flat is situated in the centre of the suburban area, close to the shops, post office and other facilities but far from other Suryoyo families who, all 50 of them, live in blocks near each other in nice low houses with pretty yards between them where they can meet and carry on a daily social life and maintain the traditional village culture.

'Do you know *the nun*'? A social worker asks me that question during a conference. No, I don't know anything about any 'nun' in Örebro or elsewhere. Some months later when I have moved to the suburban area where Inci and the four families live, I am contacted by a Suryoyo woman. She wants me to come and see her friend who lives alone, is seriously handicapped and has many personal problems. After I overcome the initial feeling of hesitation about getting involved, I decide to go with her to the woman on the following day to interview Inci and listen to what she has to stay about 'the problem'. The following biographical material on Inci's life and surroundings is based on recorded conversations I had with her over a time span. It was during this period that I began to appreciate the realm of interaction between Inci and the Swedish welfare system.

Inci - 'The Pearl' and the Person

The following notes by a social worker provides a contemporary profile of Inci and her current sufferings:

> because of her disease, and as Inci regards herself as a nun and follows a strict religious life combined with the absence of relatives, she feels very isolated.

In many aspects the care staff fail to understand and comprehend properly what it is that **Inci** wants from **her** life. According to her own interpretation, Inci knows that the staff who look after her believe that 'she should live more like Swedish' and that 'she lives in the dark' or 'that she lives silly'. Inci has tried many times to explain her religion to the staff and why she lives and thinks as she does. Her words hardly reach the staff. They end up asking her all the time Why? Why? They can't understand why, for instance, she does not want to be taken in a wheelchair by men. This is because of her faith and that she has promised God to adopt a special way of life. When Inci refuses help from men, the staff get angry with her.
Inci emphasises that her situation and her disease would be easier to bear if the authorities permitted her family to come to Sweden. The isolation and the pressure makes her frightened of getting mentally ill. She feels miserable inside. She prays to God and thinks He will help her to get her mother, stepfather and stepbrother to Sweden. When Inci tells the staff that she longs for her family and that the quality of her life would improve if they came, the staff do not understand the meaning of this deeply felt longing.

> Inci has very little contact with the Suryoyo community in the area and almost no contact with Swedish people. Her handicap and her strict religion makes her very isolated' *(Interview by the social worker 10.4.87).*

'Inci' is the Turkish word for 'pearl'. What are the necessary conditions for a pearl to become a pearl and remain a pearl and grow and develop? A pearl needs a grain of sand, a firm ground, a soft environment, the mussel, and a shelter, the shell. Just as a pearl needs protection to grow, so does Inci. As a handicapped person, she needs the kind of support which will provide her the optimum quality of life. She has the right to this quality according to legislation and ideological formulations within the healthcare system. The trend during the last decades in Sweden, deriving from World Health Organisation recommendations concerning disability and handicap, physical or mental, is towards a 'relational' approach:

> A handicap is not a property of a person or a disease per se. A handicap is on the contrary a *relation* between the injury or disease and the person's environment *(Swedish handicap policy, 1981).*

Instead of focusing on the injury or disease it is of great importance to pay attention to *limitations* in the relations between the handicapped person and the environment. This also means to pay attention to the *power relations* at different levels between the individual, the client, or the minority group he or she represents and individuals who represent these institutions.

Concerning *care in* general, the law that was introduced in 1983 (Hälso-och Sjukvårds Lagen), underlines the connection between treatment and the needs as expressed by the patient. It also underlines the importance of looking upon the patient as a whole person and a unique person. In accordance with the law, care should be of good quality, based on respect for the patient's autonomy and integrity and encouraging good relations between the patient and the nursing staff.

'What I need is my Mother'

Inci points out that her situation would be much easier if her relatives were permitted to come to Sweden. The isolation and the mental strain makes her afraid of getting mentally ill (Interview 10.4.87).

The need Inci expresses above is a real need and points out a realistic comprehension of her own situation. She is aware of the fact that her disease will make her more and more dependent on the Swedish staff and the Swedish health care system. Her mother and the step-family living with her should make it possible to live a Suryoyo life - her own food, her own language, her own customs etc. would be a part of her daily life. Most importantly, it would provide her with a miniature Suryoyo context within which to observe her religious precepts and practices and to sustain her integrity as a nun. The family could move to the Suryoyo part of the suburban area and join the Suryoyo network.

However, the Swedish immigration authorities have again and again refused asylum for the mother and her family in spite of the multitude of humanitarian reasons which are very explicit in Inci's case[5]. Despite the adopted ideology in the immigration policy and its connection with the immigrant and refugee policy and despite the legislation governing the health and social system, Inci's voice is not listened to.

Do the walls of the welfare state and notions of 'human rights' imprison Inci and her family? This is a question which needs some discussion from a holistic perspective and from the values of 'quality of life' and 'equality'. The following discussion goes some way towards explaining the nature of ideological network within which Inci finds herself enmeshed.

Ideology and Legislation: Some Contradictions

One can envisage Inci in Sweden as a person who stands in the centre of a circle. The ideological component of this circle emphasises freedom, equality and individual choice within the context of democratic solidarity and growth of a socio-economic and welfare system to improve the quality of life for all citizens. It is important to underline that from where Inci stands, parts of the circle appear inconsistent and even contradictory. The contradiction between ideology and practices, as it is expressed in restrictive legislation is apparent in an example like this.   It is categorical that the ideology prescribes optimum welfare for Inci. However, the state apparatus and the legislative system do not allow Inci to achieve the kind of fulfilment which would transform the quality of her life - especially if the conception of this quality is not conceived merely in terms of everyday material comforts but more in terms of genuine needs of human beings in distress.   The effects of this contradiction are clearly manifest in Inci's case.   It is evident that the Swedish authorities have applied immigration rules somewhat rigidly to her case without taking into account what it is that is in Inci's best interest from her point of view.   The care givers have appeared to have accepted *a priori* the logic of law and have extended little or no support to Inci and her desire to be reunited with her mother.   They have not conveyed her views and deep-seated anxiety to the authorities to represent *her* views.   As far as her human need is concerned, one can not help but conclude that both immigration and welfare authorities have failed to respond to Inci's need to have her mother living with her.   The fact that she has lived in Sweden for more than 10 years seems to have little influence on those who can, if they want, help her to improve her life.   Lack of sensitivity to her needs clearly reflects the nature of more restrictive change that has occurred in the implementation of both immigration and social welfare policy.   It is doubtful if the authorities will pay much attention to Inci's own views and her real needs. Therefore the individuals in her situation are bound to feel treated less fairly.

The Cultural Clash Explanation

In the Suryoyo culture there are obvious 'important others'.   These significant others have no counter part in Swedish culture.   The nurses are usually unaware of what a person like Inci may regard as significant others.   Those nurses who look after Inci are often very young and have no information or education on culture in general or the Suryoyo culture in particular.

That God and her religion and its values as well as the old mother are important significant others for Inci is something which is unfamiliar if not strange to Swedish nurses.   However, the secular culture in Sweden is not without religious foundations.   Roots of this culture lie in a Christian, Lutheran religious tradition since the 16th century.   But 'religion' as a phenomenon is based on individual choice.   Secondly, in the Swedish social structure 'church' is separated from 'state' and spiritual values are separated from secular values - the kind of separation which is relatively unfamiliar to Inci and her Suryoyo associates.

The mother asks for asylum several years after Inci's exile.   Why did she not ask for admission at an earlier point?   This was a negative factor when Inci's mother's case was brought to the attention of the immigration authorities.

The reason for Inci's mother not to seek entry earlier can be explained in terms of logic of cultural values which influence her willingness to come later rather than earlier.   The code says that the mother in the first place has responsibility for her own old mother and mother-in-law (Inci's grandmothers).   When these two are dead, the mother might seek asylum without losing her and her husband's honour. When following up Inci's case during this fairly long period, I have been able to undo the cultural puzzle behind the process. My role as a researcher has thus been to comprehend Inci's situation with empathy and to channel these cultural findings to the immigration authorities and to the staff and their supervisor. The information and elucidations brought into the case have not been considered or looked upon as 'humanitarian reasons'. The humanitarian dimension of social policy in Europe may become less and less easy to achieve with the current trends which seem to be much more hostile towards outsiders throughout Europe.

The Gender Perspective Explanation

As a handicapped woman in a simple and patriarchal culture Inci is subordinated and oppressed in several different ways. For a woman to be respected and earn status there are three fundamental criteria: one has to marry to produce children and to work. The woman is expected to be reproductive as well as productive. It is obvious that Inci has no capacity to fulfil the expected role as she is physically disabled. How can she save her honour and earn status? It is her religion which provides an answer to this dilemma. According to Suryoyo religious precepts, Inci can be the one who is chosen by God. She then surrenders to religious rules fully and devotionally which is to be 'a nun'. Being a nun through her belief system provides her a position through which she can achieve honour which is independent of her reproductive and productive capacities and acknowledged by the members of her community. By adopting a lifestyle that corresponds with the central elements in the religious and gender related family culture, she can save her own honour as well as that of her family.

In daily human and cultural encounters in Sweden two subordinate groups meet. Inci represents the Suryoyo minority with a low structural position in the Swedish society and a low status in the suburban area. The home nurses, most of them women, represent a low status group within the labour market. Having no information or education that would make their task easier in communicating with Inci and other Suryoyos in the area, they have been partly forced to do an unprofessional job. The outcome is marked by a communication gap and mutual misunderstanding. Nurses feel impatient with Inci while Inci continues to suffer in her deeply felt need to find a realm of meaningfulness which will sustain her long term settlement in her own community in Sweden.

The Cumulative Power Explanation: Some Theoretical Clues

The sociological conception of power and authority as it is exercised through a wide range of institutions is equally relevant for explaining the position of Inci in Swedish society. The outline of this case study demonstrates clearly that immigrants in general, but women in particular, and in Inci's case a woman who is further disadvantaged by a crippling disease, are relatively powerless to exercise what they consider to be their basic human rights. Inci needs her mother for practical help as well as a significant other who will empower her to sustain her identity as a Suryoyo woman.

However, Inci like thousands of other individual women and men have to contend with changes in Europe which are unfavourable to immigrants from Middle Eastern, Asian and African countries. Resentment and hostility against immigrants from outside has increased all over Europe. In keeping with this trend, this paper has illustrated that although Swedish values emphasise individual freedom, human rights and justice, in practice, politicians, immigration authorities and the personnel concerned with the welfare of migrants tend to contradict the ideals and fail to recognise genuine human needs of individuals like Inci and their deeply felt social and cultural aspirations.

Footnotes

1   *Svensk Invandrar - och flyktingpolitik*, Arbetsmarknadsdepartementet, 1988.
2   Official Government Reports (SOU) 1974: 69.
3   Among the Suryoyos, two denominations denote two factions within the ethnic group and church tradition. The case discussed here, as my whole study 'Identity, exile and cultural encounter - The Suryoyo case in Sweden' deals with the Suryoyo faction belonging to the Syrich Church and the Jacobite, monophysic tradition. The relations between the two factions are complicated with regard to language, church history and political identity. In the Swedish exile there has been a lot of debates between the two factions and the Swedish authorities. It is outside the scope of this paper to discuss these conflicts and positions concerned.
4   Historically in this Islamic cultural area the Christian groups have developed a limited autonomy during the Ottomon period - the millet system - supporting the groups with regard to language, confession and nationalism: 'The Christian and Jewish communities thus formed states within the state, only connected with the government at their summits' (Knutsson, 1982). These communities have changed during the post-Ottoman era after 1923. Since the Second World War, the two minorities, Kurds and Suryoyos are the only two ethnic minorities who have lost their autonomy and have been forced into conflicts between themselves and the central power.
5   During the research period, I have discussed the case with several lawyers and humanitarian organisations.

References

Arbetsmarknadsdepartementet, *Svensk Invandrar - och flyktingpolitik* (1988), Stockholm.
Björklund, U. (1981) *North to another country*, Swedish Commission on Immigration Research, Stockholm.

182   Marianne Freyne-Lindhagen

Glaser, B. and Strauss A. (1967) *Discovery of Grounded Theory*, Chicago: Aldine.
Invandrarutredningen, SOU 1974: 90.
Knutsson, B. (1982) *Assur eller Aram*, Statens Invandrarverk, Linköping.
Ornbrant B. (1981) *Möte med välfärdens byråkrater*, Stockholm: Swedish
    Commission on Immigrant Research.
Socialstyrelsen redovisar, 1979:6, *I utlandet Sverige*.
Strauss, A. (1987) *Qualitative Analysis for Social Scientists*, Cambridge.

14

Responding to Adversity: Mental Illness, Religion and Social Change among British Asians

Bernard Ineichen

This chapter will consider the extent to which religion has any influence on changing aspects of mental health of British Asians. Comparisons between religious groups such as Hindus and Muslims are significant. They deserve further exploration to determine the connection between religious belief and dimensions of mental health.

A recent estimate puts the number of British Asians (i.e. people whose cultural and ethnic origins lie in the Indian sub-continent, but are permanent residents of the U.K.) at 1,323,000, 2.4% of the British population. Of these 787,000 (60%) were Indian, mostly Sikh and Hindu; 428,000 (32%) Pakistani and 108,000 (8%) Bangladeshi, predominantly Muslim. About 485,000 (37%) were under 16, and unlike the majority of adults, the great majority of children were born in the UK (*Social Trends* 21, 1991, Table 1.4, p. 25).

Their health has been reviewed on a number of occasions: Adelstein and Marmot (1989) review causes of death, Ahmad *et.al.* (1989) tuberculosis, rickets and osteomalacia, maternal and child health and mental health; mental health is discussed at greater length by Ineichen (1984, 1987 and 1990), London (1986) and Leff (1988).

A recent review of over 30 papers concerning the mental health of British Asians (Ineichen, 1990) concluded that it appeared better than that of the rest of the British population. However, given the heterogeneity of the populations examined, the techniques used to measure mental health, and the variety of psychiatric diagnosis considered, more precise conclusions are difficult.

Few writers have tried to contrast the mental health of different British Asian groups. A rare attempt was made by Glover (1990) in Newham, East London, who found psychiatric hospital admission rates of 332 per 100,000 for Muslims, 215 for Hindus and 98 for Sikhs in 1982. In a subsequent analysis of the same material, he pointed out that their combined rates equalled the admission rates from the whole study, so that these differences would not have been apparent if 'Asian' had been used as a blanket term (Glover, 1991). The importance of these differences can not be underemphasised given the cultural diversity within the South Asian population.

Bhatt *et.al.* (1989) compared English, Gujarati and Urdu speakers visiting their GP in Manchester. English speakers were more likely than the other two groups to mention physical complaints, acknowledged more anxiety, and showed less concern about their health. Gujarati speakers had fewer psychosocial complaints, showed less anxiety, worried more about their health, and were more likely to attribute their symptoms to physical causes. The GPs felt they were more likely to be suffering from minor physical disorders (not always brought up during the consultation) and much less likely to suffer from a mental disorder. The small group of Urdu speakers were intermediate on many of these measures. Both Asian groups, the researchers felt, were sometimes inhibited by shame from talking about interpersonal problems.

Even carefully controlled studies like these two must be treated with caution. The social class composition of different ethnic groups in Newham is unlikely to be identical; almost certainly this will influence hospital admission statistics. The sub-sample of Bhatt *et.al.* differed significantly by age, sex, marital status and unemployment.

Responding to Adversity

One area of life in which religion might be expected to contribute is that of responding to adversity, but among British Asians very little empirical work on the subject has been reported. Beliappa (1991) asked a sample of British Asians (mostly migrants from India living in Haringey) what were the adversities they feared. 88 admitted at least one. Answers are shown in Table 1.

McCarthy and Craissati (1989) compared small samples of indigenous residents with Bengalis born in Bangladesh in inner city East London. The Bengalis reported more adversities overall, and there were marked differences in the types of adversities reported as reported in Table 2. The Bengalis also showed more emotional distress according to the Self Reporting Questionnaire, a measure of minor psychiatric morbidity, which identified 50 per cent of the Bengalis and 29 per cent of the indigenous group as possible psychiatric cases. The Bengalis reported more psychological distress than the indigenous group for each level of adversity.

Much more information is available about specific mental illness diagnoses. Three conditions: depression, attempted suicide and suicide are particularly useful markers of adversity within a society.

Depression

Depression is a recognised psychiatric diagnosis. Its universality has been the subject of debate (Rack, 1982 p.111), as an absence of hospitalised cases in some locations led some to believe that it was not experienced in some cultures. A growing emphasis on psychiatric research beyond the walls of hospitals has changed opinion towards its universality: its presence is now recognised in all populations and cultures. However, practices of help seeking among depressed individuals and their families are almost certainly still heavily influenced by cultural factors.

Only a small number of depressed individuals enter psychiatric hospitals, so admission rate studies are of limited value. There are also methodological difficulties: some writers lump depression together with other forms of neurosis; affective disorders may include manic-depressive illnesses; place of birth does not necessarily equate with ethnicity.

Early studies of psychiatric hospital admissions report conflicting findings. Cochrane (1977) found low rates for neurosis overall for those born in India and Pakistan. Dean *et.al.* (1981) found high rates overall for Indians, but low for Pakistanis. However, these studies rely solely on place of birth and have a further methodological difficulty, on account of the large amount of incomplete data. Carpenter and Brockington (1980) found an over-representation of Asians (Indians and Pakistanis combined) among admissions for depressive neurosis in Manchester.

Studies of depression in the community are complicated by the variety of forms in which it manifests itself. The importance of somatisation in the clinical picture has been frequently noted. Rack (1982) feels British Asian patients are unlikely to bring solely psychological problems to their doctor: these are considered more appropriately the province of helpful relatives or other non-medical sources of advice. Fernando (1986: 111) provides confirmation from Sri Lankan studies. Currer (1986) describes that among Pathan women (originating from Northwest Pakistan) adversity provokes a response of silence and stoical endurance. Purdah may act as a protection in these circumstances. Urdu speakers would talk of "a sinking heart", a concept whose relationship with depression is described by Krause (1989). Mumford *et.al.* (1991) have created an inventory of somatic symptoms associated with anxiety and depression in both English and Urdu. They point out that while depression is often presented somatically, much less is known of the prevalence of symptoms.

Venkoba Rao (1986) discusses how depressive illness manifests itself in India: somatic presentation of distress may mask a depressive mood. Guilt is less apparent: suffering may be attributed to the misdeeds of a past life, according to the law of *Karma*, which mitigates guilt through rationalisation (see also Rack, 1982: 112). Ndetei and Vadher(1984) feel this is true of less educated Indians; those with more education, like English people, tend to individualise the guilt. Drawing on hospital-based studies, Ndetei and Vadher found somatic symptoms, hypocondriasis, agitation and anxiety commoner in Indian studies and obsessional and paranoid symptoms commoner in British ones.

Cultural differences sometimes produce glaring differences in symptomatology. Rack (1982) gives an example of teenage behaviour in England and rural Pakistan. In a Pakistani village:

> A teenage girl who exhibits signs of madness is certain to get the rest of the
> family rushing about in alarm and paying a lot of attention to her needs,

which they might not have done if she had merely sat in a corner looking gloomy. The opposite applies to the English girl.

Thus the different manifestations of distress may lead to different diagnoses; hysterical pseudo-psychosis in Pakistan, reactive depression in England.

The prevalence of depression in the Indian sub-continent cannot be measured with any confidence on the evidence currently available. Sen and Williams (1987) estimate a clinical prevalence rate of 3 to 5 per cent from previous community surveys; several surveys of primary medical practice produce figures of around 20 per cent; their own survey in Calcutta produced a figure of 42.6 per cent of attenders at a primary health clinic identified as 'presenting clinically recognisable depressive phenomena, ranging in intensity from mild to marked'.

The paucity of psychiatric services means that much pathology goes unrecognised. Carstairs and Kapur (1976) claim depression is common in villages. But an urban survey (Shamasundar et.al., 1986) found that only a quarter of probable psychiatric cases were being recognised by general practitioners.

Suicide

Both the epidemiology and the cultural context of suicide have been discussed widely. Frequency in Britain can be ascertained reasonably accurately from coroners' verdicts, although doubts remain e.g. about accidental poisonings or 'undetermined deaths'. Suicide may be social and institutional or individual and personal. The institutional type is formalised both in terms of its occasion and often, its form (Farberow, 1975). *Sati*, the ceremonial death of a bereaved widow, is a Hindu example, although this now takes place only rarely (Chadda et.al., 1991).

The influence of religion has been studied in a tradition going back to Durkheim (1897) who concluded that Catholic rates for suicide were lower because Catholicism offered a greater 'Society' to its believers than did Protestantism:

> What constitutes this society is the existence of a certain number of beliefs and practices common to all the faithful, traditional and thus obligatory. The more numerous and strong these collective states of mind are, the stronger the integration of the religious community, and also the greater its preservation value. The details of dogma and rites are secondary. The essential thing is that they are capable of supporting a sufficiently intensive collective life. And because the Protestant church has less consistency than the others it has less moderating effect on suicide (Durkheim, 1987: 170).

If this Durkheimian perspective was relevant, for many British Asians of both rural and urban origin, settlement in Britain may involve social change that reduces involvement in a residentially based collective life. The stress and anxiety which less communal pattern of settlement engenders is partially modified by recreation of religious groups and organisations. However, it may be that change and stress influence some individuals to take their own life.

High rates for suicide among British Asians have been reported based on officially reported suicides between 1970 and 1978 of people born in the Indian sub-continent, using names to identify ethnic origins. The total sample numbered 145 men and 86 women, 1.8% and 2.7% of male and female deaths among the Indian (subcontinent) born. In the same period suicide accounted for 0.8 per cent and 0.6 per cent of male and female deaths nationally.

Ratios were low for Indian men overall (71) and for all male age groups except 15-24. Ratios were high (108) for women overall, and very high for women under 35; they were below 100 for all age groups of women over 35. Although figures for the youngest groups (15-24 years) were higher than for all older age groups for both men and women, numbers were quite small: 25 of each sex. See Table 3. Indian women were more likely to choose burning or hanging than other women.

Using names to identify religion suggested that Hindus had relatively higher rates than Muslims as identified in Table 4.

One piece of evidence suggests that suicides among young British Asians may still be rare: Glover, et.al. (1989) report none of Asians aged 10 to 24 in NE London between 1980 and 1984.

Suicide in India itself may be commoner than official statistics suggest. Deaths of young women in cities may be reported as 'kitchen accidents'. Pitchford (1991) quotes official figures of 11,259 dowry-related deaths of young Indian women between 1988 and 1990, of which 4038 were suicides. Despite the apparent disappearance of *sati*, death by burning appears a popular method for women both in India and among British Asians (Soni Raleigh et.al., 1990). It appears to be virtually absent in Karachi, Pakistan (Ahmed and Zuberi, 1981).

Soni Raleigh et.al. (1990) conclude that suicide levels and patterns among Asian immigrants are quite different from those prevalent in the general U.K population. In the general population rates are higher among men, the elderly, the widowed and the divorced; among Asians the highest rates are in women, the young and especially young married women. These findings reflect the circumstances of suicide in India, found by other researchers, where suicide rates are highest among those aged 15-30 generally, especially young married women, and low among the elderly. A clustering of suicides among the young, as part of a very low overall rate, has also been reported from Karachi (Ahmed and Zuberi, 1981).

The Hindu scriptures are divided on the subject of suicide: the Vedas say suicide is good, the best kind of sacrifice; the Upanishads condemn it (Venkoba Rao, 1975). Islam, on the other hand, condemns suicide as contrary to the divine will (Fareberow, 1975). Peng and Choo (1990) found confirmation of these statements, comparing rates for a dozen countries. They went on to compare the rates for different ethnic groups in Singapore, finding a much higher rate among Chinese and Indians than among Muslim Malays, and confirming the differentials reported by Tsoi and Kua (1987) for 1980: see Table 5. Ahmed and Zuberi (1981) also report a very low rate from Muslim Karachi, with a marked decline from 1959-63 to 1974-8.

Attempted Suicide

Suicidal gestures have become so popular in modern British society as an attention-seeking device that they have been described as a modern epidemic (Rack, 1982: 142). Many cases appear in hospital casualty departments. Few serious attempts are likely to avoid medical detection altogether.

A number of studies of attempted suicide among British Asians have been reported.

Burke (1976), found a lower rate than expected in Birmingham in the early 1970s, but noted that the techniques used resembled those of British people, rather than those used in India.

Further research from Birmingham has been reported (Wright *et.al.*, 1981, Merrill and Owens, 1986, 1988). Asians in this research are predominantly Indian Sikhs. Their attempted suicide rates are higher than two studies reported from Asia, although Carstairs and Kapur (1976) suggest that in rural India many attempts go unrecorded. Rates for Asian men are about half the English rate; rates for women non-significantly higher. Young women appear to be at particular risk. Rates are far higher than Burke found. Many cases centre around family disputes over Asian versus Western life-style, especially arranged marriages. Some of these marriages highlight the difference and change between generations and can cause much distress and anguish to the young as well as to the old. Asians seem to be learning to overdose from the host population: episodes are increasing faster and affecting a younger population than among whites.

Two studies are reported from London. Lockhart and Baron (1987) note the recent appearance of Asian self-poisoners. Glover *et.al.* (1989) report an excess of female Asian teenagers from among self-poisoners at the London Hospital, where between 1980 and 1984 they constituted 16% of female admissions aged 15 to 19, against 7% of that population. Rack (1982) considers suicidal gestures may have as equivalent hysterical collapses, including hallucinations, in Pakistan.

Peng and Choo (1990) report a similar pattern for parasuicide in Singapore in 1986 that they report for suicide: high among Chinese and Indians, low for Muslim Malays. Similar differentials are reported from Singapore (Tsoi and Kua, 1987) and Cameron Highlands, Malaysia (Maniam, 1988). A very low rate is also reported from Karachi, Pakistan (Ahmed and Zuberi, 1981).

Conclusion: The Role of Religion

Let me first attempt some remarks on the various Asian religious groups.

i.   *Muslims*

Most British Muslims originate in Pakistan and Bangladesh, and there may be major differences between these two groups. The Bengalis interviewed by McCarthy and Craissati (1989) for instance are among the poorest, least educated and more recently arrived groups of British Asians. There may be even larger social and health related differences between fundamentalists and other Islamic groups. Fundamentalists may see British society as essentially morally decadent. Evidence from studies of suicide and attempted suicide both in Britain and elsewhere suggests that Islam, like Catholicism is an active discouragement to suicide. However, women who in traditional families are likely to stay at home and not go out may feel trapped and isolated, with a resulting high but hidden rate of depression. Domestic troubles are given as the reason for 79 per cent of male and 82 per cent of female suicides, and (along with 'failure in love') 47 per cent of male and 90 per cent of female attempted suicides in Karachi between 1974 and 1978 (Ahmed and Zuberi, 1981).

ii. *Hindus*

As with British Muslims, there is not enough evidence to suggest for Hindus whether or not rates for mental illness overall, or depression in particular, are higher than for other groups in Britain. However, suicide rates appear to be high, and if the pattern for Singapore reported by Tsoi and Kua (1987) and Peng and Choo (1990) holds, rates for attempted suicide are also likely to be high. High suicide rates among Indian (mostly Hindu) women have also been reported from Fiji (Haynes, 1984; 1987) and both suicide and attempted suicide among both Indian males and females in Cameron Highlands, Malaysia (Maniam, 1988). The influence of Hindu religious philosophy on these rates remains uncertain. Studies from Hindu populations in other locations would be welcome.

Young Hindu wives appear to be a group who suffer from social isolation. In many instances it may mask hidden depression. Many of them may experience stresses surrounding dowry payments. For them this may constitute a source of deep anxiety making them even more vulnerable than their Muslim counterparts.

iii. *Sikhs*

My personal impression is that the very low rate for mental hospital admissions reported earlier from Newham, East London, by Glover (1990) reflects a genuinely low level of psychiatric disturbance among this group. Membership of a Gurdwara provides both practical and psychological assistance which as in Durkheim's "greater Society" supports a sufficiently intensive life. Cochrane and Stopes-Roe's (1981) investigation of good psychological adjustment among British Asians in Birmingham actually referred to a sample comprising largely Sikhs.

A final thought is that despite differences between groups of British Asians which have been emphasised throughout this paper, similarities may be even more important. The most significant influences on responses to adversity and levels of mental health may be those of family and generation.

The oldest generation of British Asians is one of migrants who have brought with them traditional values of respect for family authority. Such authority inhibits deviance (Rack, 1982: 43). The UK born and educated younger generation may be less willing than previous generations to defer to the authority of family elders. The sample interviewed by Beliappa who reported childrens' upbringing as the commonest cause of concern (see Table 1) were 95 per cent foreign-born.

The salience of cultural conflict, and specifically conflicts around dowry payments with arranged marriages, have been identified in India as contributory factors in suicide (Soni Raleigh, *et.al.* 1990). Much the same may be happening in Britain. Intergenerational conflicts may come to a head around the question of marriage: the choice of marriage partner (specifically the right of parents to choose partners for their children in arranged marriages), dowry payments, and the role of daughters-in-law, are topics around which very different views may be held within Asian communities. In the 1990s, care of frail and dependent elderly relatives may be added to such a list. The ease with which such intensely personal conflicts are resolved may be the most influential factor in determining future rates of mental illness within British Asian communities. The extent to which religion and religious values influence these changes among British Asians is a topic which calls for a more detailed study.

TABLE 1: **Subjects of Concern**

32%	Children's upbringing
21%	Health
18%	Money
11%	Employment
5%	Marriage

Source: Beliappa (1991)

TABLE 2: **Frequency of adversity among survey respondents**

Type of Adversity	Bangladeshi % (n=26)	Group Indigenous % (n=44)	Difference (chi-square)
Life events:			
Major illness	31	27	0.00
Deaths	23	20	0.0
Marital Problems	0	14	2.33
Problems with neighbours	27	23	0.01
Employment	38	20	1.85
Financial difficulties	50	23	4.34*
Problems with police	27	0	10.34***
Serious theft	12	16	0.02
Chronic difficulties:			
Racial harassment	42	2	15.73***
Discrimination over housing	31	9	4.00*
Overcrowded housing	12	23	0.71

* $P < 0.05$;
*** $P < 0.001$

Source: McCarthy and Craissati (1989)

TABLE 3:   **UK Suicides among people born in India, Pakistan, Bangladesh and Sri Lanka 1970-78**

Age(years)	Males		Females	
	Age specific ratios[1]	Observed deaths	Age specific ratios[1]	Observed deaths
15-24	118	25	181*	25
25-34	78	39	126	29
35-44	63*	42	82	15
45-54	58*	25	65	9
55-64	70	11	91	7
65+	47	3	34	1
All ages	71*	145	108	86

1   Using age-sex specific rates for the general population as the standard

* $p < 0.05$

Source: V. Soni Raleigh *et.al.*, 1990, Table II, p.47

TABLE 4:   **Suicides in UK 1970-8.   Religions of those born in India, Pakistan, Bangladesh and Sri Lanka**

		% Hindu/ Sikh	% Muslim
Male suicides	1970-77	69	26
Female suicides	1970-77	83	15
All male deaths	1975-77		41
All female deaths	1975-77		26

Source: V. Soni Raleigh *et.al.*, 1990, p.49

TABLE 5:   **Rates per 100,000 population of suicide and parasuicide by ethnic groups in Singapore**

	Suicide	Parasuicide	Parasuicide
	(1986)	(1986)	(1980)
Indians	24.2	223	185
Chinese	17.4	107	65
Malays	2.5	55	23

Source: Tsoi and Kua (1987) for 1980.
Peng and Choo (1990) for 1986.

References

Adelstein, A. M. and Marmot, M. G. (1989) 'The Health of Migrants in England and Wales: Causes of Death', in Cruickshank, J. K. and Beevers, D. G. *Ethnic Factors in Health and Disease*, London: Wright, pp.39-47.

Ahmed, S. H. and Zuberi, H. (1981) 'Changing Patterns of Suicide and Parasuicide in Karachi', *Journal of Pakistan Medical Association* 31: pp.76-78.

Ahmad, W. I. U. *et.al.* (1989) 'Health of British Asians: a research review', *Community Medicine*, 11(1): pp.49-56.

Beliappa, J. (1991) *Illness or Distress? Alternative Models of Mental Health*, London: Confederation of Indian Organisations.

Bhatt, A., Tomenson, B., and Benjamin, S. (1989) 'Transcultural Patterns of Somatisation in Primary Care: A preliminary report', *Journal of Psychosomatic Research*, 33(6): pp.671-680.

Burke, A. W. (1976) 'Attempted Suicide among Asian immigrants in Birmingham', *British Journal of Psychiatry* 128: pp.528-533.

Carpenter, L. and Brockington, I. F. (1980) 'A study of mental illness in Asians, West Indians and Africans living in Manchester', *British Journal of Psychiatry* 137: pp.201-205.

Carstairs, G. M. and Kapur, R. L. (1976) *The Great Universe of Kota, London*: Hogarth.

Chadda, R. K. *et.al.* (1991). 'Suicide in Indian women' (letter), *British Journal of Psychiatry*, 158: p.434.

Cochrane, R. (1977) 'Mental illness in immigrants to England and Wales: an analysis of mental hospital admissions', 1971, *Social Psychiatry* 12: pp.25-35.

Cochrane, R. and Stopes-Roe, M. (1981) 'Psychological Symptom levels in Indian immigrants to England: a comparison with native English' *Psychological Medicine* 11: pp.319-327.

Currer, C. (1986) 'Concepts of mental well- and ill-being: the case of Pathan mothers in Britain', in C Currer and M Stacey (eds) *Concepts of Health, Illness and Disease*, New York: Berg.

Dean, G. *et.al.* (1981) 'First admissions of native-born and immigrants to psychiatric hospitals in South-East England' 1976, *British Journal of Psychiatry* 139: pp.506-512.

Durkheim, E. (1897) *Le Suicide*, English translation, Glencoe: Free Press 1951, p.170.

Farberow, N. L. (1975) 'Cultural History of Suicide', in Farberow, N. (Ed) *Suicide in Different Cultures*, Baltimore: University Park Press, pp.1-15.

Fernando, S. (1986) 'Depression in Ethnic Minorities' in Cox, J. L. (Ed) *Transcultural Psychiatry*, London: Croom Helm pp.107-138.

Glover, G. (1987) '993W: Birthplace not stated or born at sea', *Psychological Medicine* 17: pp.1009-1012.

Glover, G. (1990) 'Mental Health of Asians in Britain' (letter), *British Medical Journal* 301: pp.239-40.

Glover, G. (1991). 'The Use of Inpatient Psychiatric Care by Immigrants in a London Borough'. *International Journal of Social Psychiatry* 37(2): pp.121-134.

Glover, G., Marks, F., Nowers, M. (1989) 'Parasuicide in young Asian Women' (letter), *British Journal of Psychiatry*, 154: pp.271-2.

Haynes, R. M. (1984) 'Suicide in Fiji: a preliminary study'. *British Journal of Psychiatry*, 145: 433-438.

Haynes, R. M. (1987) 'Suicide and Social Response in Fiji: a historical survey', *British Journal of Psychiatry*, 151: 21-26.

Ineichen, B. (1984) 'Mental Illness among New Commonwealth Immigrants to Britain' in Boyce, A. J. (Ed) *Mobility and Migration: Biosocial Aspects of Human Movement*, London: Taylor and Francis, pp.257-274.

Ineichen, B. (1987) 'The Mental Health of Asians in Britain: a research note', *New Community* 14(1/2), pp.136-141.

Ineichen, B. (1990) 'The Mental Health of Asians in Britain: Little Disease or Under-reporting?' *British Medical Journal*, 300: pp.1669-70.

Krause, I. B. (1989) 'Sinking Heart: a Punjabi Communication of Distress', *Social Science Medicine* 29(4): pp.563-575.

Leff, J. (1988) *Psychiatry Around the Globe: A Transcultural View*, London: Gaskell/Royal College of Psychiatrists, 2nd Ed.

Lockhart, S. P. and Baron, J. H. (1987) 'Changing Ethnic and Social Characteristics of Patients Admitted for Self-poisoning in West London during 1971/72 and 1983/4', *Journal of the Royal Society of Medicine*, 80(3): pp.145-8.

London, M. (1986) 'Mental Illness among Immigrant Minorities in the UK', *British Journal of Psychiatry* 149: pp.265-273.

Maniam, T. (1988) 'Suicide and Parasuicide in a Hill Resort in Malaysia', *British Journal of Psychiatry*. 153: pp.222-225.

McCarthy, B. and Craissati, J. (1989) 'Ethnic differences in responses to adversity'. *Social Psychiatry and Psychiatric Epidemiology*, 24: pp.196-201.

Merrill, J. and Owens, J. (1986) 'Ethnic Differences in Self-poisoning: a comparison of Asian and White Groups', *British Journal of Psychiatry*, 148: pp.708-712.

Merrill, J. and Owens, J. (1988) 'Self-poisoning among Four Immigrant Groups', *Acta Psychiatrica Scandinavica*, 77(1): pp.77-80.

Mumford, D. et.al. (1991) 'The Bradford Somatic Inventory', *British Journal of Psychiatry*, 158: pp.379-386.

Ndetei, D. M. and Vadher, A. (1984) 'A cross-cultural comparative study of patterns of depression in a hospital based population', *Acta Psychiatrica Scandinavika*, 70: pp.62-68.

Peng, K. L. and Choo, A. S. (1990). 'Suicide and Parasuicide in Singapore 1986' *Medicine, Science and Law* 30(3): pp.225-233.

Pitchford, R. (1991) 'Blood money'. *The Guardian*, 7 August

Rack, P. (1982) *Race, Culture and Mental Disorder*, London: Tavistock.

Sen, B. and Williams, P. (1987) 'The Extent and Nature of Depressive Phenomena in Primary Health Care: a study in Calcutta, India', *British Journal of Psychiatry*, 151: pp.486-493.

Shamasundar, C. *et.al.* (1986) 'Psychiatric Morbidity in General Practice', *British Medical Journal*, 292: pp.1713-5.

Social Trends 21, (1991), London: HMSO.

Soni, Raleigh V. S., Bulusu, L. and Balarajan, R. (1990). 'Suicides among immigrants from the Indian sub-continent', *British Journal of Psychiatry*, 156: pp.46-50.

Tsoi, W. F. and Kua E. H. (1987) 'Suicide following parasuicide in Singapore', *British Journal of Psychiatry* 151: pp.543-545.

Venkoba, Rao A. (1975) 'Suicide in India' in Farberow, N. L. (Ed) *Suicide in Different Cultures*, Baltimore: University Park Press, pp.231-8.

Venkoba, Rao A. (1986) 'Indian and Western Psychiatry: a comparison', in Cox J. L. (Ed) *Transcultural Psychiatry*, London: Croom Helm, pp.291-305.

Wright, N., Trethowan W. N., and Owens J. (1981) 'Ethnic differences in Self-poisoning', *Postgraduate Medical Journal*, 57: pp.792-3.

Author Index

Subject Index

Actors' Frame of Reference 1
Adaptation 2
Africa 9
Anglicisation 3
Anglo-Indian Conservative
    Association 105, 108
Aryan Superiority 6
Associations 8
- of immigrants 55
- of Ukrainians 159
Azad Kashmir 23
Bangladesh High Commission 29
Bangladesh War 70
Bangladesh Welfare Association 29
Bangladeshis
- community 40
- the largest ethnic minority 28
- Tower Hamlets 28
Being English/British 41
Bengali Lascars 28
Bengalis in Britain 4
Black British Immigrants 22
Brick Lane, Spitalfields 28
British Asians 183
- mental health of 183
- middle class professional 135n
British Board of Jewish Deputies 14
British Indians 135n, 153
British Missionary Activity 163
British Raj in India 11
- its effect on ethnicity in Punjab
    88f.
British Social Structure 9
Buddhism 18, 23
Calvinism 17-18
Caribbean 9, 20
Children
- Christian 156
- Punjabi 157, 163
- Hindu 157
- Ukrainian 160
Christianity 13, 19, 22, 23, 150
- Lutheran 54
- Non-Conformist denominations
    21
- Roman Catholic Churches 34
Christianity and Ethnicity
- Asian Christian Fellowship 163
- Assyrians 53
- Irish Catholics 12, 157f
- Greek Cypriot Orthodox 158f,
    165, 166n

- Punjabi Christians 12, 162-164
- Suryoyos 170
  - Association 170
  - Culture 179
  - families 170
  - factions 181n
  - Inci 172-174, 176-178
  - immigration to Sweden 174-
    175
  - Orebro 170
- Ukrainian Catholics 159f, 166n
Christians 17, 157
- Gujaratis 168n
Church of England Sunday School
    162
Churches
- Separate churches 165
Citizenship rights 8
Civil Society 8
Class
- differences Sweden 44
- fraction West Indians 21
- history West Indians 20
- language and socialist political
    discourse 39
- relations 4
- Secular politics and socialist
    values 9
Communalism
- a basis for identity 135n
- Hindu-Muslim tensions 135n
Communist Party 96
Communities in urban space 28
Confucianism 17
Congress Party 96
Conservationist lobby 31
Danes 45
Depression 184-186
Dual Socialisation 3
East Africa 20, 35
Edinburgh Indian Association 124
Endogamy
- Cypriots 164
- Ukrainians 164
Ethnic
- boundary 5, 123
- Class 19
- Community 164
- Competition 144
- enterprise 147
- group and category 4
- Identity - Secular 146